The
Bell Witch

The Full Account

Pat Fitzhugh

The Armand Press
Nashville

This book is a work of both history and fiction. The names, places, and dates mentioned herein are the product of extensive research and are believed to be accurate. The individual stories contained herein were either given to the author by other parties or handed down over the years as folklore, either of which may or may not be true. The dialogue spoken by the various characters in this book are a product of the author's imagination and are used for the purpose of bringing the characters and story to life. Most locations mentioned in this book are on private property; do not visit them without permission.

Cover art by Kris Stuart-Crump
Photography by Pat Fitzhugh
Book design by The Armand Press

ISBN: 0-9705156-0-X
Printed in the United States of America

CONTENTS

CONTENTS

CONTENTS

CONTENTS

CONTENTS

CONTENTS

CONTENTS

CONTENTS

CONTENTS

CONTENTS

CONTENTS

PROLOGUE

THIS IS THE STORY OF AN ENTITY that terrorized a pioneer family, drove a man to his death, and held an entire community in its maligned grasp of terror. The astonishing events that took place in the Red River Settlement of Robertson County, Tennessee between 1817 and 1828 have baffled scholars and researchers for nearly two centuries.

First appearing to farmer John Bell in the form of a small animal in his field, the sinister entity grew to knock on the walls of Bell's log home at night and pull the bedcovers from his children as they lay sleeping. Soon, the sounds of rats gnawing at bedposts and chains being dragged across the floor were commonplace in the Bell home.

After a year of being terrorized by the entity's noises and removal of their bedcovers, the children began to experience physical abuse when they tried to resist. The force was getting stronger. One target in particular was John Bell's youngest daughter, Elizabeth, who was barely twelve years old at the time. Night after night, the entity pulled her hair, tied it in knots, and slapped her face as she tried to pull away. This was only the beginning.

With the passage of time, the entity developed a voice that began in whispering and crying tones, and later developed the strength to be understood. The entity's intelligence was remarkable. It knew every passage in the Bible, everything about a person's past, and what people on the opposite side of the world were doing at any point in time.

The entity's character was enigmatic. It assumed various physical forms and spoke with multiple, disembodied voices — often using reverse speech. It never gave a straightforward answer when asked about its purpose, only stating that it would torment John Bell to a slow, painful death and ensure that Elizabeth never married her suitor, Joshua Gardner. On one occasion, however, the entity claimed to be the "witch" of Kate Batts, an eccentric woman who lived near the Bell farm. This proclamation earned the entity its infamous nickname, "Kate."

While Kate fostered strong hatred for many, she showed adoration for a select few. When John Bell's wife Lucy once became ill, Kate sang and fed her hazelnuts out of thin air to give her strength and lift her spirits. While Lucy Bell was benefiting from Kate's benevolence, John Bell came down with a mysterious ailment and Elizabeth began experiencing fainting and seizure-like episodes while being tortured at the hands of Kate.

After terrorizing the Bell home and the Red River Settlement for some four years, "Kate" left and stayed gone for seven years, returning in 1828. During her short return-visit, it is said that she had a series of discussions with John Bell, Jr., where she predicted the Civil War, the Great Depression, and World War I. "Kate" promised to return 107 years after she bade farewell to John Bell, Jr. Did she ever leave?

Things have not been right in the area since Kate first appeared in 1817. Over the years, the written eyewitness accounts of those who experienced her have become collectively known as the legend of the "Bell Witch." The legend has been published several times over the last century, with each author sharing his or her unique perspective on the case.

This book is no different in some regards; however, I have researched the legend for over twenty years, utilizing all available resources to put the historical aspects of the legend into the proper context. My resources include interviews with descendants of those who actually experienced the events, public records in five different states, family Bibles and memoranda, church records, other published (and unpublished) accounts, and personal visits to the actual sites that figured into the legend.

Perhaps the most intriguing element of this epic tale of terror is that it involves real people, places, and dates. The victims were honest, educated, and prominent citizens of their day, who walked the same ground as you and I, but at a time in history so far-distanced from our own that their plight is beyond our comprehension. The remarkable events that took place in the Red River Settlement between 1817 and 1828 changed their lives forever. This is the story of those people and their legacy.

The stories of specific encounters with the so-called "Bell Witch" have undoubtedly been distorted and embellished with the passage of time; however, the basic framework remains constant — there was something very wrong in the Red River Settlement of Robertson County, Tennessee during the early 1800's, and it was very real to the men, women, and children who experienced it.

In addition to the many stories I am about tell you, some of which seem to hold greater veracity than others, I have incorporated into this book a number of historical facts and related information that I feel is invaluable in the pursuit of understanding the legend of the "Bell Witch."   While some of the following stories might be best classified as "folklore," the historical facts I am now bringing to light should serve to bind fiction and reality together and strike a reasonable balance.

Parapsychologists and scholars have considered this AUTHENTIC haunting to be one of the greatest supernatural phenomena known to the world. Even though the people who experienced "Kate" are long gone, their sworn affidavits, manuscripts, and legacies live on — and this, dear reader, is their story.

Pat Fitzhugh
Nashville, Tennessee

A WORD OF THANKS

I AM SO FORTUNATE to have so many people to thank. The following list is by no means complete, but it starts where it should start: with you, the reader. If you have wondered whether an author would ever think enough of you to say "THANK YOU!" – you can stop wondering. This book is for YOU.

First, I would like to thank my family for the love, support, and perseverance they gave me as I worked on this book day and night for more than a year. Also my parents, who now live in Heaven; I miss them terribly and know they would love this book. My friends, colleagues, and neighbors who have provided moral support along the way — thank you for believing in me. Event planners, who have facilitated my "Bell Witch" lectures and workshops, I am so grateful.

A very special thank-you to Kris Stuart-Crump, whose wonderful artistic abilities adorn the cover of this book; and, to Shae Kelly and Courtney Winstead, whose faces are manifested in Kris' digital artwork. I am eternally grateful.

I would also like to thank Tim Henson, James Humphries, Jim Brooks, and all of the other fine people who provided me with valuable insight into this thing called the "Bell Witch."   I am equally grateful to Bims Eden, who shared many stories with me during his later years.   Also, to the many people who shared valuable information but chose to remain anonymous — you know who you are, and I sincerely thank you for instilling your trust in me.

This book would not have been possible without the expert knowledge of Nancy Williams-Lewis, Jim Brooks, Phillip Norfleet, and Walter Bell, whose knowledge of the Bell, Gunn, Powell, Batts, and Johnston families has proved to be invaluable.

I would also like to thank those who granted me permission to visit and photograph the few remaining sites that are of "Bell Witch" significance and the graves of those who figured into the legend — your allowing the legend of the "Bell Witch" to be rendered in a serious and historically-enlightened manner is greatly appreciated.   In addition, I wish to thank the hard-working people in the many public records offices I visited during the years of my research.   You saved me countless hours and I am eternally grateful.

A personal word of thanks goes to those who enthusiastically support my literary and research efforts.   You know who you are, and your support is the catalyst for my continued work.   To those I may have left out inadvertently, I offer you my apologies and a big word of thanks for all you have done.

AUTHOR'S NOTE

IN WRITING THIS BOOK, I have made limited use of several previously-published works that are regarded as being primary sources of information about the "Bell Witch." Those works are, "Authenticated History of the Bell Witch," by Martin Ingram (1894), "The Bell Witch: A Mysterious Spirit," by Dr. Charles Bailey Bell (1934), and "Echoes of the Bell Witch in the Twentieth Century," by H.C. Brehm (1979). Some quotes from Ingram's book appear in chapters 16 and 17, some quotes from Dr. Bell's book appear in chapter 18, and one paraphrase from Brehm's book appears in chapter 21.

All other Twentieth Century stories were obtained through personal experiences, letters sent by others, and discussions with "Bims" Eden before his death (many of which appear in other books as well). Footnotes throughout the book disclose the sources of my information, and author's notes at the end provide additional discussion.

CHAPTER ONE

Early History of the Bells

THE CLAN John Bell was descended from originated in the West Marché of Scotland's Border in Dumfriesshire, which in 1609 became Middleby Parish.   The Clan and its chief, William Bell, later moved across the river Kirtle to Blackethouse. [1]

Between the 1600s and early 1800s, many members of this clan emigrated to America as a result of differences in beliefs between their Protestant religion and the predominant Roman Catholic Church.   After landing in New England, many of the Bells migrated southward to Virginia and North Carolina as land grants became available.

Settling in Isle of Wight County, Virginia was Arthur Bell, John Bell's grandfather. [a]   One of his sons, William Bell, married Ann Jones in 1721 and started a family. [2]   Several years later, they

---

[1] *Abstracts of Surnames, "Bell,"* 1978.
[2] *Isle of Wight County, Virginia, Great Book 2,* p.84.

moved to Edgecombe County, North Carolina. [3] Most
of their land holdings were in Edgecombe and
Halifax counties near the Tarboro Settlement, where
they were successful planters and prominent
citizens.

John Bell was born in 1750 to William and Ann
Jones Bell, both of whom died in the next few years. [4]
He spent his childhood in Edgecombe and Halifax
Counties learning the popular trade of barrel
making, then later joined Union Baptist Church, [5]
also known as Towne Creek Baptist Church, which
was led in part by the Fort family that figures
prominently into later chapters of this book. It was
there where Bell met his future wife, Lucy Williams,
the daughter of wealthy Edgecombe County planters
John and Mourning Williams.

John and Lucy Bell married in 1782 and acquired
a 323-acre farm on the south side of Kehukee
Swamp, near Blackman's Branch. [6] They worked
hard for many years, accumulating several slaves,
acquiring additional land, and turning their farm into
one of the best in the area.

The Bell Farm in North Carolina

The farm had rows of cotton, corn, and tobacco
that stretched as far as the eye could see, and
abounded with mules, cows, and hogs. Despite the
Bells' receiving a slave from Lucy Bell's father's
estate settlement in 1793, the farm's growth still
made it so that Bell could no longer manage the
many day-to-day tasks by himself — he would be up
and working hard by daybreak each day, often not
retiring until past eleven o'clock in the evening. This

---

[3] *Edgecombe Precinct, North Carolina, Deed Book 1*, p.73.
[4] *North Carolina Secretary of State Wills, Book 8*, pp. 107-108.
[5] Kehukee Baptist Association records.
[6] *Halifax County, North Carolina, Deed Book 13*, p.157.

routine continued until Bell finally decided to hire someone to oversee and help with the various, day-to-day tasks on the farm.

After the overseer had taken over many of the day-to-day farming matters, Bell was able to spend more time with his family and managing the farm's finances and dealing with markets.   The stress associated with Bell's once-daily routine soon became a thing of the past, and he did not regret his decision to hire an overseer.   It was not long, however, until Bell was once again plagued by problems; only this time they were of a different nature.

The Evil Overseer

Although the overseer was knowledgeable about farming matters and was a very hard worker, he had difficulties getting along with other people. Known as a quick-tempered man who seemed to find fault with everyone except himself, and who treated the slaves with severe cruelty, the overseer quickly made enemies all around the Settlement. He often argued with John Bell about matters that they did not see eye-to-eye on.

These arguments often led to the overseer's shouting threats and words of disrespect to Bell. After such arguments, the overseer typically took out his frustration with Bell on the slaves by severely beating them, knowing it was the only way he could hit a person without fear of repercussion.

The arguments between Bell and the overseer continued with increasing frequency and severity as time went on, often making Bell feel compelled to reconsider his decision to hire this man as the overseer of his farm. Lucy Bell seemed to think the overseer's problems stemmed from his young age and that despite this one shortcoming, he had great farming knowledge and lots of potential.

One evening after a rough day, John Bell stormed into the house exclaiming, "Lucy, you must understand that it's more than profit which is at stake here. Black's cruelty to our slaves and his bad reputation in the settlement is eroding the respect and good name we have worked so long and hard to build. There are other overseers just as wise and hardworking as Black, and who can treat slaves and his fellow man like human beings. Can't you see, Lucy, John Black is destroying everything we stand for; and that before long we will see not only our good name tarnished, but also a lack of profits as the result? Humans who are beaten to the point they can hardly walk are not producers, and those who must watch these inhumane acts day in and day out grow to resent their own work even more. What effect do you think that has on profits?"

Lucy then replied, "But John, he is a very young man and will soon grow out of his immature ways. I know he will! I've seen positive changes in his attitude and character just in the short time he has been working for us. I realize it is a very hard decision, but please, John, give him time. You have seen with your own eyes what he has done for this farm and the profit we have to show for it. Don't broach the subject of productivity with me when the arguments you two have take you away from what you should be doing and never solve anything in the first place. You are his boss, so don't argue with the lad; just firmly and politely tell him what you expect. But please, don't get rid of him now." "Okay, Lucy. I will hope and pray that you are right. In the morning, I will once again attempt diplomacy."

At daybreak the next morning, Bell went out into the field to meet the overseer and discuss the problems between them and what he expected. The next few weeks were quiet and uneventful, and then, the arguments started again. Another source of problems between John Bell and the overseer was the overseer's fondness for Bell's daughter, Mary, which was not well-received by Bell.

John Bell Shoots the Overseer

While taking his customary walk around the farm one morning, John Bell briefly stopped to check something in one of the outbuildings. While inside the building, he heard the overseer and several of the slaves talking as they passed by on their way to another field. The overseer was ridiculing and engaging the slaves in insulting conversation as he did each day. This day, the subject was Mary Bell.

"I seen you boys eyballin' Miss Mary yesterday. Yeah, quite a delightful site if I say so myself...Miss Mary, with huh pretty long hair ridin' in the wind; those beautiful blue eyes and devilish smile downright chom the energy right out of a man, if ya know what I mean. Whatcha' don't know is that Miss Mary is all mine; she even told me so. And the next time I see you cast yoah eyes upon huh like that, I'll hang yoah stinkin' carcasses in the woods and throw a party for the buzzards."

Speechless and overcome by his own anger, Bell sat down to "cool off" a bit before confronting the overseer about what he had just overheard. After the overseer and the slaves had walked a fair distance past the outbuilding, Bell emerged and yelled for the overseer to come back and have a quick word with him inside the building. As the overseer entered the building, he reached for his pocket where he usually kept his pistol. A shot was fired, and Bell emerged from the building unscathed, as the overseer lay in a puddle of his own blood just inside the door.

Bell faced legal charges over the incident and was found not guilty because he had acted in self-defense. Mary Bell soon married and moved away. Not long after having been cleared of any wrongdoing in the incident, Bell hired a new overseer who had roughly the same farming knowledge that John Black did. The two years that followed were plagued with many different problems, which resulted in financial losses – ultimately forcing Bell to sell his farm and leave the area. [7]

The Farm's Downfall

Despite the success of other planters' crops in the area that year, Bell's cotton, tobacco, and corn crops failed. The financial impact of this crop failure forced Bell to sell several slaves in order to have money to live on until the next crop season. Between crop seasons, John and Lucy Bell had more bad luck – the mules died of colic, and the cows and hogs became sick with an incurable disease. Bell was forced to sell even more slaves, keeping only a few for the next crop season.

Money was now a major concern for the Bells, as were several buildings on the farm that were in bad need of repair. To that end, the Bells' future and livelihood depended solely on the next crop season. Despite fervid prayer and much hard work, the crop season once again failed miserably.

Against his will, Bell decided to sell the farm to another planter, William Rawls, and move to the new land in the west and start over. [8] This was no easy decision, especially for a man of Bell's strong pride and character.

---

[7] Source does not wish to be disclosed.
[8] *Halifax County, North Carolina, Deed Book 19*, p.164.

The Bells Leave North Carolina

Over the years leading up to the farm's downfall, John and Lucy Bell received letters from many friends who had moved to the western lands from North Carolina. Several of these families, such as the Forts and Gunns, settled in middle Tennessee near the Red River at the edge of an area known as the "Barren Plains." In their letters, they described this land as being the most beautiful and fertile land anywhere, yielding plentiful returns for the many families who emigrated from the east.

Elias Fort had been a clerk with the Tar River Association, a religious advocacy group in North Carolina that included John and Lucy Bell's church. Soon after arriving in the new land, Fort and two other clergymen successfully started a Baptist church in the Red River area. Given the opportunity to be reunited with old friends, and to start a new farm in an area known for its fertility, John and Lucy Bell decided to move their family to this land.

In the winter of 1803-1804, John Bell and his family set out across the mountains of North Carolina and east Tennessee, on their way to middle Tennessee. They settled in the Red River bottomland area, located in what is now the western end of Robertson County, Tennessee. The travel party was large, consisting of John and Lucy Bell, and their children, Jesse, John Jr., Drewry, Esther, and Zadok.

Along with their family, John and Lucy Bell brought several slaves, including a woman named Chloe and her son, Dean. Dean played a big role in getting the Bell family from North Carolina to Tennessee safely, and later became the most valuable slave on the Bell plantation.

CHAPTER TWO

The Bells' New Home

THE BELLS PURCHASED 220 ACRES of land bordering the south side of the Red River from William Crawford, an earlier settler. [9] On the property was a double-log, weather boarded house with six large and comfortable rooms. The house stood about 100 yards down a fenced lane, which led to the Brown's Ford and Springfield Road.

It was one of the finest farms in the community at the time, boasting a large pear orchard in the back and several pear trees on the front lawn. The well was about 100 yards north of the house, and the family cemetery was located atop a cedar-covered hill about 300 yards to the northwest. Several large fields had been cleared before the Bells moved to the area, beyond which were dense forests that flourished with wild plants and berries, deer, rabbits and other animals.

---

[9] *Robertson County, Tennessee, Deed Book E*, p. 126.

The Red River Community

Thought by many to be the prettiest stream in the country, nearby Red River abounded with game fish and carried the beautiful and melodic sounds of swirls and ripples. The fields and sparse forests lining the river made excellent planting areas and gathering places for families to picnic and play.

A number of other families lived in the community; including, James Johnston and his brother, William; the Forts, Frederick and Kate Batts, Jeremiah Batts, Benjamin Batts, the Gardners, the Porters, James Byrns, and Frank Miles. Bordering the Bell farm on the east side was the Johnston family farm, consisting of James Johnston and his two sons, John and Calvin.

The Johnstons were the Bells' closest neighbors. James Johnston was an old and devout Christian and the founder of Johnston's Campground, located at the confluence of Johnston Spring and Sturgeon Creek. Families came to the campground from all over the countryside, staying for weeks at a time to sing hymns and praise the Almighty.

The Gunns and the Forts, two prominent families of religious leaders in the community, frequently held revivals and other worship services at the campground. John and Calvin Johnston continued to maintain Johnston's Campground up until the mid 1850's.

Doctors were scarce, with most being located at major trading centers. The community doctor was Dr. George Hopson of Port Royal. [b] While quite a distance from most other settlements, Hopson was said to have always been where he was needed in the blink of an eye.

There was one school in the area, located on James Johnston's farm near the Bell property line.

Johnston had donated this particular tract of land to be used as a school. The first class was held in 1812 and was taught by Reverend James Gunn, who had recently moved to the area. Among his pupils were Jeremiah Batts, Jr., Thomas and William Martin, James Christy, and James, Joseph, William and Edward Gunn. The tuition paid was 50 cents per month. [10]

Several of the Bell children were later educated at this school under the tutelage of Professor Richard Powell, a bright, young mathematician who came to the area about 1815 from Halifax County, North Carolina. Powell was known to be very strict on his students, often detaining them after school and on into the evening until they had fully understood and completed the day's lesson. He was also one of the very few teachers in Tennessee at the time that was educated beyond the basic level of schooling.

Tennessee Historian Albert Virgil Goodpasture describes what schools were like in the early days of Robertson County, Tennessee:

"In the early days of the county there were no schools which afforded more than an elementary education. They were usually taught in rude log houses built in some old field, and were supported by subscription, or the tuition of pupils.
The curriculum embraced reading, writing, arithmetic, grammar, and geography, with the first three receiving the greater part of the attention. The teachers were frequently of very limited education, and one who could take a

---

[10] Albert Virgil Goodpasture, *Goodspeed History of Tennessee – Robertson County*, 1886, p. 861.

class through the ordinary arithmetic was considered an excellent scholar." [11]

There were several towns in the general vicinity of the Bell farm, including Port Royal, Springfield, Clarksville, and Nashville, all in Tennessee. Just over the Kentucky state line and only a few miles away were Keysburg and Adairville, Kentucky.

Port Royal, situated on the Red River about seven miles upstream from the Bell farm, was the principal trading center of Robertson County at the time. More navigable in those days, the Red River was an important steamboat route to New Orleans and other ports by way of the Cumberland, Ohio, and Mississippi rivers. In addition to being a stop along a key stage route, Port Royal was also the point of convergence for several roads major roads connecting Adairville, Clarksville, and Springfield.

The significance of Port Royal as a trade center diminished after the Edgefield and Kentucky Railroad, which later became the Louisville and Nashville Railroad, was built in 1859 to serve nearby Adams Station and Springfield. By 1879, steamboats had stopped calling on Port Royal and the once-thriving trade center became a "ghost town." Port Royal is now a state park in Montgomery County, Tennessee near Clarksville.

Religion

John Bell was accepted into Red River Baptist Church in 1805 by a letter of dismission issued from his former church in North Carolina. [12]

Ministers John Taylor and Ambrose Dudley of

---

[11] Albert Virgil Goodpasture, *Goodspeed History of Tennessee – Robertson County*, 1886, p. 860.
[12] *Red River Baptist Church Minutes (1791-1826)*, P. 161.

Kentucky, along with Elias Fort and William Prince, established the Red River Baptist Church in 1791 near the confluence of the Red River and Sulphur Fork Creek in Port Royal. The church has changed its location five times since its inception, and is currently located in Adams, Tennessee.

Red River Baptist Church in Adams, Tennessee as it appears today.

The first leaders of Red River Baptist Church were the Forts, who emigrated to middle Tennessee from North Carolina in 1788 and settled between the Red River and Elk Fork Creek. Elias Fort had been actively involved with the Tar River Association in North Carolina before moving to Tennessee, and was one of many friends who wrote letters to the Bells telling them about the beauty and fertility of the Red River bottomland.

Two of Fort's sons, Josiah and Sugg, served as clerk of Red River Baptist Church at different times during the church's early years. [c] Sugg Fort eventually became the church's pastor. As families continued to migrate to the area, more churches sprang into existence; and the area became evenly split between the Baptist and Methodist faiths.

Most families who professed the Methodist faith worshiped at nearby Bethel Methodist Church with Reverend James Gunn.   Reverend James and Reverend Thomas Gunn were the pioneers of Methodism in the area.   The Gunns preached to various congregations that comprised "circuits," some of which still exist today.

The fact that the Bell family was of a different religious faith than the Gunns did not preclude a lifelong friendship between the two families. Reverend Thomas Gunn officiated at several of the Bell children's weddings, and his daughters, Martha and Elizabeth, married sons of John Bell.

Both the Red River Baptist Church and Bethel Methodist Churches continued to grow, with families from all over Robertson and Montgomery Counties increasing their participation in worship services and invigorating revivals.   Sugg Fort's ministerial duties now encompassed both Red River Baptist Church and newly formed Drake's Pond Baptist Church near the present town of Guthrie, Kentucky. [d]

In addition to traditional worship services, church members often congregated in homes throughout the community to read scripture, sing hymns, and pray to the Almighty.

The Bells Prosper

John and Lucy Bell had three more children — Elizabeth, Richard Williams, and Joel Egbert Bell, in the years following their emigration to Tennessee. Around 1814, the Bells' two oldest sons, Jesse and John Jr., joined the 2nd Tennessee Regiment and fought under then Major General Andrew Jackson, at Horseshoe Bend in 1814 and New Orleans in 1815.

During this time, the Bells also patented an additional 100-acre tract of land, which increased the size of their farm to 320 acres. [13] Along with Dean and the other slaves, Bell and his sons cleared new fields and planted orchards that still exist today.

John Jr. and Drewry Bell, along with neighbor Alex Gunn, engaged in flatboating between Port Royal and New Orleans. During the summer, they built flatboats and loaded them with goods and produce to sell for high dollar in New Orleans. When the Red River rose enough for safe passage, usually in the spring, they would begin their journey up the Red River to the Cumberland, then to the Ohio and Mississippi rivers, landing in New Orleans some weeks later. After selling their goods, they would sell the scrap lumber from their flatboats for extra money to return home on.

The first marriages in the Bell family took place in 1817 when daughter Esther and son Jesse married their neighborhood sweethearts, Alex Porter and Martha Gunn, respectively.

Because of their acts of kindness, fair business dealings, and strong religious convictions, the Bells became a family of great prominence and enjoyed a good rapport with other families in the community. John Bell was a man of great wealth and influence in the community, eventually becoming an elder of Red River Baptist Church, an honor that he and his family held in the highest regards. [14] The Bell home was the site of many social gatherings where the Johnstons, Gunns, Forts, Frank Miles, and others frequently gathered for dinner, chat and worship.

One of the most frequent visitors to the Bell home was Professor Richard Powell. A man of knowledge

---

[13] *Tennessee Grant Book K*, p. 403.
[14] *Red River Baptist Church Minutes (1791-1826)*.

and polite manner, Powell always made it a point to visit the Bells when he was in the area. He always began his visits by praising Elizabeth's progress in school, and often spoke of her irresistible charm and beauty.

Another frequent visitor to the Bell home was Joshua Gardner, a handsome and well-mannered young man who lived on a farm that bordered the south side of the Bell property. It seemed the only thing Gardner and Professor Powell shared in common was their unmistakable fondness for Elizabeth Bell.

Joshua Gardner, six years Elizabeth's senior, was known as one of the brightest and most outspoken young men in the community, and never once attempted to hide his fondness for her. The Bells were very fond of Gardner and his family, and had no problems with his visiting Elizabeth on a regular basis. At the young age of 12, Elizabeth was not yet ready for serious courtship and spent much of her time with other girls.

Elizabeth's two closest friends were Rebecca Porter and Partheny (Theny) Thorn. Rebecca Porter was the younger sister of Alex Porter, who married Elizabeth's older sister, Esther. Theny Thorn was the adopted daughter of James and Jane Johnston. The three girls were the best of friends, and often slumbered, went on picnics, and took hikes together through the forest and along the Red River.

CHAPTER THREE

Trouble Begins

A LARGE AND HAPPY FAMILY, the Bells enjoyed everything life had to offer — until one day in 1817. What happened on that cool, fall day would remain with John Bell's family for the next eleven years, inflicting terror and humiliation that would alter their lives forever and baffle the most learned of scholars.

Strange Animals and People Appear

John Bell was walking through one of his cornfields when he came upon a strange-looking animal standing in a corn row. Its body was unmistakably that of a dog, but the head closely resembled that of a rabbit and had bright, green eyes. Unlike anything Bell had ever seen before, the creature stared at him for several minutes without moving.

Baffled and somewhat frightened, Bell loaded his shotgun and took aim at the creature. As quickly as he could put his finger on the trigger, the creature ran away. He looked through every corn row for the creature but found nothing, not even a track. Although he could not easily forget the sinister look that the creature gave him, Bell decided it was probably a mix-bred dog that had strayed into the cornfield.

Bell thought nothing more of the incident until dinner one evening about a week later when Elizabeth and Drewry mentioned having seen an old woman walking in the orchard and mysteriously disappearing after a short time.

Upon hearing this, he told them that who they saw was probably a new neighbor who had accidentally wandered onto the property and quickly exited upon seeing them and realizing their trespass. Given the large number of people migrating to the area at the time, this was a reasonable explanation and nothing more was mentioned about the incident.

They continued with dinner until John Jr. asked, "Father, why have you not eaten for several minutes? It's not like you to sit at dinner with a half-empty plate before you; and, you look like you are worried. Is something wrong?" John Bell replied, "Thank you for your concern, son, but all is well. This has been a very busy week, and I was thinking about some things I hadn't had time to think about until now. I offer my apology if this has disrupted your dinner." "John, you do look very tired; perhaps you should retire early this evening and get some rest," suggested Lucy Bell. "I think it would do me some good," he replied. The family finished dinner and John Bell retired shortly thereafter.

About halfway through dinner the next evening, Drewry Bell walked in and exclaimed, "Father, you won't ever guess what I just saw! It was the largest bird I've ever seen, sitting right on the fence out by the lane! I thought it was a wild turkey, so I fetched my gun; but it flew away as soon as I aimed at it. I watched it for a good distance, and I swear it was either the world's largest wild turkey or some type of big, ancient bird!"

"Are you sure it wasn't an eagle, son?" John Bell inquired, "you know eagles can get very big, and they are very plentiful in these parts." "No, father; I'm sure this wasn't an eagle, it didn't have the grace nor the wingspan of an eagle. I will look around the farm in the morning and see if I can see it again," replied Drewry. "So just what did this magnificent bird say to you, brother?" asked Elizabeth. "It said that you're not at all funny, little sister!" exclaimed Drewry. "Okay, enough of the foolishness; you need to eat your dinner before it gets cold," Lucy Bell remarked.

Philis, one of the house slaves, spoke up and said she had heard her older brother, Dean, speak of a large, black dog that followed him when he visited his wife at the Gunn farm each night. The dog jumped out of the bushes at the same place each night, and would follow him to the Gunn property line before running away. "Well, Dean is a very good and honest man, Philis, but his imagination is sometimes as big as Kate Batts' stomach," John Jr. said laughingly. After some family conversation and a long prayer later that evening, the Bells retired.

Knocks on the Walls

Several weeks elapsed without incident, and then the Bells began hearing faint, knocking sounds on the door and outside walls of their house after dark. After being victimized by this seeming "prank" for several evenings in a row, John Bell and his sons rushed outside whenever they heard these sounds, hoping to catch the culprit.   They kept up this routine   night   after   night...always   returning frustrated and without an explanation.

The force and frequency of the knocking sounds grew with the passing of each night, and fear began to set in as hopes of finding an explanation for the "pranks" quickly faded.   Something was terribly wrong, and the Bells now knew it.   The Bell children found it increasingly hard to go outside after dark, and John Bell himself often initiated important conversations with his sons just prior to going outside, so they often followed him to continue the conversation.   The rest of the family knew this was out of character for Bell and that he was very troubled about something.

Bedcovers Pulled from Children

As the nights grew colder, the noises that once occurred outside the Bell home moved inside.   The Bell children began waking in the middle of the night, extremely frightened and complaining of noises that sounded like rats gnawing relentlessly at their bedposts.

The noises would temporarily stop when a candle was lit, but quickly started up again as soon as the candle was blown out.   After these noises had been heard inside the Bell home each night for about a week, the children began to feel light jerking at their pillows and sheets as they were about to doze off. When they tried to hold on to their sheets or hide underneath them, the jerking became considerably stronger — often pulling the sheets off the beds and leaving the children freezing and trembling with bone-chilling fear.

Sometimes when trying to resist this unknown force pulling at their sheets, the Bell children were slapped in their faces by a seemingly invisible hand. John and Lucy Bell always rushed to the children's bedsides to comfort them when such disturbances occurred, but even this level of comfort and consoling was not enough. The harder the Bells tried to resist the mysterious force, the more restless and vicious it became.

The disturbances occurred very late at night, sometimes not ending until after 3 o'clock in the morning. When awakened, the Bells searched every room of the house in hopes of finding a reasonable explanation for the humiliation and torment that was being inflicted upon them by this mysterious entity, seemingly at its own will. When they searched one room, the noises began in another room. When they ran to the other room hoping to find the culprit, the noises ceased and soon started up in yet another room.

Over time, the once light gnawing at the bedposts became louder and sounded like a dog grinding its paws into the floor beneath the bed. The Bells also began hearing the sounds of stones falling and chains being dragged across the floor late at night.

These disturbances took not only an emotional toll on the Bells, but a physical one as well. Work on the farm still had to be done, which meant rising before daybreak each day. Since the Bells often did not get to sleep until after 3 o'clock in the morning, they grew tired quickly each morning and the days soon became longer.

The Bells seldom spoke of the disturbances while working during the day or having dinner in the evening because their exhaustion and level of emotional stress were beyond anything they had ever experienced. By this time, it was clear in the minds of John and Lucy Bell that the disturbances were the work of an entity that possessed much greater power than their own, and which seemingly had a mind of its own.

When the Bells occasionally spoke of the disturbances among themselves, the only possible explanations that came to mind were acts of the Almighty or fallout from the New Madrid earthquakes that occurred in west Tennessee several years earlier.

Elizabeth is Tortured

Shortly after retiring one evening, the entire family was awakened by ear-piercing screams coming from Elizabeth's room. When John and Lucy Bell arrived at their daughter's bedside, they found her crying, her hair in knots, and her face covered with welts.

"Oh God, my dear child, what has happened to you? I've never seen a human being in as much fear as you appear to be in now. Please, tell your father and I what happened to you." Elizabeth's words were not understandable, as she was still crying and gasping for breath. Her body cold and trembling from head to toe, she tried very hard to speak, but the chattering of her teeth muffled her words.

Lucy Bell lay beside her while John Bell rubbed her head and repeatedly told her everything was going to be all right. "Your mother and I don't have all the answers about why these things are happening, but I promise you in the name of the Lord God Almighty that your mother and I will always do everything we can not to let anything bad happen to you. We love you very much, Elizabeth." He then knelt on the floor next to the bed, looked upward, and cried, "My God, why...why is our beloved and innocent daughter, Elizabeth, being subjected to such evil and painful torture? What has she done to deserve this? Even a horse thief does not deserve treatment as cruel and sinister as this, yet with my own eyes I see it being inflicted on an innocent child barely twelve years of age! Why, dear God, why?"

Now much calmer, Elizabeth turned to her father and said, "Thank you, father; I love you and mother as much as life itself, and it deeply hurts me to know that you are suffering my pain; but God will see us through it, He always does." She gave her father a kiss on the cheek, and he and her mother tucked her in and left the room. Less than a minute had elapsed when Elizabeth began screaming again. John and Lucy Bell rushed back to her room and found her holding her ears as tightly as she could with her now blood-soaked hands. "Oh God! What is it, Elizabeth? Who or what did this to you?" Bell inquired.

"Father, did you not hear that!" "We didn't hear a thing...what did you hear?" "A scream, a very loud scream in both my ears and the pain is unbearable! It was louder than anything I've ever heard before. Please, I beg of you, stay in here with me for the rest of the night. I'm very scared." Lucy Bell crawled under the covers and spent the rest of the night with Elizabeth. The next morning, Elizabeth's face was covered with welts and bruises, and she could barely hear a thing. John Jr. and Drewry comforted and talked with her to help get the events of the previous night off her mind. After these most recent events, it became obvious to the Bells that they were not dealing with the Almighty, but a sinister entity with powers stronger than they could comprehend.

After much thought and discussion, the Bells decided to see whether the mysterious entity possessed intelligence. Late one night they began asking questions that required numbers for answers, such as "How many miles to Port Royal?" The entity answered the question correctly by rapping on the wall seven times. When asked the question, "How many slaves do we own?" the entity correctly rapped nine times on a bedpost. From this point on, the Bells considered the entity to be not only an evil being, but an intelligent being as well. From this point in time, they referred to the entity as, "The Spirit."

John Bell feared greatly the skepticism and scrutiny of the community and church that would befall him when others in the community learned of his family's encounters with the "Spirit." There was also the fear that if someone came and proved the encounters to be a hoax, the credibility of John Bell and his family would suffer irreparable damage. It was for those reasons that John Bell swore his family to complete secrecy in the matter of the "Spirit." e

Up to this point, the apparitions that had occurred were more mysterious than frightening; however, as time went on, mysticism gave way to all-out terror and fright.

CHAPTER FOUR

Terror Takes Over

ONE MORNING, Elizabeth took her younger brothers, Richard and Joel, on a hike through the woods nearby. It was a beautiful spring morning with the sound of cheerful birds and ripples from the Red River filling the air with beautiful music. Enjoying every step of the way, they often stopped to smell the wildflowers or watch a deer or rabbit darting through the woods. They continued towards the Red River as they planned a contest to see who could skip a rock the farthest across the river.

As they approached a large sinkhole near the bluff overlooking the river, a cold and unwelcome feeling began quickly taking their breath and energy away. Dark clouds quickly set in and the temperature dropped several degrees in the matter of what seemed like only a minute. What had been the perfect spring day only a moment before was now a cold and gloomy day. As they neared the sinkhole, they noticed something in the distance that appeared to be greenish in color and hanging from a tree at the sinkhole's crest.

Now feeling very uneasy, Richard asked, "Are we really supposed to be here?" Joel replied, "Well, I don't feel good at all any more. It feels almost as if we're unwelcome here and are being watched from the woods. Something is not right here; I can feel it. What about you, Elizabeth, why are you shaking?" "I don't know, Joel; I guess that sudden gust of wind just caught my senses a little off guard. Let's keep walking; we're almost to the river and I'm sure the bad weather will blow over soon."

"So, what's in that big hole anyway?" asked Richard. "It formed many thousands of years ago and leads down to the back of the cave that we sometimes use for storage during the summer. It is cold in the cave all year, so that's why we keep food and other things there," replied Elizabeth. "Father took me into that cave once, and I didn't like it...the air was hard to breathe and a bad feeling came over me, which seemed to get worse the farther back in the cave we went," exclaimed Richard; "Father told me there are hundreds of Indians buried in the hill above it. What is the green thing up ahead? It's way too big to be a leaf, and it doesn't look like a part of the woods!" "Then just stop talking about it, and let's go see for ourselves," exclaimed Elizabeth.

A Lifeless Body in a Tree

As they moved closer to the green object, they began to make out the image of the lifeless body of a young, dark-haired woman hanging from the limb of an oak tree. Her face was very pale, and she was wearing a green dress. Elizabeth and her brothers cautiously inched forward for a closer look. Although the young woman was dead, there appeared to be small drops of water running down her cheeks as if she was crying.

Overcome by fear and the strong power radiating from the lifeless figure, the children stood motionless and speechless, as they wanted to leave but no longer had the strength to. The power this figure possessed seemed to sap all of their energy. The cold breeze they had felt just moments before was now completely unbearable, and their faces were as pale as that of the young woman hanging from the tree.

Sweating and trembling from head to toe, they once again tried to run and finally succeeded. As they made their way through the woods and toward their house, all three children turned for one last look at the woman. The body was no longer there, and the weather had returned to that wonderful, spring day it was only moments earlier.

Upon returning home, they told the rest of the family about their encounter with the woman hanging from the oak tree. Drewry mentioned that on several occasions, he and some of the farm hands had seen what looked like dirt being thrown at them while on their way in from the fields, and that they sometimes saw snakes and other animals in places they wouldn't expect to find them. Joel added that while walking past that same oak tree on the way to school, rocks and sticks were often thrown at him and Richard from thickets in the woods. They tried throwing them back into the thickets on several occasions, but the rocks and sticks would be thrown back as soon as they resumed their walk. They tried unsuccessfully to find the source of these pranks, but became frustrated and gave up after a short time.

Faint Whistles and Whispers

After the pranks and disturbances had continued for some time, the Bells began hearing faint, whistling sounds coming from the walls and ceilings of their house. These sounds soon grew into faint whispers that sounded like an old woman crying. Unlike most of the disturbances up to that point, the whispers could be heard during the day as well as at night, and were no longer confined to the house. The faint whispers seemed to follow the Bells everywhere they went, and sounded as if "something" was trying desperately to tell them something.

Mysterious Lights in the Dell

After dinner one evening, John Bell, Lucy, John Jr., and Drewry gathered in the family room to discuss the two sons' upcoming flatboat trip to New Orleans and their plans for returning home. After a few moments of conversation, Lucy Bell frightfully exclaimed, "Look! Look at those lights outside the window in the dell and along the lane. I've never seen anything like that before. They are so beautiful...the lights along the lane are flickering slowly, and the lights in the dell look like candles dancing! Where did they come from, John?" "I haven't seen them before, Lucy, but the slaves are probably just having some fun; they worked very hard today and need to have a little fun. I think I'll go out and pay them a compliment," John Bell said as began walking out front door where he immediately discovered that the lights along the lane and in the dell were gone. He was perplexed as to how the lights could have been blown out in the short time it took him to leave the room and walk to the porch.

Bell wandered across the property to the slave quarters, where he found everyone but Dean fast asleep. "Dean, why are you still awake when all the others are sleeping? You and the others worked very hard today, for which I am grateful; but you need your rest." Noticing that Dean's body was trembling, Bell continued, "You look like you've just seen a ghost! Is there anything wrong?" "I think I have, Mister Bell!" Dean replied. "I was getting ready to crawl under the covers when I saw all those light things in front of your house and in the dell. I thought it was you and your family walking around with candles, but when I went to take a closer look they disappeared right in front of me!"

"That wasn't us, Dean," replied John Bell; "have you or any of the other servants seen things that you weren't really sure what was?" "Yes, Mister Bell. We have seen some frightening things around here lately. My mother says it is probably that old "witch" that Philis has been hearing some of you talk about at dinner," Dean remarked. "We don't know what it is, Dean; but tell the other servants not to say anything about what they've witnessed or heard my family discuss. It's very important that we keep this a secret," Bell said. "Yes sir, I will," Dean replied.

John Bell walked back to the house and rejoined the conversation in the family room. After discussing John Jr. and Drewry's upcoming flatboat trip for several minutes, a loud, whispering sound filled the room. Much louder than it had been up until this point, the Spirit seemed to be trying hard to say something important. "What do you want? Is there something you are trying to tell us?" asked John Bell. The whispering became louder but remained unintelligible.

A cold, strong draft was felt, followed by several pieces of furniture being tossed about the room as though the Spirit had become very angry. John Bell fell to the floor as his chair was kicked out from under him while Lucy and Drewry sat watching in a state of total fear. John Jr.'s reaction was much different, however. Springing from his chair, he exclaimed, "You are nothing but a demon that was cast out from the depths of hell, here to humiliate our family and torture father and Elizabeth. If you are so strong and mighty, then leave father and Elizabeth out of it altogether and torture me, instead. I am not a coward, but you are. I know exactly what you are, and you know that I will never be afraid of you!"

The strong draft and loud whispers stopped when John Jr. finished speaking, and he and Drewry put the furniture back in place.

Elizabeth's Bed Catches on Fire

Before they could resume the conversation, loud screams were heard coming from Elizabeth's room. John Jr. and Drewry quickly rushed up the stairs where they found Elizabeth crying and trembling with fear. She screamed loudly, "It was on fire! Fire! I saw it with my own two eyes when I walked in! I know what I saw...it was completely engulfed flames!"

"Sister, what did you see burning?" Drewry asked. "It was my bed, Drewry, and it just burned and burned...never changing form or color. It was like my bed was protected in some way, but flames were rising from all around it and the top of it. When I screamed, I looked back and the flames were gone," exclaimed Elizabeth. "So I see you're still afraid to pick on someone your own size!" John Jr. screamed at the top of his lungs.

From the walls of Elizabeth's room came a faint,

understandable voice that the Bells had not heard before, which uttered, "Oh come now, John. If you really know Spirits like you told those witch doctors down in New Orleans last year, then you should know the emotional pain you suffer when you see your father and sister hurt is much, much greater than any physical pain I could ever inflict on you. And John, that type of pain is the worst of all — It penetrates your mind and erodes away your very soul."

"I do not believe you! You epitomize all things evil and are nothing more than a demon; even lower in character than other demons, which is why you were cast out of hell. Go back there and never come back!" John Jr. shouted. As was usually the case, his words silenced the Spirit. The silence was short-lived this time, however.

A Voice is Heard

Over time, the Spirit's voice gained strength and articulation, developing characteristics that differed according to its emotional state at any given time. When angry or excited, the Spirit spoke in a high-pitched tone that often brought ringing or blood to peoples' ears. When content, the Spirit spoke in a low-pitched tone, similar to the sound of low-pitched musical notes. Despite the fact that the Spirit displayed intelligence and could now speak, the Bells' futile attempts to determine its origin, identity and purpose continued.

John Bell's Mysterious Illness

Also during this time, John Bell found it increasingly difficult to swallow, and often complained about what he said felt like a stick lodged sideways in his mouth, pushing outward against his cheeks and making it hard for him to control his tongue and jaw motions. Dr. Hopson tried administering several medications to Bell, all to no avail — a mysterious, untreatable affliction had set in.

It was said that John Bell occasionally declined neighbors' invitations to dinner because he feared he would have an episode with his tongue and disrupt the meal. On one occasion, he traveled to nearby Cedar Hill to discuss a business matter with Magistrate James Byrns and several other men. Dinner was almost ready by the time they finished their discussion, and Byrns asked the men to stay for dinner. All took him up on the offer except Bell, who remained quiet and stared at the floor before excusing himself and leaving. Bell went back to see Byrns the next morning, explaining the problems with his tongue and jaw and apologizing for his abrupt exit the evening before.

More than a year having elapsed since John Bell's fateful day in the cornfield, the disturbances still gained in force and frequency with each day that passed, taking a devastating toll on John Bell and his family.

While Lucy Bell had not had any unpleasant encounters with the Spirit, the emotional strain she endured day-in and day-out eventually took its toll on her in the form of frequent minor illnesses. Elizabeth Bell had reached the point where she suffered prolonged spells of unconsciousness and fatigue after being beaten by the "Spirit." Elizabeth was seldom able to see Joshua Gardner because of the bruises, scratches and welts that frequently covered her face and arms. Had anyone outside the family seen her like this, it would have raised the question of "who and why," which was something the Bells had vowed not to discuss outside the family.

CHAPTER FIVE

The Bells Share the Secret

JOHN BELL'S AFFLICTION WORSENED. Only a short time after he was stricken, he became unable to eat without almost choking, and the nervous pressure that started in his jaw affected his entire head. After giving the matter much thought, Bell decided that the time had come to share the "family secret" with his closest friend and neighbor, James Johnston.

John Bell visited James Johnston early one morning and told him about the Spirit and why he had felt it best to keep it a secret as long as possible. For hours, Johnston listened attentively as Bell tearfully described the painful events that had taken place over the past year.

Shocked by what Bell had told him, Johnston said a prayer for the Bells and offered to help in any way he could. "James, I would like you to experience this first-hand and tell me what you think it is. You and Jane are welcome to stay the night with us any time you want to," Bell announced. "We would be glad to,

John. We could hold a prayer meeting in your home tonight and Jane and I will spend the night afterward," replied Johnston. John Bell thanked him for his time and concern, then mounted his horse and rode home.

James Johnston led the worship that evening at the Bell home, reading scripture, leading hymns, and praying.   He   prayed   fervently   for   the   Bells' deliverance from the mastery of the maleficent Spirit, and that its identity and purpose would soon be made known. Not long after everyone retired, the disturbances commenced — gnawing, scratching, beating on the walls, pillows being jerked, and other mysterious actions began occurring all throughout the Bell home. It seemed as if the Spirit was aware of the Johnstons' presence and was putting on a "show" for them. Despite his and his wife's intense fear, James Johnston listened carefully to the Spirit.

Hearing the sounds of air being blown and lips smacking together, he decided that the Spirit possessed some form of human-like intelligence. Curious about the Spirit's ability to communicate, Johnston asked, "In the name of the Lord, what or who are you? What do you want and why are you here?" This question silenced the Spirit for a short time; however, the disturbances soon started again and with a much greater force. The Johnstons spent the remainder of the night listening to Elizabeth scream from being pinched and slapped.

Friends Vow to Help

While eating breakfast the next morning, James Johnston remarked, "I've now experienced what your family has been experiencing for the past year. It is different from anything I have ever seen or heard about, and certainly well beyond my comprehension.

The fact that it stopped when I spoke tells me it possesses human-like character and intelligence."

"What do you think we can do about it, James? Lucy and I have tried everything we know to try, and the disturbances just get worse. As you can easily see for yourself, they've taken quite a heavy toll on Elizabeth," Bell responded. "John, I know you won't see fit to do this but I feel that others need to know about these disturbances so they can help, too. We're not dealing with coincidence, movements of the earth, or a prankster here; we are dealing with a demonic Spirit, a minion of the devil that possesses intelligence and power that is much greater than our own — just like the Bible talks about!"

John Bell then responded, "But James, you must understand that if someone proves this to be a hoax, my entire family will look like a bunch of fools. And, there is the church to consider. The alleged presence of an evil Spirit in our home would cast a dark shadow over my family and our religious convictions, which would get us labeled as "outcasts." I don't want that to happen." "John, Almighty God is on your side. The first people outside your family who should be told of this Spirit are the preachers. The Gunns and Reverend Fort are devout Christians and men of great courage who always have compassion for their fellow man."

Just as Johnston finished talking, a feeble voice filled the room and exclaimed, "Ol' Sugar Mouth is right. The Gunns and the Reverend Fort are fine Christian men who are very understanding and compassionate. They are among the best men in the land, just as is Ol' Sugar Mouth himself." Dead silence filled the room as everyone who heard the voice became wide-eyed and overcome with fear.

Holding his Bible high in the air and looking around the room, James Johnston said a prayer.

Joel Bell broke out in laughter, as he had not heard the Spirit call anyone by a nickname before. "Ol' Sugar Mouth" would become the Spirit's nickname for James Johnston from this point forward.

John Bell and James Johnston mounted their horses and quickly rode to the home of Reverend Sugg Fort, where they told him in painful detail of the disturbances that had been plaguing the Bells for the past year, and what Johnston himself witnessed just the night before. Fort listened attentively just as Johnston had the day before. He said a prayer for the Bells' deliverance, then suggested they all go and explain the situation to the Gunns. The three men set out to visit Revs. Thomas and James Gunn.

After explaining to the Gunns what had been taking place in the Bell home, the men joined in prayer. Reverend Fort then said to John Bell, "John, regardless of anything bad that may happen to you or your family, Brothers Gunn, James Johnston, and I will always lend you and your family the same type of support, Spiritual guidance and compassion that we would our own families during such a difficult time. And above all, John, remember that the Lord will always be with you."

Neighbors Encounter the Spirit

The word spread, and after about two weeks, there was nobody in the community who was not aware of the disturbances going on at the Bell place. Instead of approaching the disturbances with skepticism, most of the Bells' neighbors became genuinely concerned about the matter and offered to help in any way they could.

Since James and Jane Johnston's experiences at the Bell home confirmed that the disturbances were not just confined to the Bell family members and their slaves, many neighbors began visiting the Bell home hoping to have an encounter with the Spirit to see what all of "the talk" was about. The Spirit seldom failed to create a disturbance, either. On many occasions, the visitors got exactly what they wanted and left hurriedly, never to return. Some neighbors were braver than others, however. James Johnston's sons, John and Calvin, spent considerable time at the Bell home engaging the Spirit in conversations and frightening demonstrations.

Calvin Johnston Shakes an Invisible Hand

While both brothers were devout Christians and upstanding citizens of the community, the Spirit openly expressed its distrust of John Johnston because it seemed that he was always trying to trick or outsmart the Spirit with leading questions and conversation.

John Johnston was said to have been the shrewder of the two brothers, and the "Sprit" pointed out on several occasions that his motives were never of an earnest nature and were only a ploy to investigate and expose as much as he could. Calvin Johnston, on the other hand, was of a much different character than his brother. He was very plain and straightforward about his intentions and never asked the Spirit leading or "trick" questions.

One evening while visiting the Bells, Calvin Johnston asked, "What do you use to slap the children? The sounds are loud and high-pitched, and the children say the slaps feel like stings." The Spirit replied, "Why my hand, what else?" After much discussion and pleading from Johnston, the Spirit agreed to shake hands with him provided he agreed not to squeeze or hold its hand. Johnston stretched out his arm and felt a soft, delicate hand press against his hand for a few seconds.

Then, Calvin's brother John begged the Spirit to shake hands; to which the Spirit quickly responded, "No, you only want a chance to catch me!" Kneeling on the floor, Johnston pleaded his case once more. "Please let me shake your hand; I promise in the name of the Lord that my intentions are sincere!" "I know you, Ol' Jack Johnston; you are a grand rascal, trying to find me out, and I will not trust you!" the Spirit exclaimed. While the Spirit stuck to its word and never let John Johnston shake its hand, Johnston did manage to engage the Spirit in many interesting and thought-provoking discussions.

John Johnston Tests the Spirit

While spending an evening at the Bell home conversing with the Spirit, John Johnston decided to conduct some simple tests to see just how much it knew about him and his family. His first question was, "What does my Dutch step-grandmother in North Carolina say when one of her slaves does something wrong?" Speaking in the woman's own voice and using her Dutch accent, the Spirit replied, "Hut, tut. What has happened now?" *Hut tut* is a Dutch term meaning, "No-no," and is used as a chiding expression — almost a term of endearment. Johnston later told others of this encounter and how the Spirit knew the correct phrase and could imitate his step-grandmother perfectly.

During another late-night discussion with Johnston, the Spirit became angry and threatened to kill him. He noticed the shadow of a long, sharp knife just behind his head while walking home the following morning. Knowing Kate was about to make good on her threat, Johnston thought to himself, "If the Lord wants me to die, then I will die; I will not run." He stood patiently in his tracks, waiting to see what fate would deal him. The knife continued to dangle behind his head.

After standing still for some time, he began looking around and soon discovered that the "knife" was actually the shadow of a cornstalk blade blowing in the wind. Johnston hypothesized that many so-called "encounters with Kate" were logical things like the shadow of the cornstalk blade, but that most people ran away without analyzing their surroundings and finding the true sources of what they saw.

On another occasion, Johnston asked the Spirit, "Can you tell me what my wife has been doing lately?" "Yes I can. She has been baking cakes for you to carry along to eat on your trip to Nashville, where you intend starting tomorrow," the Spirit replied. Like many other things the Spirit told Johnston, only his immediate family knew of this fact.

One of the most important things John Johnston learned of the Spirit was its inability to read peoples' minds. He asked the Spirit on several occasions what he was thinking about, but a correct answer was never given. But what remained a mystery to Johnston and others was whether the Spirit was *really* incapable of reading minds, or was only making people think that was the case. Johnston took solace in knowing that he was not the Bells' only friend whom the Spirit expressed a strong dislike for. One of his neighbors on Sturgeon Creek, Frank Miles, was also strongly disliked by the Spirit.

Frank Miles is No Match

Frank Miles was one of the Bell family's closest

friends and was especially good friends with John Jr. Elizabeth Bell remarked later in life, "Of all of our friends, none were thought of more highly than Frank Miles. Brother John and he would have died for each other without hesitation." [15]

Standing well over six feet tall and weighing close to 250 pounds, Frank Miles was thought to be the strongest and most fearless man in Robertson County at the time. Where it would require two men to carry one end of a large log, Miles easily carried the opposite end by himself. It was also said that he could uproot a tree more than one foot in diameter with his bare hands. Like his best friend, John Jr., Miles strongly disliked the way Elizabeth was treated by the Spirit and readily made it known.

As was the case with other friends of the Bells, Frank Miles spent many nights at their home distracting the Spirit with conversation so they could sleep. It seemed that the Sprit would leave the Bells alone when it Spirit had someone to pester and gab with. Miles sometimes tried to sleep over, but rarely ever slept because the Spirit pulled the covers from his bed as fast as he could pull them back up. On one occasion, he tried holding the covers in place with all of his weight and strength. Despite his weight and great strength, Miles' efforts were useless. The covers flew off the bed and he was left holding small pieces of ripped fabric in his hands.

As is the case with anyone who has a temper problem, Miles' temper was his worst enemy. The Spirit took great pleasure in taunting him as he ran around the room with his arms extended in hopes of catching it, exclaiming repeatedly, "You ol' fiend from hell, just stay still long enough fer me to git my arms around ya, an I'll crush the life out of ya!"

---

[15] Dr. Charles Bailey Bell, *The Bell Witch: A Mysterious Spirit*, 1934.

In response to Miles' frequent outbursts, the Spirit would strike him all over his body. When he turned in one direction, the Spirit would kick him in his posterior region; then, when he quickly turned around to "catch" the Spirit, it slapped his face and began laughing — just before telling him he had better leave the house before he gets knocked unconscious. Frank Miles never succeeded in catching the Spirit; and if anything, only made matters worse for both Elizabeth and him when he mouthed off.

After arriving at the Bell home one evening, Miles called out to Elizabeth, "Come, sit by me, lil' sis; I've come to give ya' a good rest; nuthin' will bother ya' while I'm here." The Spirit's loud and angry voice was then heard all over the house, "You go home; you can do no good here!" Instantly, the Spirit grabbed Elizabeth's hair and pulled her to the floor, pinching her cheeks until they bled.

In a fiery rage, Miles jumped up and began pacing the room as he cursed the Spirit and demanding that it assume a shape so he could "choke the life" out of it. The Spirit fired back screaming, "You have no business here; leave Betsy alone and mind your own affairs before I put you away for good." "You're the biggest wuss ever; to visit this earth and torture a child little not much more than just a baby!" Miles yelled. "She is not a baby, Frank; she is a young woman," the Spirit responded. Miles then shouted, "Why don't ya mess with me, ya ol' fiend from hell," to which the Spirit promptly replied, "well at least I still have my teeth, and that's a whole lot more than I can say for you, Ol' Frank Miles. You are already acquainted with the least I can do to you. And even you, as you sit there as dumb as a sack of turnips, should recognize that it's in your best interest to leave here now!"

It took little time for Miles to realize that the angrier he became, the worse the Spirit would treat Elizabeth. Although he continued regularly visiting the Bells, the Spirit seemed much calmer once Miles learned to bite his tongue.

Later in life, Elizabeth Bell spoke of the kindness and concern that Frank Miles' showed during her times of need. "Frank was always tender and good to me and to all the family. He was never forgotten by any of us; and as long as there are Bells in the world, I hope they will never forget the man who I know meant what he said when he offered to fight a fiend of hell for the Bell family, even though he might die on the spot." [16]

---

[16] Dr. Charles Bailey Bell, *The Bell Witch: A Mysterious Spirit*, 1934.

CHAPTER SIX

Visitors from Near and Far

THE BELLS began receiving a steady stream of visitors both day and night as word of the Spirit traveled beyond the Red River community. There were horses tied to every fencepost along the lane leading to the Bell home, and the Bells rarely had fewer than four overnight guests at any given time.

Skepticism

It was suggested by some that the Bells were staging the hauntings in an attempt to make money; however, the Bells never charged visitors a cent and always offered them food and lodging if they stayed long enough. The economic conditions in the Red River area at the time, coupled with John Bell's documented financial condition, make this notion highly unlikely. [f]

Another popular opinion among skeptics was that while in New Orleans during the War of 1812 and on later flatboat trips, John Jr. and Drewry learned ventriloquism and the mystical arts, and then transferred their knowledge to Elizabeth and a select few neighbors. A Dr. William Fort traveled all the way from Missouri to the Bell farm in an attempt to prove this theory.

Dr. Fort sat in the front room with the family one evening when the Spirit began its nightly routine of gabbing, singing hymns, and physically abusing people. He placed his hands over the mouths of Elizabeth and several of the other Bell children as the Spirit spoke. Not once did the Spirit stop speaking or change its voice in any way. Fort concluded that the Spirit's demonstrations were not the product of ventriloquism and left early the next morning without further comment.

The Spirit treated visitors differently depending on their character and intentions. People of good character were treated with respect, whereas those of questionable character were quickly exposed and ridiculed, often leaving quickly. The thing that seemed to frighten visitors most was the Spirit's propensity to divulge their deepest and darkest secrets, which usually embarrassed them.

On one such occasion, four visitors who had traveled a great distance arrived late one night at the Bell home and were greeted by John Bell. As they began introducing themselves, the Spirit called one of them by name and proclaimed, "He is the grand rascal who stole his wife. He pulled her out of her father's house through a window, and hurt her arm, making her cry; then he whispered to her, 'hush honey don't cry, it will soon get well.'"

As the four dumbfounded men quickly proceeded to the door, one asked, "Is what we just heard true?" The man who had been accused replied, "Yes, every single word of it."

Peddlers and Quacks

The most unwelcome visitors to the Bell farm were peddlers, skeptics, and those who claimed the ability to rid the place of the Spirit. Visitors who had the misfortune of belonging to one of these groups quickly fell victim to the Spirit's pranks and ridicule, and in some cases, even physical abuse.

Peddlers, such as the Shakers, were met by the dogs and turned away as soon as they were seen coming down the lane, often having to hold their wide-brim hats on because their horses ran away so quickly. Those who claimed to possess supernatural powers or psychic abilities were referred to as "witch doctors" by the Bells and others in the community. [g] The Spirit took great pleasure in ridiculing, abusing, and exposing these "frauds" as it liked to call them.

Skeptics were forced to endure ear-piercing noises, the mimicked screams and voices of their families, and color visions that caused significant mental disorientation. The minds of skeptics who visited the Bell farm succumbed to a temporary form of psychosis until enough courage could be mustered to step outside the door and leave.

The Englishman

One afternoon, an Englishman visiting relatives in nearby Kentucky came to visit the Bells and see what all the talk of "a Spirit" was about. Sitting in the family room, he told John Bell, "I have heard of such Spirits before in my home country and have done extensive research on their origin and purpose. I assure you that there is a rational explanation for what is going on in your home, Mr. Bell. There is always a rational explanation for such things, and I intend to seek out and share with you the explanation for what has been happening here. With your permission, Mr. Bell, I wish to stay here for the next three nights until I have to begin my journey back to England. That should give me more than ample time to determine what is really happening here."

"You are more than welcome to stay here and look around the farm all you want to, even if it takes more than three nights," Bell replied. "Thank you, Mr. Bell. That is most generous of you, and I appreciate your hospitality," replied the Englishman. "I am missing my parents dearly and they must be missing me too; so I think I will be on my way after three nights."

Suddenly, the disembodied voices of a male and female with British accents were heard. "Oh, Phillip, I am missing Charles more and more each day; I do hope we hear from him soon." "So do I, my dear Anne. It takes a long time for a letter to travel across the world, but I am sure we will hear from him soon." Now very pale and trembling from head to toe, the Englishman turned to John Bell and exclaimed, "Those were the voices of my parents! How can that be! They are on the other side of the world, and nobody in this household knows their voices. Did you hear that, Mr. Bell?"

"Indeed I did," Bell replied with a mischievous grin on his face; "Well Charles, I shall leave you alone now. It seems you have your work cut out for you and I need to check on Lucy and the children. If you need me, don't hesitate to let me know." Charles wiped the perspiration from his forehead and continued sitting in the family room, not falling asleep until almost 5 o'clock in the morning when he was awakened by his mother's screaming voice some three thousand miles away.

"Charles, my God! I don't know what has happened to you or if I am losing my mind, but I just distinctly heard you say 'Those were the voices of my parents! How can that be? They are on the other side of the world, and nobody in this household knows their voices. Did you hear that, Mr. Bell?' I don't know where you are now, or if there is a Mister Bell, but I am very worried about you; your father is concerned that I am beginning to lose my mind! I do know what I just heard. For God's sake, Charles, come home quickly and tell me I am not losing my mind!"

Upon hearing this, Charles quickly proceeded to change into some new clothes, which were now a necessity, and leave the Bell farm before anyone knew what happened. The Bells received a letter from him some two months later, stating that his mother had indeed heard his voice and that the conversation he heard repeated at the Bell home did actually take place. He went on to concede that there was not, nor would there ever be, a rational explanation of the goings-on at the Bell farm. He also went to great lengths to apologize for acting so arrogantly during his visit.

Mr. Williams

While some visitors left the Bell farm at the first inkling of trouble, others stayed and tried to either determine the Spirit's identity or prove the disturbances to be a hoax. Detectives traveled great distances to investigate the disturbances, often with hopes of furthering their careers by exposing some type of hoax" and the masterminds behind it.

One such detective was a Mr. Williams, who had gained great notoriety as a detective in the northern part of the United States. Upon his arrival at the Bell home, Williams shook hands with John Bell and proclaimed, "I am a professional detective and have heard much about the mysterious disturbances that are taking place here.   I do not believe in supernatural things, and I am an expert in detecting jugglery, ventriloquism, and the like.   Having had extensive experience in solving mysteries, I would like to stay here and investigate the matter, with your permission of course."   Bell replied, "Then you are just the man we have been needing here for some time.   Make my house your home, and make free with everything here as your own as long as you think it proper to stay."   Williams unpacked his belongings and ate a hearty dinner that evening.

As was usually the case after dinner, several visitors from around the community visited the Bells to pray, sing hymns, and witness the Spirit's demonstrations.   Everyone sat in the family room for hours listening to Mr. Williams describe his various encounters in the detective business, where at many points he insisted that he would quickly expose the disturbances at the Bell farm.   The Spirit did not appear in any form that night or the next night.   All was quiet, and Williams became very impatient.

Speaking to several other men, Williams commented that he was convinced the disturbances were a series of tricks performed by the Bells in an attempt to make money, and that they were afraid to do any tricks while he was there for fear of being exposed.   John Bell got word of what Williams had said and became angry.   When he began pondering the idea of ordering Williams to leave, he heard the Spirit's voice say, "No you don't, Ol' Jack, let him stay; I will attend to the gentleman and satisfy him that he is not as smart as he thinks."

The Bells had many visitors that evening, each wanting to witness the Spirit's demonstrations.   As was the case the last two evenings, the crowd sat in the family room talking until late at night without hearing anything from the Spirit, as if it had decided to leave and never come back. Disappointed but relieved, everyone finally retired after the long evening of praying, singing and waiting. The candles were blown out, and the sounds of bedtime conversation soon gave way to snores. A short time later, everyone was awakened by Mr. Williams' loud screaming.

His shoulders were pinned to the floor and his face was being slapped repeatedly, back and forth. The slapping continued as Williams, unable to move his body, pleaded for his life. The slapping stopped only long enough for an angry voice to ask, "So, which one of the Bells do you think I am?" The slapping resumed with more force, then stopped several minutes later. Williams sat in a chair and held a burning candle by his side for the rest of the night.

Williams heard the mysterious voice insult and ridicule him every few minutes, repeatedly ordering him to answer the question about which one of the Bells "it" was, and whether he was satisfied with the findings of his investigation. No longer able to speak, Williams sat trembling and gasping for breath while occasionally being kicked onto the floor where he was beaten, choked, and stabbed with pins by the angry, invisible force.

When day broke, Mr. Williams loaded his saddlebags and bade John Bell and his family a quick goodbye. The horse would not move forward. Williams kicked, whipped, and yelled at the horse, but it continued raring up and kicking in its tracks. He began petting and consoling the horse, hoping to calm whatever fear had developed. Upon mounting the horse again several minutes later, he found that it still would not go. Suddenly, a voice that seemingly came with the wind exclaimed, "I can make that horse go. Let me get on behind!"

The horse took off in a wild rage; galloping in a circle around the yard with the Spirit yelling, "Hold on old man, hold on!"   After several circles around the yard, the horse ran to the gate and down the lane with Mr. Williams clinging tightly to its neck and screaming for his life. For the next week, the Spirit told of the incident with much glee and laughter. "Lord Jesus, I scared that old man nearly to death. I stuck him full of brass pins. He will spit brass pins and foxfire for the next six months. Lord Jesus, how he did beg. I told the old scoundrel that he came here to kill me, and I was not going to let him off easy. He said if I would let him alone, he would never come here again. I broke him from trying that caper anymore!

Dr. Mize the Witch Hunter

Nothing that had been asked or tried thus far yielded a definitive clue with respect to the Spirit's identity and purpose, and everyone involved was overwhelmed by the perplexity that resulted from its astonishing and terrifying demonstrations. Those who came from far-away places and claimed there was no Spirit, or acknowledged the Spirit but could not get rid of it, numbered in the hundreds. Their predictable antics and the consequences that followed were all pretty much the same, and the Bells quickly grew tired of these so-called, "witch hunters."

One evening when John Bell, James Johnston, and Drewry Bell were discussing the Spirit, they concluded that the time had come to bring in an outside party — someone knowledgeable about evil Spirits and possessing the ability to remove them.

"I've asked many of our guests if they knew of any man who is knowledgeable about such matters and can lay claim to having actually removed evil Spirits," commented Drewry, "and a good many have told me that if any man can do it, it is a 'Dr. Mize' of Franklin, Kentucky." "From where or what power does this man derive his authority to eradicate evil Spirits?" inquired James Johnston; "evil Spirits are mentioned all throughout the Bible, and I firmly believe that the Almighty Creator is the only power that can eradicate them." "I know not from where his authority comes," replied Drewry, "but he is known as both a magician and master of the surreal world. Some very fine people have recommended him."

"James, it's worth a try. This man is certainly not God, but neither is the Spirit. Let us fight fire with fire and see what happens. As a family, we are at the end of our wits," John Bell exclaimed, "and, these disturbances have gone on for a long time without an explanation; we can't take it any longer. I am willing to try anything that might rid my family, my house and my soul of this terrifying and demonic creature from Hell." Johnston responded, "John, I agree. No family anywhere, for any reason, deserves this kind of treatment; so to that end, I will go along with your wishes even though I still believe that only the Almighty can eradicate evil Spirits."

Drewry then suggested, "If it will make you feel any better, I would like for you to journey with me to Franklin, Kentucky and discuss our trouble with 'Dr. Mize.' Although he comes highly-recommended, father and I would feel uncomfortable having him as a guest here without your first discussing the topic of religion with him." "I would feel most honored to join you, Drew; that is, provided your father has no objections," replied Johnston. "Not at all, James; I appreciate your continued sympathy and concern during in this unfortunate time of need," John Bell responded.

"We need as little interference from the Spirit as possible, so I would recommend that we leave around three o'clock in the morning so we can be well out of the area by daybreak," advised Drewry; "the Spirit has never manifested itself during that time." "Three o'clock is quickly approaching; you'd better get some sleep now," suggested John Bell.

At three o'clock the next morning, Drewry Bell and James Johnston met at the Bell-Johnston property line and headed toward Springfield, where they picked up the main trail to Franklin, Kentucky. When day broke, they were well beyond Springfield and galloping up the trail to Franklin when they happened upon what looked to be a sick rabbit lying in the middle of the trail.

They stopped to give the rabbit a chance to move out of the way, but it lay still. James Johnston jokingly remarked, "Well, Drewry, I guess that's your 'Spirit' there; take her up in our lap, she looks tired!" "If the thing didn't look so sick, I'd shoot it and fry it up," Drewry responded. As they proceeded to guide their horses around the rabbit, it slowly hopped off the trail and into the woods. They arrived in Franklin by eight o'clock that morning to look for Dr. Mize, who was easy to find because of his popularity in the area.

Greeting them at his front door, Dr. Mize asked Bell and Johnston what brought them to the area. They took a seat and proceeded to describe in vivid detail everything from when the Spirit first appeared up until the present. Mize listened carefully as the men told story after story of the Spirit's remarkable demonstrations and how it mercilessly and relentlessly tortured the Bells and terrified everyone in the community.

"Well, gentlemen, I must say that I have heard so many different versions of this story in the past that I was convinced it was a ploy to entice people into visiting that area to engage in the constant and fervent worship it is known for; however, I am now of a different opinion after hearing these remarkable stories from one of the Bell family and a close neighbor." Mize continued, "The 'sprit' you speak of is outside the realm of ordinary phenomena, but I am confident that with my experience in wizardry and exorcism, I can rid your home of this horrible creature. With your permission, I would like to visit the farm in about ten days to spend about one week conducting experiments."

"Yes, by all means!" exclaimed Drewry; "you are most welcome in our home, and father and I will see to it that you get anything you need to conduct your experiments." They thanked Dr. Mize for his time and left for Springfield where they had business the next morning. The men returned to the Bell home the following evening to find the Spirit gleefully telling everyone present about their trip to visit Dr. Mize, repeating their exact words in their own voices.

"I knew something was amiss that morning when Drewry wasn't at breakfast and nobody could tell me where he was. I got on his track and caught up with him and Ol' Sugar Mouth about twenty miles out and overtook them. I followed them a long way, listening to them talk about how they were going to approach the old fool when they got to Kentucky. I finally hopped out in front of them like an old, sick rabbit," the Spirit exclaimed, "Ol' Sugar Mouth told Drewry, 'There is your Spirit; take her up in your lap, she looks tired!' Then Drewry said, 'If it didn't look so sick, I'd shoot it and fry it up.'"

Both men confirmed that what the Spirit said was indeed true, and Johnston insisted he was only joking when he mentioned the Spirit after seeing the rabbit.

Mize arrived at the Bell farm ten days later, boasting of his ability to cast out demons and evil Spirits. John Bell and other family members were not impressed by his comments as they had already heard essentially the same claims made by others before him. Mize was nevertheless welcomed into the Bell home and extended the same hospitality that all other guests received.

After three days elapsed with no sign of the Spirit, Dr. Mize located an old shotgun and proclaimed that it did not work because the Spirit had placed a "hex" on it. He began cleaning the gun and adjusting its trigger mechanism as he uttered several words in a seemingly unknown tongue. He later took the gun outside and fired several shots, proclaiming that the gun worked because he had managed to remove the hex that the Spirit placed on it. Mize then informed John Bell that, because Spirits were "scared" of him, the Spirit would probably never return to the Bell farm.

Dr. Mize stayed another night at the farm, mixing strange concoctions and performing various incantations to the amusement of the Bells and the other guests.

After the Spirit had all it could take of Mize's antics and pseudo-rituals, it finally spoke, asking a long series of irrelevant questions as if it was trying to annoy him. Despite his look of fear and worry, Dr. Mize continued performing his strange pseudo-rituals and incantations. After the questions had continued for several minutes, Mize exclaimed, "This is not any of your business, and you have no knowledge of what I am doing." "Oh?" exclaimed the Spirit; "well you have omitted some very important ingredients from your mixture." "And just what is that?" inquired the terrified wizard. "If you were a witch doctor you would know how to aerify that mess so as to pass into the aeriform state and see the Spirit that talks to you, and without asking all of those silly questions," the Spirit responded. "What do you know about this business, anyhow?" inquired an astonished Dr. Mize. "You are nothing but an old fool, and you know nothing about what you're pretending to do," the Spirit replied.

Overcome by fear and embarrassment, Dr. Mize reluctantly said to John Bell, "That 'thing' knows much more about the supernatural than I do, and I am sorry to say there is absolutely nothing I can do for you." Mize mounted his horse early the next morning in anticipation of leaving the Bell farm as quickly as he could. However, his horse refused to move forward — rearing, snorting, and occasionally walking in small circles.

The Spirit's voice suddenly and gently blew through the treetops, "Oh, don't worry you old rotten heap of donkey droppings, I'll get that horse going for you." The horse suddenly began to run fast, carrying Dr. Mize down the lane and to the road, then across the Red River as he clung to the horse's mane for dear life.

When the Spirit paid its customary visit to the Bells that evening, it gleefully told about how it had accompanied Dr. Mize on his way home and played all sorts of tricks on the "old fraud." Several weeks later, Mize wrote a letter to the Bells confirming all of what the Spirit had told them. Dr. Solomon Mize was never seen or heard from again in that part of the country.

CHAPTER SEVEN

The Spirit Loved to Gab

BESIDES TORMENTING SKEPTICS and exposing the truth about so-called "experts" like Dr. Mize, the Spirit took pleasure in arguing with people about various issues of the day. When someone tried to make a point that the Spirit disagreed with, it expressed disagreement and reminded the person of acts committed in their past which would discredit their point.   There was no pulling the wool over the Spirit's eyes.

The Spirit's favorite topic seemed to be religion, as it spent considerable time discussing and arguing religious topics with preachers and anyone else who would listen.   Richard Williams Bell tells of the Spirit's fondness for religion:

"The first exhibition of a religious nature was the assimilation of Mr. James Johnston's character and worship, repeating the song and prayer, uttering precisely the same petition made by the old gentleman the night himself and wife came for the purpose of investigation, and the impersonation of Mr. Johnston was so perfect that it appeared like himself present. It was not uncommon after this for the witch to introduce worship, by lining a hymn, as was the custom, singing it through, and then repeat Mr. Johnston's prayer, or the petitions of some one of the ministers. It could sing any song in the hymnbooks of that time, and quote any passage of Scripture in the Bible from Genesis to Revelations.

The propensity for religious discussion was strongly manifested, and in quoting Scripture the text was invariably correctly cited, and if any one misquoted a verse, they would be promptly corrected. It could quote Scripture as fast as it could talk, one text after another, citing the book, chapter, and number of the verse. It was a common test to open the Bible at any chapter, and call on the Spirit to repeat a certain verse, and this was done accurately, as fast as the leaves were turned from one chapter of the book to another.

It delighted in taking issue on religious subjects, with those well-versed in Scripture, and was sure to get the best of the argument, being always quick with a passage to sustain its point. This manifest knowledge of Scripture on the part of the witch was unmistakable, and was the most mystifying of all the developments, and strangers who came from a long distance were eager to engage the seer in religious discussions, and were is often confounded; and they were no less astounded when the witch would remind them of events and circumstances in their history in a way that was marvelous.

Just here one circumstance I call to mind. The discussion had turned on the command against covetousness and theft. A man, whose name I will call John, put in remarking that he did not believe there was any sin in stealing something to eat when one was reduced to hunger, and could not obtain food for his labor. Instantly the witch perniciously inquired of John 'if he ate that sheepskin.' This settled John. He was dumb as an oyster, and as soon as the subject was changed he left the company, and was conspicuously absent after that. The result was the revival of an old scandal, so long past that it had been forgotten, in which John was accused of stealing a sheepskin." [17]

Gossip

The Spirit also enjoyed gossiping about various goings-on in the community, most of the time embarrassing the people who were involved. The Spirit often bragged to Revs. Thomas and James Gunn about putting the community on its best behavior by publicly telling of people's personal shortcomings such as marital disputes, coming home drunk, dozing during church services, and skipping church to go fishing.

The Spirit checked on peoples' activities and whereabouts when asked, and reported all of the details back to the person who asked. Other than the incident with the Englishman, where the Spirit repeated voices on opposite sides of the world, one of the most astonishing demonstrations of this type occurred when the Spirit told Lucy Bell of the whereabouts and actions of one of her sons, Jesse.

---

[17] Richard Williams Bell, *Our Family Trouble*, 1846 (Mini-Histories: Nashville, 1985).

The Spirit Reveals Jesse's Whereabouts

One evening, the Bells gathered in the family room after dinner to talk and pray, as was customary. "Have any of you seen Jesse lately?" asked Lucy Bell. John Jr. replied, "Brother told me last week that he would be in Kentucky on business this week and probably wouldn't return until sometime today or tomorrow. If he has already returned, he's probably spending some time with his family and will come to visit us tomorrow."

"I know your brother is a very busy man, but ever since he got married and moved into a home of his own he hasn't made his presence known very much around here. I really miss him sometimes, and it's at times like this that I worry about him a great deal. I suppose it's just a natural thing for a mother to miss her children when they move away," remarked Lucy Bell.

A short time later, the Spirit declared, "I know you are worried about him, Luce. Wait a minute, and I will go and see for you." The Spirit returned in less than one minute, reporting that Jesse was at home with his wife, tired from his business trip and reading a book by candlelight. Lucy thanked the Spirit and retired for the evening knowing that Jesse was safe at home. Early the next morning, Jesse Bell and his wife visited his parents and siblings, just as John Jr. had predicted.

He told of his successful business trip and about a strange thing that happened at his house the previous evening. "Martha had retired for the evening, and I was so tired from my trip that I couldn't seem to muster enough energy to walk to the bedroom. I sat down and began to catch up on my reading when I suddenly noticed the candle flickering and felt a cool draft coming from the door.

I looked up and noticed that the door had opened all by itself. It stayed open less than a minute and then closed, as quickly and quietly as it opened!"

This did not surprise the Bells, as it had become a common thing for the Spirit to keep tabs on family members and report their activities to Lucy Bell. In addition to keeping Mrs. Bell apprised of her own family's whereabouts, the Spirit kept her abreast of important news regarding her friends and the family's business interests in North Carolina.

John Bell, Jr.'s Business Trip

One Sunday night the Bells and some guests sat in the front room discussing John Jr.'s trip to North Carolina the following day. He was to collect his father's share of an estate settlement. John Bell gave him specific instructions regarding the matter and several of the guests gave him advice about surviving the long journey over the mountains and through hostile Indian territory.

After a lengthy discussion, the Spirit spoke up and began trying to talk John Jr. out of the trip. "John, your trip will be a very long and hard one, and you'll return with nothing. The estate has not been settled, and will not be for months after you return home."

"First of all," exclaimed John Jr., "none of us asked for your opinion; so silence yourself and let us finish our discussion. Secondly, I believe nothing you tell me. Your pointless remarks are nothing more than your self-serving way of getting the attention of others so that your sinister, demonic power will gain in strength and enable you to destroy more lives." He continued, "And, if travel is one of your concerns, then I suggest that you do a little of it yourself. Let's see how long it takes you to get back to the depths of hell whence you came!"

"But John," the Spirit responded, "a very beautiful and charming lady is on her way from Virginia at this very moment to visit some of your neighbors. She is witty and wealthy, and possesses more slaves than both your father and Ol' Sugar Mouth put together. You and this woman were meant to be together and have the potential to enjoy a lifetime of happiness together; but if you make that trip to North Carolina, you will never meet her."

"Now that's one of the most ridiculous yet creative things I have heard you say! I did not think that a minion of the devil could possess such creativity," John Jr. laughingly exclaimed. "Then tell me that in six months!" replied the Spirit.

John Jr. left for North Carolina the following morning as planned. He returned six months later, exhausted and empty-handed, only to learn that a beautiful, young woman from Virginia had arrived in the neighborhood the day after his departure and stayed six months, leaving the day before he arrived back home.

As the Spirit was keeping an eye on everyone in the community and what was happening in North Carolina, an increasing number of people, mostly those who were members of Red River Baptist Church, were keeping a close eye on John Bell.

CHAPTER EIGHT

John Bell is Scrutinized

THE NOTION THAT AN EVIL SPIRIT had taken up residence in John Bell's home did not settle well with many members and elders of the church. Many questions were being asked about the disturbances at the Bell farm, to which the elders had no answers.

Dispute with Benjamin Batts

Reverend Sugg Fort, the church's pastor and a very influential man, had vowed to stand behind Bell throughout the disturbances; however, the elders ran the church, and it was they who felt something needed to be done. To complicate matters, John Bell had been involved in a business dispute with a neighbor and fellow church member a few years earlier, around June of 1816.

This dispute was recorded in the church minutes, as follows:

"Brother Bell informed the church, that there was a report in circulation, that he, had taken unlawful interest from money lent Benjamin Batts; which report Brother Bell says is false; in as much as he never lent Mr. Batts a cent of money or received a cent of interest from him at all.

Brother Bell was then called on, to inform the church what he supposed gave rise to said report. He said sometime about the first of June past, he purchased a Negro slave girl from said Batts for which he gave said Batts $100. But did not get possession of said Negro for several days afterwards, Batts insisted the Negro was worth more and insisted to have liberty to sell her again. At last Brother Bell told him if he then sold the Negro he must pay him (Bell) $150. Bell then had the Negro in possession & a bill of sale for her. Some days afterwards, Mr. Batts & Mr. Boggan went to the Bell's house and gave him they said $150.

Bell counted out $120 and observed he was satisfied with that. He then gave up the Negro & burnt the bill of sale. After more talk on the matter, it was postponed for consideration till tomorrow." [18]

The outcome of the subsequent meeting was recorded in the church minutes as, follows:

---

[18] *Red River Baptist Church Minutes (1791-1826)*, p. 180.

"The church with the Brethren who were present unanimously justified Brother Bell in what he did agreeable to the evidence that came to them." [19]

Unsatisfied with the church's action, Batts took it up in a court of law, where in 1817, John Bell was tried and convicted of "usury." [h] Being that Bell was an elder of the church, the news of his conviction spread quickly throughout the Red River community, Port Royal, Springfield, and Drake's Pond.

Dispute with Josiah Fort

Aside from his dispute with Benjamin Batts and having the Spirit in his house, John Bell had also been involved in a theological dispute with Reverend Sugg Fort's older brother, Josiah Fort. Very little is known about this dispute other than it began around August of 1815 and was the subject of the subject of church discussion and a private hearing the following December. [20]

The outcome of the hearing is not known; however, Josiah Fort requested and received a letter of dismission from Red River Baptist Church at the church meeting following the hearing. [i] It is not known whether Fort's leaving the congregation had to do with his dispute with John Bell, the death of his wife the previous month, or other reasons. [21]

Bell had also been involved in a dispute with another member of the community to whom he had loaned his best slave, Dean. The man became angry with Dean and beat him relentlessly, bursting his head open. This made John Bell furious. The men settled their differences and Dean carried the scar on

---

[19] *Red River Baptist Church Minutes (1791-1826)*, p. 181.
[20] *Red River Baptist Church Minutes (1791-1826)*, pp. 165-166.
[21] *Red River Baptist Church Minutes (1791-1826)*, pp. 167-169.

his forehead for the remainder of his life, insisting that it was inflicted by the Spirit while on a 'possum hunting trip. [22]

John Bell's Excommunication

After the news of John Bell's court conviction in the Benjamin Batts dispute, which took place after the events listed above, things were not looking good for him in a number of ways.   Because of the negative publicity given the church as the result of his being convicted in a court of law, the church decided to "reconsider" Bell's usury case — the same case in which he had already been tried and unanimously justified by the church.   The following was recorded in the church minutes of the November 15, 1817 church meeting:

"On motion agreed to reconsider the case of Brother Bell, as decided in July 1816. On motion agreed to set Brother Bell, as decided, aside for a hearing, on the matter of taking USURY.   He having been found guilty by the Jury, in the Circuit Court, for the County of Robertson, as such we think the cause of Religion or the Religious cause suffers in his hands." [23]

At a later meeting, a poll was taken to see whether church members felt the charges against John Bell were supported.   A majority of those present abstained from voting; however, the majority of those who did vote said the charges were not supported. [24]

At the January 1818 meeting of Red River Baptist Church, John Bell's religious fate was decided based

---

[22] M.V. Ingram, *Authenticated History of the Bell Witch*, 1894, p. 219.

[23] *Red River Baptist Church Minutes (1791-1826)*, p. 189.

[24] *Red River Baptist Church Minutes (1791-1826)*, p. 190.

on the charges of "covetousness" and "contempt" that were formally brought against him at the December meeting.

The charge of "covetousness" carried one specification, that being Bell's having been found guilty of usury in a court of law. The charge of "contempt" carried three specifications, the first of which was Bell's allegedly saying that the church had received a member who did not walk according to the apostolic order. The second specification of contempt stemmed from Bell's allegedly having said "harsh contemptuous words" against the church, and the third specification stemmed from Bell's allegedly having threatened to withdraw his membership from the church.

After reviewing John Bell's case, the church made the following decisions, as recorded in the church minutes:

"Brother Bell was found guilty of the first charge but gave satisfaction for the second charge & the specifications. The question was taken whether Bell's acknowledgements for the 1st charge were satisfactory? Answer, No. Whereupon the vote was taken, and he the said John Bell was excommunicated from our fellowship." [25]

Many believed, and still believe, that the real reason behind Bell's excommunication from Red River Baptist Church was that the Spirit visited and tormented his family.

John Bell lived at a time in history when there was much superstition regarding the unexplained, the Spiritual world, and witchcraft. The widespread theological turmoil already inherent to the era, when

---

[25] *Red River Baptist Church Minutes (1791-1826)*, p. 191.

coupled with these superstitions, led many to believe that people, places, and events of a mystical nature were manifestations of God's dissatisfaction with the world, and that the devil was robbing Christian souls in exchange for the satisfaction of seeing the demise of Christianity.

It should come as no surprise that someone like John Bell, known to have an evil Spirit living around his home, would be excommunicated from any church in the land at the time. As a side note, Benjamin Batts himself was excommunicated from Red River Baptist Church in March of 1825. [26]

John Bell's most prestigious honor, that of being an elder of Red River Baptist Church, had been taken away from him. Even a minor reprimand by the church would have been considered an embarrassment, but the idea of an elder being barred from the church was unthinkable.

As Bell's feelings of embarrassment and depression were evident in his every word and action, his family did everything they could to raise his Spirits. Bell kept to himself for most of the remaining year, only speaking to visitors and the slaves when he felt he had to. It was a time for him to think about how he was going to get his spiritual life back together and regain the respect he lost. Bell's demeanor showed signs of improvement toward the end of the year, and in January of 1819 he made it a point to participate in Elizabeth's thirteenth birthday party and socialize with her friends and their parents.

The Spirit Attends Elizabeth's Party

People from all over the community brought lots of food and gifts to the party. The parents socialized

---

[26] *Red River Baptist Church Minutes (1791-1826)*, p. 241.

inside while the children played games outside in the snow that had fallen the night before. Sitting near the house was a slide used in the late summer to haul heavy loads of tobacco from the fields to the barn. The slide had runners on the bottom and made for an excellent sleigh during the winter, so the children decided to take a ride around the farm.

As soon as the children had gotten situated on the slide, the Spirit yelled, "Hold tight when we get to the corner!" The slide immediately took off without the horses attached, circling the house several times before returning and stopping where the ride first began.

All of the children were scared, but in amazement nonetheless. After another ride, this time with the horses attached to the sleigh, they went inside to quench their appetites and tell of the amazing ride around the house on a sleigh pulled by an "invisible horse."

As they sat down and prepared to eat, the Spirit spoke up and announced, "I have something for you! Look behind you!" Curious, the children turned around and found lots of wild fruits and berries, most of which had never been seen in Robertson County. As they began peeling fruit, the Spirit remarked, "Those came from the West Indies. I brought them myself. Now eat and be merry!"

This was one of the few times that the Spirit treated Elizabeth nicely, which came as a very pleasant and welcome surprise to Elizabeth. This was certainly better than having her face slapped, her hair pulled, and being forced to vomit brass pins.

The Bells enjoyed a quiet afternoon together in the family room after the party was over. All of the visitors except Joshua Gardner had left, and it was a time for them to pray together and thank the Almighty for allowing others to see fit in socializing with John Bell. Up to this point, the Bells had very little reason to believe that others in the community would associate with Bell because of his excommunication from the church a year earlier.

As the afternoon ended and the aroma of dinner began filling the house, they heard a knock at the door. Much to their surprise and astonishment, the visitor was Reverend Sugg Fort. Being viewed as an outcast in the eyes of the church, John Bell did not understand why Reverend Fort would be visiting his home, or how he should act when greeting him at the door.

Rev. Fort Keeps his Vow to Help

Before Bell had time to fully open the door and address him, Reverend Fort said, "John, I've not been to see you as of late because I know you've been feeling bad and have needed time to yourself. In hopes that you would get to feeling better, I held off as long as the Lord and my conscience would let me; but John, as your friend I consider this to be very important and can't continue to let my feelings about your Spiritual matter remain silent.

"I want you to know, John, that despite all which has happened to you in the church, the vow made by myself and the Gunns to fully support you and your family throughout these disturbances still holds true, and our feelings are just as strong now as they were the day you first told us about them. Everything happens for a reason, and mortals like us don't always understand the Lord's reasons. His word and teachings make it incumbent upon us to accept these things regardless, as they are His will and done for a reason.

"Please understand that the Gunns and I will continue to do everything in our power to support and comfort you during this most difficult time. Our love for you and your family has not changed, and we continue to pray for each of you."

With a tear in his eye, Bell replied, "Thank you, Reverend Fort. You do not know how much we appreciate what you just said. Lucy and I have always believed that we would never be able to conquer this evil Spirit without the help of God and men like you, the Gunns, and James Johnston. Please come in and make yourself at home. We would like very much for you to stay and have dinner with us this evening if you see fit. It should be on the table in a few minutes."

John Bell Tortured at Dinner

Reverend Fort graciously accepted the invitation and they all soon sat down for a hearty dinner. About halfway through the meal, John Bell felt the onset of an episode with his tongue and stopped eating. He continued talking with Reverend Fort as he waited for the episode to pass, but not more than a minute later, his chair forcefully flew out from under him — sending him to the floor where he began trembling and vomiting.

Reverend Fort and Drewry Bell quickly rushed to his side, where they remained until the episode had passed. After Bell began regaining his color, they helped him back into his chair. Several mysterious, laughing voices began to fill the room. Coming from the walls and ceiling, these voices sounded as if they were making fun of John Bell.

Another disembodied voice began speaking in reverse, saying, "Bell Jack Ol', beginning the only is this. You just wait and see what's in store for you. I will kill you and make sure you die the slowest and most horrible death anyone could ever think of."

Reverend Fort began saying a prayer. Tears now rolling down his face and overtaken by fear, John Bell interrupted Reverend Fort's prayer with a prayer of his own. "Why, dear God? Why is this happening to our family? What have we done to deserve this? What? We have always tried to live according to your word! My family and I cannot continue living this life of pain, delusion, and torment. If it means I must go, then so be it; I would give my own life in but a minute if it meant the well being of Lucy and the children. Please, dear God, have deliver us from this evil and sinister force before it's too late; please, I beg of you!"

Immediately after Bell's prayer, a strong draft blew through the room and put out the candles as the voice of a small child was heard saying, "We will see you in hell, and that's where you will rot, Ol' Jack Bell." The candles then mysteriously started burning again all by themselves and the child's voice faded into the fierce and howling January wind that swept around the outside the house.

Sounds that resembled whips popping were then heard and John Bell fell to the floor screaming. When Reverend Fort and Bell's sons tried to help him, they found his face and arms covered with reddish, purple marks from where he had been struck by a seemingly invisible whip. "A whip just slapped both sides of my face and both my arms! I have never felt such pain, and I pray that it never happens again to Elizabeth, me, or anyone else," Bell cried loudly. Reverend James Gunn was in the area later that evening and stopped to pay the Bells a visit.

The Spirit Quotes Two Sermons

Reverend Gunn, Reverend Fort, John Jr., and

Lucy Bell went to the family room after dinner for some conversation and prayer. After they had conversed for some time, they the Spirit spoke up and asking Reverend Gunn about several points he had made in a recent sermon.

Reverend Gunn angrily responded, "And just how do you know what I preached about that morning?" "I was present and I heard you," replied the Spirit. "That is impossible! You were not there, and there's no way you could know what my sermon was about!" Gunn exclaimed. The Spirit proceeded to quote Reverend Gunn's entire sermon and closing prayer using his own voice, word for word.

Amazed by the Spirit's rendition of Reverend Gunn's sermon, Lucy Bell remarked that Reverend Fort had the advantage because having attended Reverend Gunn's sermon, there was no way the Spirit could have known anything about Reverend Fort's sermon. "Oh, Yes I do!" exclaimed the Spirit; "I was there and heard him." Assimilating the voice and character of Reverend Fort, the Spirit quoted his sermon and closing prayer, word for word.

The most astonishing aspect of this demonstration was that at precisely eleven o'clock in the morning, Reverend Gunn preached at Bethel Methodist Church, six miles southeast of the Bell home, and Reverend Fort preached at Drake's Pond Baptist Church, seven miles northwest of the Bell home. Both ministers confirmed that the Spirit had quoted their sermons correctly.

The Spirit Tells About a Wedding

The group began discussing a similar incident that had taken place a few weeks prior, when Reverend Thomas Gunn took ill and was unable to marry a couple he had promised to. In a letter to Martin

Ingram, Mr. Henry Pickering, son of Major Garaldus Pickering, ʲ relayed his father's account of this remarkable incident:

> "While the family and guests were at supper, the subject of a wedding that was to take place at that hour came up. Father stated the names of the contracting parties, which I have forgotten, but remember the circumstance very distinctly, as it impressed me at the time.
>
> However, some one remarked that the hour for the marriage had about passed, and the parties were no doubt then man and wife. Another remarked that Reverend Thomas Gunn performed the ceremony. The witch then spoke, exclaiming, 'No, he did not marry them.' 'Yes, but you are mistaken this time,' replied one, 'Brother Gunn was engaged to tie the knot, and he never fails.' 'He failed this time,' returned the witch, 'Brother Gunn was taken very sick and could not go, and the wedding was about to be a failure, but they sent off for Squire Byrns and he married them.'
>
> No one present believed it possible for the witch to know the facts so soon, but this was ascertained on the following day to be the truth of the case in every particular." [27]

The Spirit's recital of Reverend Fort and Reverend James Gunn's simultaneous sermons, along with the discussion about Reverend Thomas Gunn's missing a wedding, sent Reverend James Gunn into a fit of anger, prompting him to ask the age-old question of the Spirit's identity and purpose.

---

[27] M.V. Ingram, *Authenticated History of the Bell Witch*, 1894.

CHAPTER NINE

The Spirit's Identities and Forms

REVEREND GUNN SPRANG TO HIS FEET and shouted, "So you are able to quote sermons, argue about the scripture, and beat people within inches of their lives; yet you will not tell us what you are and why you are here! Like the others present here and all over the country this evening, I want an answer and I want it now!" The Spirit responded, "I am a Spirit who was once very happy, but have been disturbed and made unhappy." "How were you disturbed, and what makes you unhappy?" inquired Gunn inquired.

Spirit Looking for a Lost Tooth

The Spirit then provided what seemed to be the explanation everyone had been waiting for; changing its voice from loud and angry to a soft, feeble tone, the Spirit stated, "I am the Spirit of a person who was buried in the woods near by, and the grave has been disturbed, my bones disinterred and scattered, and one of my teeth was lost under this house, and I am here looking for that tooth. The incident has been long-forgotten by everyone but me." John Jr. and Lucy Bell quickly recalled the incident referred to by the Spirit.

A few years earlier, the farm hands found several Indian graves in a small mound while clearing a plot of land near the Red River. Following John Bell's orders, the hands worked carefully around the mound so not to disturb it. Several days later, Corban Hall, a friend of Drewry's, stopped for a visit and Drewry told him of the new discovery. They discussed the possibility of there being valuable relics in the mound and decided to unearth a grave to see what they could find.

They found nothing but the bones they had disturbed while searching for relics. They brought a jawbone back to the house as a souvenir, where Hall jokingly threw it against one of the walls next to the front porch. The impact of the jawbone hitting the wall jarred one of the teeth loose and it fell between the cracks of the porch. When John Bell walked through the passageway and saw what Drewry and Corban had done, he scolded them severely and had one of the slaves take the jawbone back to the mound and re-seal the grave.

After hearing the Spirit's claim and recalling the incident with the jawbone several years earlier, John Jr. decided that it would be best to search the ground underneath the porch for the missing tooth.

Early the next morning John Bell, John Jr., and Drewry removed the porch section where the tooth had fallen. They sifted through the dirt for hours but found nothing. As they were putting the porch section back into place, a loud voice exclaimed with laughter, "I just said that to fool you. It was all a joke, and the joke is on you, Ol' Jack Bell!"

This prank would later prove to be the first of many. The Spirit once told Calvin Johnston that it was the Spirit of a child buried in North Carolina, and on another occasion told James Johnston that it was the "witch" of his stepmother.

The Spirit's false claims to an identity continued, and it took pleasure in sending people on long and fruitless escapades. Fearing sinister repercussions, everyone participated in these escapades even though they knew they were only for the Spirit's laughter and enjoyment. One such escapade took place shortly after Reverend James Gunn learned that the search for the tooth had been a prank.

A Search for Buried Treasure

After giving the Spirit's deceitfulness much thought, Reverend Gunn one day became angry and visited the Bell farm for no purpose other than to confront the Spirit. Upon his arrival, Gunn expressed his concerns to John and Lucy Bell, insisting that he would get the truth out of the Spirit one way or another. They sat on the front porch and discussed the previous day's search for the tooth, agreeing that even though it was probably still under the porch, it had nothing to do with the Spirit's claim to have been looking for it.

Throwing his hands up and looking off into the distance, Reverend Gunn angrily exclaimed, "I don't know. I don't know what you are or why you are here ridiculing visitors and torturing John Bell's family. But one day soon, we will all know the truth." Through the wind that blew through the large pear trees came the voice of an old woman, who said, "I am the Spirit of an early immigrant who brought a large sum of money and buried my treasure for safe keeping until needed. In the meanwhile I died without divulging the location, and I have returned for the purpose of making known the hiding place; and I want Betsy Bell to have the money." The name, "Betsy," was the nickname given to Elizabeth Bell by the Spirit.

"Where is this money buried?" asked Reverend Gunn. The Spirit replied, "I shall not tell anyone until certain conditions are met. Drewry Bell and Alex Porter must agree to do the digging, and 'Old Sugar Mouth' must go along to supervise and take charge of the money for Betsy." After giving the proposition some thought, Reverend Gunn approached Drewry Bell, Alex Porter, and James Johnston to inform them of the Spirit's proposition. All agreed to the conditions and the Spirit agreed to describe the location of the buried money. "The money is buried under a large, flat rock at the mouth of the spring that empties into the Red River on the southeast corner of the farm," the Spirit advised.

Early the next morning, the three men proceeded to the spring and easily found everything the Spirit had described. They spent several hours digging around the enormous rock so they could slide poles underneath it and move it out of the way. After lots of hard work and continuing encouragement from James Johnston, Bell and Porter finally managed to move the large rock to its side. Much to their chagrin, they found nothing underneath but dirt.

After taking a much-needed break and discussing what their next step would be, they began digging a hole where the rock had been, assuming the money might have been buried several feet below the ground. Drewry Bell sifted through the dirt as Alex Porter dug. The hole had become almost six feet deep by the end of the day and no money had been found.

Very hungry and frustrated, the men returned

home where that evening, the Spirit laughed about how the men had been fooled into performing the laborious task of removing the large rock and digging a deep hole. Using the men's own voices, the Spirit recited the exact words said by each that day and described how they groaned, perspired and prayed. The Spirit gleefully told all of the Bells' visitors over the next several weeks about this prank.

The Spirit Assumed Many Forms

The Spirit often claimed that it could be all things to all people, possessing the power to assume any character or form it desired. When John Johnston asked the question, "Where do you live?" the Spirit replied, "I live in the woods, in the air, in the water, in houses with people; I live in heaven and in hell; I am all things and any thing I want to be. I'm in the water you drink and the air you breathe."

The Spirit frequently manifested itself in the form of multiple, disembodied voices coming from the walls the ceiling, the wind, and the trees. There were also occasions on which the Spirit hopped onto peoples' horses and rode with them. One such occasion was when Billy Wall, from nearby Montgomery County, decided to visit the Bells and see what all the "Spirit talk" was about.

The Spirit Rides a Horse

Wall mounted his large horse and set out on his journey, but only to be stopped a mile short of the Bell home by a voice he heard coming from the bushes beside the road. "Hello Ol' Billy Wall, are you going to see the witch?" the voice asked. "Yeah, that's where I'm going; why?" Wall responded. "I am going there too, and I believe I will ride behind you on that fat horse," exclaimed the voice. "Alright, then come on out of the bushes and hop up," Wall said. Nothing came out of the bushes, but Wall suddenly felt his horse begin to squat and jerk, and then make strange sounds as if it was in pain.

Reaching both hands behind his back, he felt nothing behind him. He could still hear the voice, which by that time sounded as if it had gotten on the horse and was right behind him. The voice again spoke, "Why Billy, this sure is a fine horse; you ought to be proud of him just like that nice head of hair you have." "What? Who are you and why can't I see you? I never saw you move. You're still supposed to be over there in the bushes!" Wall exclaimed.

The voice then began laughing and telling Wall that he looked like a statesman because his hair was standing up so high. The horse finally moved and Wall reached the Bell farm a short time later, where upon arriving the voice said, "Mr. Wall, hitch your horse to the rack and go in; I will be in pretty soon and will entertain you." Shortly after Wall hitched his horse and entered the Bell home, the noises commenced as promised.

Although a disembodied voice seemed to be the Spirit's favorite form in which to manifest, it also took great pleasure in assuming the form of a rabbit hopping through the grass, across the road, and other places where people were.

The Playful Rabbit

Richard Williams Bell, Joshua Gardner, Alex Gooch, Elizabeth Bell, and Theny Thorn one day decided to go for a stroll through the countryside and see if their dogs could jump any rabbits. The dogs jumped a rabbit and began chasing it shortly after they were let loose in the dell. The children ran alongside the rabbit in hopes of cornering it so the dogs could catch it more easily.   Something was different about this rabbit, however.

The rabbit seemed wilder than any they had seen, running in circles and going up and down a hill several times.   Instead of quickly hopping into a thicket as most rabbits would, this rabbit remained in the wide-open field as if it was trying to play "games" with the children.

The children and their dogs became exhausted and gave up after several minutes of chasing the rabbit. They saw the rabbit stand still and stare at them, then slowly hop into a nearby thicket as they sat on the ground catching their breath.   That evening, the Spirit made much adieu about the rabbit chase, exclaiming, "Josh can sure run like a dog.   I almost had to dodge between his legs.   The rabbit you were chasing was really I!" k

When the Spirit took the form of an animal other than a rabbit, it was most often the form of a dog or bird.   On one such occasion, a dog began talking to Dean and later appeared to him with two heads.

The Spirit Appears as a Dog

Dean was one of the Bell family's slaves who came from North Carolina along his mother, Chloe, and in the winter of 1803-1804.   Dean was known for his skill with the axe and maul, and was considered the best log splitter in Robertson County.   Small in physical stature, he was very muscular, hardworking and honest — and as such was John Bell's most valued slave.   Dean's wife, Kate, worked at Alex Gunn's farm, nearby.

After most days ended, Dean went to the Gunn farm and visited with his wife.   While on his way to the Gunn farm one evening, he saw a black dog jump out of the bushes and into his path. The dog followed him all the way to the Gunn farm, and then disappeared. The dog continued this pattern of behavior for several nights in a row, meeting Dean at the same place in the path and following him all the way to the Gunn farm before disappearing.

Dean grew suspicious and told his wife about the mysterious dog. Together, they decided that the dog must have been the "old witch" that had caused so many problems for the Bells. His wife made him a magic "witch ball" out of her hair and several ingredients believed to scare away evil Spirits.

The next evening, Dean came down the path whistling happily and carrying his "witch ball" in his pocket. He was no longer worried about the mysterious dog. As he approached the place in the path where the dog had appeared the last several evenings, the voice of an old lady asked, "Dean, what makes you whistle?" "Because I'm going to see my wife," he replied. "Dean, what's that you have in your pocket?" the voice inquired. "Nothing," replied Dean. The voice exclaimed in an angry tone, "Dean, you know that is a lie. You have your wife's hair and some yarn wrapped up in a ball to pester me. I'll show you, Mister Smarty, you can't bother me with that." He was terrified.

As Dean knelt down and began to pray, the voice said, "Lord Jesus, Dean, what a fool you are; don't you know you can't pray like Ol' Sugar Mouth? Get up from there!" "What, in the name of the Lord, are you going to do to me?" asked Dean. "Unless you give me that ball, I am going to turn you into a horse and ride you across the river to the stillhouse!" His hands trembling in fear, Dean pulled the "witch ball" out of his pocket and accidentally dropped it. As soon as the "witch ball" hit the ground, it caught fire and emitted smoke so strong that it almost took his breath away. Just as he caught his breath, he heard a crackling noise behind him and looked around to see what it was.

Dean saw what had become a familiar sight — the mysterious black dog. It came from the bushes where he heard the old lady's voice a minute earlier, just as it had before; only this time its mouth was open and it was walking slowly towards him. As the dog came within a few feet, Dean swung his axe and split its head in two. After rolling over and kicking for several minutes, the dog jumped into the air and fell to the ground beside the burning "witch ball." The ball shot up into the air and was never seen again.

After sitting on the ground for several minutes catching his breath, Dean looked up and saw the dog he thought was dead slowly get up and walk back into the bushes. Only this time, it had two heads instead of one.

Not long after Dean split the dog's head in two and lost his "witch ball," his wife make him another one. "Now listen here...as long as you keep this ball in your pocket, nothing is going to bother you. But if you don't, you might as well consider yourself a goner," she warned. Heeding his wife's warning, Dean carried the new "witch ball" with him everywhere he went.

One evening while going to see his wife, Dean once again encountered the mysterious dog — still with two heads. It walked from behind a tree and into the path directly in front of him. With its mouths wide open, the dog gazed at Dean for several minutes with its fiery, red eyes. He finally got up enough nerve to try to communicate with the dog, asking, "In the name of the Lord, what's that?" "Dean, you can't pass here unless you give me that ball in your pocket," replied the dog, which was still using with

the voice of an old lady. "What's your name?" asked
Dean. "My name is Blackdog; you know me, you
rascal, because you once split my head open with
your axe," answered the dog. "I don' t have a ball;
you took it the other time!" Dean exclaimed. "You're
a liar, Dean. I know you have gone and gotten
another ball!"

"If you won't let me pass, I can go back," Dean
yelled as he slowly walked backwards until the dog
was out of sight. Thinking he could make a getaway,
he turned around to run. He saw the two-headed
dog again upon turning around, standing in front of
him and blocking his escape. "What do you want?"
he asked; to which the dog replied, "Unless you give
me that ball, I'm going to turn you into a mule and
ride you across the river to the stillhouse!" "I'm not
going to give you my ball, and I'll split your head
open all the way to the tail if you don't get out of my
way!" yelled Dean. "Say your prayers, Dean!"
exclaimed the dog.

The Spirit Turns Dean Into a Mule

Trembling and beginning to lose his strength,
Dean began feeling sick and accidentally dropped his
axe. "Alright, Dean. Get down on your hands and
knees and find that axe of yours, right now!" the dog
insisted. Dean got down on his hands and knees
and began feeling all around for his axe, which he
soon realized was missing altogether. When he tried
to get back up, he realized that he was stuck on his
hands and knees and could no longer move.

From behind Dean, the voice of a small child
exclaimed, "He's too high behind to tote double,"
followed by the old lady's voice saying, "That's
alright; level him down." Something suddenly jerked
on Dean's "tail," causing him to give a hard, one-

legged kick that resulted in the sound of something falling to the ground directly behind him. The small child's voice spoke again, "There, bad luck. He spoiled the job. He's nothing but a darned mule." "Well, you can't make anything out of a slave but a mule, no how," replied the old lady's voice.

The two voices then began arguing about who would ride on the front and who would ride on the back. The small child's voice exclaimed, "I have to ride in the front — the mule hasn't got a mane for straps and a bridle to hold to, and my arms aren't long enough to reach his ears!" The argument ended, and the two entities climbed onto Dean's back. The entity riding in the back gave Dean a swift kick to his side and yelled happily, "Now, let's ride him to hell for breakfast!" The entity riding in the front, which possessed the small child's voice, grabbed and jerked Dean's ears, making him lean his head forward and begin kicking. After giving a few hard kicks, he no longer felt the weight of the invisible entities on his back.

Almost instantly, he heard what sounded like two bodies land on the ground next to him. Now able to move, Dean rose and brushed the leaves off his pants, and then left hurriedly — never to take this path again.

The Spirit Appears as a Rabbit and a Bird

On another occasion, the Spirit manifested itself in the form of both a rabbit and a bird to Alex Porter, who lived near the Bell farm and was the husband of the Bells' oldest daughter, Esther. At the time of the apparitions, Porter did not realize that the bird and rabbit were manifestations of the Spirit. The Spirit told him of this late one night as he returned home from a visit with John and Lucy Bell.

Realizing that the Bells got very little sleep and were growing more weary by the day, Porter asked the Spirit to follow him home so the Bells could get some much-needed rest. The Spirit declined, stating, "Alex, you will kill me if I visit your house." "No I won't," replied Porter. After he had gone a fair distance down the road, the Spirit said to Porter, "Oh, but I know you. I have been to your house." "Not true," replied Porter.

"Do you remember that bird you thought sung so sweet the other morning?" asked the Spirit. "Yes, I do remember; what about it?" "Well, that was me! And Alex, didn't you see the biggest and poorest old rabbit that you ever saw in your life as you went to see Ol' Jack Bell this evening?" "Yes," replied Porter. "Well, that was also me!" the Spirit gleefully exclaimed.

Porter had almost reached his farm by this time. The Spirit had gone from a simple, question-and-answer dialog, to an uncontrolled fit of laughter that lasted until Porter reached his front porch and hurriedly locked the door. The Spirit returned to the Bell home and commenced its nightly torment and demonstrations, describing in vivid detail how it had scared "Ol' Alex Porter" on his way home.

CHAPTER TEN

The Terror Escalates

A S IF THE SPIRIT'S random demonstrations, acts of violence, and animal-like apparitions were not baffling enough, the Spirit now set its sights on further confusing the Bells and others by assimilating the voices and characters of four, distinct entities that it collectively referred to as the "witch family."

The Witch Family – Multiple Entities

In addition to assimilating the voices of people in the community and occasionally speaking in its own voices, the Spirit's introduction of the "witch family" brought new voices and characters never heard of before, which ultimate proved to be the most remarkable demonstration ever performed by the Spirit.

The first character, "Blackdog," spoke in a rough, feminine tone and was the self-proclaimed head of the "witch family." Both the characters of

"Mathematics" and "Cypocryphy" spoke with the voices of young girls, and the character of "Jerusalem" spoke with the voice of a young boy.

Almost every evening for several months, the "witch family" made its presence known by putting on "shows" at the Bell home for everyone present. Each demonstration commenced with a series of faint whispers, usually right after the candles flickered out for no apparent reason. The "witch family" began each demonstration by filling the room with the odor of corn whiskey, which "Blackdog" said they had taken from nearby Gardner's still. A reason was never given as to why the "witch family" seemed to be intoxicated during most of its demonstrations.

Often boasting slurred speech and overly festive attitudes, the "witch family" sang hymns and gabbed with the Bells and their visitors, sometimes all night long. As the self-proclaimed leader, "Blackdog" always had the final word and often shouted profanities at other members of the "witch family."

The "witch family" demonstrations were not confined just to the evening hours and at the Bell home, however. Demonstrations took place at other times and places as well, and often proved more frightening than those that took place at the Bell home. One such case of a daytime "witch family" demonstration took place when the "witch family" appeared at the farm of Alex and Esther Porter one afternoon.

Apparition at the Porter Farm

Elizabeth Bell arose one morning and decided it would be a good day to visit her sister, Esther. After a quick breakfast, she proceeded to the Porter farm where Esther greeted her at the door. Esther's husband, Alex, was away doing some construction work at nearby Fort's Mill, so Elizabeth and Esther were the only people at the farm that day. What they witnessed later that afternoon was one of the most baffling and terrifying accounts of Spirit ever told or written.

As Esther began to cross the road to collect eggs from the hen house, she casually glanced down the road and noticed a pale-looking young woman walking towards her. Eager to properly greet the woman, she quickly gathered up the eggs and returned to the road. Upon returning to the road, she approached the woman who was then standing directly in front of the house and brushing her long, dark hair.

Thinking she recognized the woman as being one of her new neighbors, Esther politely greeted her and tried to strike up a conversation. The woman stood speechless, staring off into the distance as she continued brushing her hair. After having been ignored for some time and sensing that the woman was troubled about something, Esther walked into the house and told Elizabeth about the woman. Elizabeth said she had been watching the young woman through the window and noticed that she looked to be frightened or preoccupied with something.

After a half-hour, Esther and Elizabeth looked out the window again and noticed that the woman had not moved. They both grew very frightened, as they knew something different about the young woman. Her pale skin and seemingly obscure demeanor made her like no woman they had ever seen before.

After several minutes, the woman climbed onto the fence and sat there. She tucked her hair and put her bonnet back on, and then climbed down and began walking across the road toward the hen house. She finally veered away from the hen house and walked out into the middle of a small field that contained several saplings and a large, knotty log. Neither Elizabeth nor Esther could figure out who this woman was and why she was acting so strangely.

Suddenly, and seemingly out of nowhere, came two little girls and one little boy who joined the woman in the field. Each of them, including the pale woman, grabbed a sapling and bent it in half. All four began bouncing up and down on the saplings as if they were at play.

Esther's husband was returning by this time, and she quickly ran outside and told him about what was happening in the field across the road. Taking a look for himself, Alex Porter saw the saplings bouncing up and down but not the young woman and children who were sitting on them. Esther and Elizabeth were still able see them, however. Realizing that both women were terrified, Porter suggested that the figures bouncing on the saplings were "witch" apparitions and that he would take care of the problem if Esther brought him his gun.

While Esther was fetching the gun, Elizabeth saw the woman and children jump down from the saplings and take cover behind the knotty log. When Esther returned with the gun, Elizabeth asked Alex Porter to shoot next to a large knot near the middle of the log where she had seen the little boy raise his head for a split second. Porter fired a shot but nothing happened. They found nothing but the bent saplings and a mark where Porter's shot had grazed the log upon inspecting the field a few minutes after the apparition took place.

When the "witch family" visited the Bell home that evening, "Blackdog" exclaimed, "Ol' Alex Porter sure is a good shot. He shot 'Jerusalem' from seventy-five yards and broke his arm!"

A Sick Dog at the Door

Just before retiring later that same evening, the Bells and several visitors heard a strange, panting sound coming from outside the front door. John Bell opened the door and found a stray, black dog standing on the porch, looking as if was in need of attention. As Bell held the door open, the dog slowly walked into the family room where Elizabeth and John Jr. began petting it. The dog let out several short growls and they quickly backed away from it.

Fearing that the dog was sick and a possible threat to his family's health, John Bell fetched his gun and started to take the dog outside. Lucy Bell talked him out of killing the dog, which at that very second rolled several times across the floor in the direction of the door and exited quickly. The Spirit, speaking with the voice of "Blackdog," spoke up and exclaimed, "Look out, Ol' Jack, here comes Jerusalem!"

After several uneventful minutes, John Bell inquired, "Where is Jerusalem?" "There he is, on the wall!" replied the Spirit. The Bells and their guests began looking at the walls and soon noticed a bug crawling up the side wall. "Well, if that is Jerusalem, I will kill him!" exclaimed John Bell. Bell killed the bug. Now roaring with laughter, the Spirit yelled, "Lord Jesus, what a fool I did make of Ol' Jack Bell!"

The "witch family" demonstrations were very frightening and intense when they occurred; however, it was only a short time until the "witch family" ceased its demonstrations. It was never heard from again in the 1800's.

Elizabeth's Problems Escalate

All during the period of the "witch family" demonstrations, the Spirit maintained its persistent tormenting of the Bell family. Covers were jerked, rats continued gnawing at the bedposts, John Bell was kicked and slapped from one end of the house to the other, and Elizabeth was still being beaten within inches of her life almost every night.

Over time, Elizabeth developed many scars on her arms where the Spirit pinched her repeatedly until she bled. Her face was bruised and covered with handprints most of the time as well, because the Spirit frequently slapped her face and pulled her hair. Her two closest friends, Theny Thorn and Rebecca Porter, supported and comforted her throughout her trials and tribulations and never let her down in time of need.

The Spirit Spanks a Baby

Elizabeth often spent the night with friends and neighbors in hopes of getting relief from the Spirit's constant torment, a tactic that was successful only a few times before the Spirit began following and tormenting her and others everywhere she went.

On one occasion, the Spirit followed her to the home of John and Martha Johnston, where as soon as she began to fall asleep it commenced disturbing the entire Johnston home by pulling covers, whistling, and turning over chairs. The ruckus quickly awoke the Johnstons' new baby, Nancy, and her mother assured her that everything was all right and rocked her back to sleep.

The disturbances soon started up again, and baby Nancy was once again awake and crying. Angrily, the Spirit exclaimed, "Martha, why don't you slap that child and make it behave itself? If you won't, I will!" Less than a minute later, everyone in the Johnston home heard the sounds of slapping followed by baby Nancy's ear-piercing screams. They rushed to her cradle but found nothing out of the ordinary. Baby Nancy soon stopped crying and remained quiet for the rest of the night.

It finally reached the point that Elizabeth could not spend the night with friends because her presence invited the Sprit, which in turn harmed not only her, but her friends and their families as well. Joshua Gardner eventually found out about the Spirit's torturing Elizabeth and remained supportive of her at all times. They grew closer together in a very short time, and Joshua spent many hours at the Bell home comforting Elizabeth after being abused. Elizabeth and the rest of her family were grateful to Gardner for the attention and compassion he showed her, and were thrilled about their courtship. However, not everyone was happy about it.

Powell Learns of Elizabeth's Courtship

Professor Richard Powell had the personal misfortune of finding out about Elizabeth and Joshua's courtship when he paid one of his customary, Friday afternoon visits to the Bell farm and overheard Lucy Bell happily telling some other visitors about Joshua and Elizabeth's courtship. Being eleven years Elizabeth's senior, he made every attempt to conceal his feelings for her and the heartbreak he felt upon learning of the courtship. Powell's fondness for Elizabeth had been obvious for quite some time; however, nobody ever commented about it.

The Spirit Denounces Elizabeth's Courtship

Another party was unhappy about Elizabeth and

Joshua's courtship — the Spirit. Convinced that their courtship would continue and eventually blossom into marriage, the Spirit often whispered repeatedly in a faint, melancholy voice, "Please Betsy Bell, don't have Joshua Gardner. Please Betsy Bell, don't marry Joshua Gardner." Elizabeth and Joshua could not go anywhere to be alone and talk without hearing the Spirit plead this sorrowful cry all around them, in the wind and trees, in the ripples of the Red River, and deep in the forest.

Although greatly troubled by the Spirit's disapproval of their courtship, Elizabeth and Joshua agreed to hold strong regardless of any consequences they might suffer as a result. The Spirit was often asked why it opposed their courtship, but the only answer ever given was, "Betsy Bell, you will never have happiness if you marry Joshua Gardner. It is best that you not marry him, and future generations will prove me invariably correct."

This empty, meaningless answer served very little purpose other than to further fuel the perplexity already associated with the Spirit's origin, identity, and purpose — once again eliciting the question, "Who or what are you, and what do you want?"

CHAPTER ELEVEN

The Spirit is Named "Kate"

AFTER MUCH STUDY and careful planning, Reverend James Gunn posed this question to the Spirit in a way that a truthful answer was the only option. The Spirit acknowledged that it could never lie to a preacher and that the question as posed by Reverend Gunn could not be evaded.

The Spirit Claims to be Kate Batts

The Spirit then explained, "I am nothing but Old Kate Batts' witch, determined to torment Ol' Jack Bell out of his life." After the Spirit made this startling revelation to Reverend Gunn, many people in the community came forward to say they had felt the Spirit had something to do with Kate Batts all along because of her eccentric nature and sometimes-questionable actions.

Kate and Frederick Batts lived about two miles from the Bell farm on what is now known as Bell's Cross Road. The Batts family was large — consisting of Kate and Frederick, one son, and five daughters. Mrs. Batts handled most of the family's business because her husband was an invalid.

The trees in the foreground denote where Kate and Frederick Batts' house stood.

A "large" woman with a flair for using big words out of context, Kate Batts was considered pompous and outspoken. She was frequently the subject of gossip in the community, especially when it came to the popular belief that she was looking for a man to replace her invalid husband. Although an avid churchgoer, Mrs. Batts never arrived on time because she walked everywhere she went. Before leaving her farm, she would place a blanket across her mule's back as if she was going to ride; however, she instead walked next to the mule for the entire journey.

Kate Batts' Odd Ways

Many people suspected Kate Batts of practicing

Black Magic and other forms of the occult because of her sometimes secretive ways and the strange things that often befell those who crossed her. It seemed that anyone who became involved in a dispute with Mrs. Batts soon met with a debilitating accident or sickness.

She was also known to collect a brass pin from every woman she met. It was believed by many that the collector of a brass pin held a certain "power" over the person from whom they collected the pin. The Spirit made mention of this on several occasions, exclaiming, "Ol' Kate Batts' sticks the pins in an old stump on the Bell place and then tells me who to stick with them." Both John and Elizabeth Bell often felt a stinging sensation that they described as feeling like they were being stuck with pins, and the other Bell children often found pins sticking out of their beds and pillows just before retiring in the evenings.

Mrs. Batts' actions were unpredictable and sometimes downright humorous. Several years before the Sprit came to visit the Bells, Kate Batts attended a revival and rode a man's back like a horse, causing the revival to prematurely end, and sending everyone out the door in laughter. People laughed about this incident for weeks.

Kate Batts Creates an Uproar

Revivals were very popular in the early Nineteenth Century, and everyone who attended became enthusiastic and overtaken by the Holy Spirit. One evening, Red River Baptist Church held a revival with a guest minister, Reverend Thomas Felts. Reverend Felts had a very direct way of preaching that usually had everyone in a Spiritual frenzy within minutes of his opening remarks.

At the height of the revival, Joe Edwards was down on all fours begging the Lord to forgive him for his many sins. Edwards was a known sinner and his "conversion" was of particular interest to others in the community. As he continued his crying and fervent prayer, everyone cheered him until, all of the sudden, Kate Batts entered the room and made her way over to Edwards. Without saying a word, she spread her skirt across his back and sat on him.

Not seeing what had just happened because he was facing the floor, Edwards thought that he was in a struggle with Satan and that the devil was on top of him. He screamed louder and louder, and then cried, "Oh I am sinking, sinking! Oh take my burden Jesus and make the devil turn me loose or I will go down, down, and be lost forever in torment. Oh save me, save me blessed Lord!" Concerned about Edwards' physical condition, a deacon offered to escort Mrs. Batts to a seat. She replied, "No thank you; this is so consoling to my disposition that I feel amply corrugated." "But you are crowding the mourner!" exclaimed the deacon. "Oh, that doesn't disburse my perspicuity; I'm a very plain woman and do love to homigate near the altar where the Lord is making confugation among the sinners. Yes, bless Jesus! Let him suffocate; he's getting closer to the Lord!" replied Mrs. Batts.

Edwards' arms and legs soon gave way to Mrs. Batts' enormous weight, and two deacons pulled her off his back just as he collapsed. Still not knowing what had happened, Edwards arose and fervently proclaimed his deliverance. Kate Batts then yelled, "Bless the Lord, bless my soul, Jesus is so good to devolve his poor critters from the consternation of Satan's mighty dexterity!" Reverend Felts made some closing remarks and quickly dismissed all in attendance. The entire congregation was roaring with laughter, including John Bell and his family.

As she was preparing to leave, Mrs. Batts noticed Bell's fervent laughter and walked over to confront him. "Oh yes, old John Bell, you have your broad acres and your great big home; and the future may look bright to you now, but just wait and see what changes soon befall you and another member of your family," she warned. Bell continued laughing and dismissed the incident as another one of the "lectures" that Mrs. Batts was known to give those she did not like. People all over the community laughed about Joe Edwards' encounter with Mrs. Batts for weeks.

Kate Batts is Scrutinized

The incident that most fueled the stigma associated with Kate Batts involved one of her neighbors, Emily Paine, who became frustrated after seeing no sign of butter after two hours of vigorous churning. Exhausted and already familiar with Mrs. Batts' reputation, Mrs. Paine decided that Kate Batts had probably "bewitched" the milk.

In her frustration, she threw a hot poker into the milk, exclaiming, "There, Kate Batts, you're finished!" As the day went by, Mrs. Paine could not seem to get the churn and Mrs. Batts off her mind — an unrelenting curiosity had set in. After some thought, she fabricated an excuse to visit Mrs. Batts and then proceeded to the Batts farm. Upon arriving, she found Mrs. Batts nursing a badly burned and blistered right hand. Mrs. Batts explained that she had accidentally picked up a hot poker by the wrong end earlier that morning.

The Spirit's New Nickname

As the news of Emily Paine's remarkable

encounter traveled throughout the countryside, more people became of the opinion that Kate Batts was directly involved with the disturbances at the Bell farm. People began referring to Kate Batts as a "witch" and forbade their children from going near her farm or playing with her children. She became very upset when she learned that she was the suspected culprit behind the disturbances.

Kate Batts visited everyone in the community, including the Bells, proclaiming her innocence, and vowing that she would find "the corrigendum that dared to splavicate her character with the spirifications of John Bell's 'witch,' and would show him the perspicuity in the 'constipation' of the law." Despite Mrs. Batts' pleas and a lack of any credible evidence connecting her with the disturbances, many people, including the Bells, began calling the Spirit a name that it would answer to from this point forward. No longer was the Spirit referred to as a Spirit, but was simply called, "Kate."

Despite the Spirit's apparent satisfaction with her new name, "Kate," she continued relentlessly tormenting John Bell and his family as she had been for the past two years. The only difference was that the Spirit answered to the new name.

CHAPTER TWELVE

Evil to Some and Good to Others

JOHN BELL AGED A GREAT DEAL over the two years since the disturbances began — his hair had become almost completely gray and he often carried dark circles below his eyes. Eating also became more of a problem for Bell because of his worsening affliction. Showing no mercy for Bell, Kate continued her antics of slapping and sticking pins in him, and reiterating her vow to kill him. Although John Bell and his daughter Elizabeth seemed to be the main targets of Kate's evil deeds, other members of the Bell family had their own share of problems.

"Kate" Empties the Milk Viles

One of the Bells' neighbors, Betsy Sugg, decided paid Lucy Bell a visit one day. The two ladies sat down and talked for several minutes, then Mrs. Bell asked, "Betsy, you haven't seen our new dairy house, have you?" "Why no, Lucy; I didn't even know

about it. How long have you had it?" replied Mrs.
Sugg. "John Jr., Drewry and Frank Miles built it for
me about three weeks ago," replied Mrs. Bell; "come
look at it with me, it's arranged nicely and I'm very
proud of it."   "Yes, I'd be delighted!" Mrs. Sugg
responded.

The two ladies walked across the back yard and to
the dairy house, where upon unlocking the door and
entering, Mrs. Bell exclaimed "Oh no! The milk is
gone!   And the basins have even been covered!"
"What do you think happened?" Mrs. Sugg inquired.
"Apparently some of Kate's mischief," replied Mrs.
Bell, "she is always playing some such prank as
this."

"Kate" Kicks Drewry's Chair

When inside the house, Drewry Bell frequently sat
in a chair in the corner of the family room and liked
to lean back so the top would rest at an angle against
a desk. Many times when he sat in the chair, the
desk was suddenly pulled from behind it — throwing
him to the floor and leaving his feet poised in the air.
The angle at which he leaned made no difference,
and the desk was too heavy to have accidentally slid
across the floor because of Drewry's weight. John
Jr., who was much taller and heavier than Drewry,
could lean back in the chair as far as he wanted
without the desk moving.

In addition to playing tricks with chairs and
disturbing the Bell children in other ways, Kate was
known to have spanked them on occasion. Her
spankings were always loud and intense, and
remembered forever by those at the receiving end.

Joel's Spanking

In his manuscript, "Our Family Trouble," Richard

Williams Bell gave his own eyewitness account of his younger brother, Joel, receiving a spanking at the hands of Kate:

"It happened that Joel and myself were left to occupy a room alone one night, and were troubled less than usual in the early part of the night, but Kate put in good time just before day. It was quite a cold morning, and rather too early to get up, but Kate continued pulling the cover off and jerking my hair, and I got out of bed and dressed myself.

Joel, however, was much vexed, and said some ugly things about 'Old Kate,' and gathering up the cover from the floor, he rolled himself up in it for another nap. Directly, the witch snatched it from him again. Joel became enraged, pulling at the cover while Kate seemed to be hawking and spitting in his face, and he had to turn loose the cover.

This made Joel raving mad, and he laid flat on his back, kicking with all his might and calling old Kate the meanest kind of names. 'Go away from here, you nasty old thing!' he exclaimed. Kate became furious also, exclaiming, 'You little rascal, I'll let you know who you are talking to.'

That moment, Joel felt the blows falling fast and heavy, and no boy ever received such a spanking as he got that morning, and he never forgot it. It was frightful. I could do nothing for his relief. He yelled frantically with all of his might, arousing the whole house, nor did his punisher cease spanking until father entered the door with a light, finding him almost lifeless. The blows sounded like the spanking of an open heavy hand, and certainly there was no one in the room but Joel and myself; and if there had been, there was no way of escaping except by the door which father entered, and that would have been impossible unobserved." [28]

Aside from the torment that Kate put the Bell children through, she sometimes did things that appeared to be for their own good. On one such occasion, Richard, Elizabeth, and her friend, Rebecca Porter, averted a possible tragedy by heeding Kate's warning about an approaching storm while horseback riding.

"Kate" Saves Children from Storm

They went horseback riding all around the countryside, eventually ending up the bend of the Red River on the north end of the farm. This very pretty spot boasted lots of poplar trees, wildflowers, and other plants. Dark clouds and strong winds began rolling in soon after they arrived, and limbs began falling from trees all around them.

Kate had warned them not to go because of a dangerous storm quickly approaching before they left the house that morning. The children often heard Kate say such things, only to find out later that she merely wanted them to stay inside and not go out and enjoy themselves. However, this time, the warning was genuine and certainly in their best interest.

As the bottom fell out and a cold, drenching rain began to fall, Kate yelled to the children, "If you don't cross the river right now, some of you will be killed!" Frightened by the weather and the urgency inherent in Kate's voice, the children quickly prepared to cross the river. Because of the roaring thunder, the horses

---

[28] Richard Williams Bell, *Our Family Trouble*, 1846 (Mini-Histories: Nashville, 1985).

spooked and became difficult to control — refusing to do anything but rare up and walk in the direction away from the river; the area opposite of where Kate said was safe.

"You little fools! Hold tight now and say nothing to the horses!" Kate yelled.   The horses suddenly calmed, turned around, and then carried the children across the river where they waited until the storm passed over.   Through the mist and fog brought about by the storm, the children noticed that the area they had just been in was strewn with fallen trees, some of which were more than six feet in diameter.

A Rescue in the Cave

On another occasion, Elizabeth and several of her friends went to explore the cave by the Red River on the north end of the farm and, thanks to Kate, averted a potentially tragic situation.

After entering and making their way some 500 feet back into the cave, they were forced to get on their hands and knees to continue through the narrowing passageway. The boy leading the group was walking about ten yards in front of the others. He stopped at one point to peer into a narrow opening in the wall to see what was on the other side. When he tried to look around and yell for the others to come with him, he discovered that his head was stuck in a crevice. Now very nervous and screaming for help, the boy accidentally dropped his candle and the cave became completely dark.

The others became frightened, and the echoes of the boy's screams in the darkness made it impossible for them to know where he was. Suddenly, the cave mysteriously lit up and Kate's voice exclaimed, "I'll get you out!" The boy felt something grab his feet and pull, which in turn freed his head from the crevice. This strong and invisible force did not let go of the boy until it had pulled him all the way back to the cave's entrance.

"Kate's" Adoration for Lucy Bell

Although Kate sometimes helped the children when they appeared to be in danger, she was particularly fond of Lucy Bell. She often commented, "Ol' Luce is a good woman." Kate often conversed with Mrs. Bell about issues of the day and different goings-on in the Red River community and her home state of North Carolina.

Mrs. Bell's Illness

In September of 1819, Lucy Bell experienced a bout with pleurisy and was confined to her bed for nearly three weeks. The Bell family and Dr. Hopson were very concerned about her health because she had grown weaker than was expected and had completely lost her appetite. The most concerned entity of all, however, was Kate.

Kate stayed by Lucy Bell's side day and night, saying over and over, "Luce, poor Luce, I am so sorry you are sick. Don't you feel better, Luce? What can I do for you, Luce?" She also sang beautiful hymns to Mrs. Bell to help lift her Spirits. When she asked for something, Kate always told her family or the slaves where to find the item. When Mrs. Bell awoke each morning, Kate would always ask, "How do you feel this morning, Luce? Did you rest well through the night? Don't you want to hear a song, Luce?" to which Mrs. Bell often replied, "Yes Kate, sing something sweet." Kate knew many hymns, both traditional and her own creations.

KATE'S SONG

Come my heart and let us try
For a little season
Every burden to lay by
Come and let us reason.

What is this that casts you down?
Who are those that grieve you?
Speak and let the worst be known,
Speaking may relieve you.

Christ by faith I sometimes see
And he doth relieve me,
But my fears return again,
These are they that grieve me.

Troubled like the restless sea,
Feeble, faint and fearful,
Plagued with every sore disease,
How can I be cheerful? [29]

Despite being very ill and weak, Mrs. Bell always thanked Kate for singing to her, saying, "Thank you Kate; that was so sweet and beautiful, it makes me feel better."

One day at the height of Lucy Bell's illness, Kate said to her, "Luce, poor Luce, how do you feel now? Hold out your hands, Luce, and I will give you something." As she held out her hands, hazelnuts fell from the ceiling. Witnesses were so astonished that they checked the roof to make sure there was no opening from where the nuts could have dropped.

---

[29] Dr. Charles Bailey Bell, *The Bell Witch: A Mysterious Spirit*, 1934.

After several minutes had passed without Mrs. Bell eating the hazelnuts, Kate inquired, "Say Luce, why don't you eat the hazelnuts?" "I am sorry, Kate, but I am not strong enough to crack them," Mrs. Bell replied. "Well, I will crack some for you!" exclaimed Kate. The nuts suddenly cracked open on the bed next to Mrs. Bell, where she ate a good number of them and thanked Kate for her kindness.

Another similar incident occurred the following evening when Kate came to inform Mrs. Bell about the birth of a baby at John Johnston's house. After a short conversation, grapes fell from the ceiling and landed on the bed next to Mrs. Bell, just as the hazelnuts had the day before. Despite her illness and poor appetite, Mrs. Bell ate all of the grapes and went on to fully recover from her illness a short time later. Kate was once again happy.

One evening several weeks later, the Bells and some guests were sitting in the family room discussing Kate's demonstrations with the grapes and hazelnuts when, all of the sudden, Kate's voice rang out, "Who wants some grapes?" In no time, fresh grapes began falling from the ceiling and into Elizabeth's hands. The grapes were eaten and enjoyed by all who were present. Kate's sometimes-good deeds did not stop here. She also had a fondness for Martha Bell, wife of John Bell's eldest son, Jesse.

Stockings for Martha Bell

Martha Bell was sitting on her front porch late one afternoon peeling apples when she began hearing a faint, buzzing sound nearby. Having had a number of previous encounters with Kate, she easily recognized the buzzing sounds. "What do you want, Kate? Speak out so I can understand you," asked

Martha Bell. "Pots, I have brought you a present to keep in remembrance of me when you go to your far away new home. Will you accept it?" "Why certainly, Kate, I will gladly accept any present you may bring. What is it?" [1]

Out of thin air, a neatly wrapped package fell and landed in her lap. She opened the package and found a pair of black silk stockings inside. Kate then proceeded to tell her, "I brought it, Pots; see what a nice pair of stockings. I want you to keep them for your burial, to remember me, and never wear them." After thanking Kate, Mrs. Bell examined the stockings and discovered a small strange-looking spot in one area. Kate then spoke up and declared, "That is blood! They killed a beef at Kate Batts' this morning and the blood splattered on the stocking."

Martha Bell told her husband about the incident when he returned from the fields later that afternoon. Curious about the validity of Kate's explanation of the blood, Jesse Bell paid a surprise visit to the Batts farm to see what he might learn through casual conversation and observation. Upon arriving, Mrs. Batts greeted Bell and exclaimed, "I am very glad you came to visit! I was just thinking of you and Martha earlier today. We killed a nice beef this morning and I had intended to bring some to Martha but didn't get around to it." After some general conversation, Mrs. Batts gave Jesse some of the meat and sent him on his way.

It would appear that while Kate was very kind to most women, she treated men in a cruel manner. This was not always the case, however. She treated the Johnstons, Reverend Fort, and the Gunns very kindly – often citing their strong religious convictions as being the reason why. There was, however, one man in particular who Kate held a much greater and different fondness for — William Porter.

"Kate" Sleeps with William Porter

Porter was a bachelor who lived on Sturgeon Creek not far from the Bell and Johnston farms. He was a good friend of the Bells and spent many nights in their home watching Kate's demonstrations and trying to help shed any light he could on the mystery. Over time, Kate developed a fondness for Porter and began to engage him in flirtatious and otherwise unnecessary conversations.

After building a large fire in his fireplace and climbing into bed one cold night, Porter began hearing what sounded like scratching and thumping at the side of his bed. Then, in a soft voice, Kate said to him, "Billy, I have come to sleep with you and keep you warm. It's a very cold night and I know you could use the company." Knowing there was nothing he could do to change his predicament, Porter responded by saying, "Well, okay; but you had better behave yourself."

He then felt a scaly, slithery, creature crawl up underneath the covers and lay beside him. He held onto the covers tightly as he felt them being slowly pulled away. His tight and powerful grip proved to be no match for "Kate," however; the covers were pulled completely off him and assumed the form of a human body lying beside him. Angered by Kate's insistence on hogging the covers, Porter decided to burn her, as it appeared the perfect opportunity had finally availed itself.

He quickly rose out of bed and put his arms around the covered body, then lifted it and ran towards the fireplace with it. The sheet grew heavier with each step he took, and a foul odor began emanating from it. After taking just a few more steps, Porter became so exhausted and consumed by the foul odor that he dropped the sheet just before reaching the fireplace. Wanting to finish the task, Porter quickly stepped outside to get some fresh air and regain his composure. Upon going back into the house, he found the sheet completely unraveled and no trace of the foul odor that had filled the room only minutes earlier.

CHAPTER THIRTEEN

"Kate's" Hatred for the Slaves

DESPITE HER ADORATION FOR LUCY BELL and others, Kate often reiterated her hatred for the slaves — which was nearly as strong as her hatred for John Bell. She enjoyed playing pranks on the slaves and often spoke of what she called their "foul smell." While Chloe seemed to enjoy an uneventful relationship with Kate, her relationship with Chloe's children was anything but uneventful. This was especially the case with Harry, a house servant who was responsible for starting the morning fire to warm up the house.

Harry and the Fire

Several mornings in a row, John Bell awoke to find the house unusually cold. After learning that Harry had not been starting the fire early enough, Bell scolded him. Despite Bell's scolding Harry about the fire for several days in a row, the problems continued and Bell became frustrated.

Kate apparently did not like being cold in the mornings, either. On one cold morning, she said to Bell, "Never mind, Ol' Jack, don't fret. I will attend to the rascal the next time he is belated!" After several days of being punctual, Harry was later making the fire one morning than he had ever been. As Bell harshly scolded Harry, Kate interrupted and exclaimed, "Hold on Ol' Jack, didn't I tell you not to pester? I will attend to this rascal!"

As it was, Harry was on his knees and blowing into the fireplace to make a blaze. Suddenly, something grabbed him by the neck and began beating him mercilessly. The sound of a piece of wood like a paddle was heard all throughout the Bell home. Nobody who rushed into the room saw anything that resembled a paddle; however Harry's yelling, which worsened the beating, was heard by everyone both inside and outside. Harry made the fire in plenty of time each morning from this point forward.

Harry was the only slave known to have received a beating from Kate, however his sister, Philis, received a spanking from her mother as the result of a prank played by Kate.

Philis' Legs Become Locked

Late one afternoon while waiting on dinner, the Bell children decided to test their athletic abilities by engaging in some contests of strength and agility. They rolled, jumped, and put their feet behind their heads. From the kitchen, Philis watched with amazement, as she had never seen anyone do such tricks. The next day, she decided to try the same maneuvers by herself in an upstairs room.

After trying for some time and finally getting her feet behind her head, she realized that they were stuck and she could not move. After spending several minutes trying to free herself but to no avail, Philis heard her mother calling from downstairs. Embarrassed, she responded, "I'll be there in just a minute, I promise!" After calling several more times, her mother became frustrated and went upstairs to spank her. Finding Philis in a position more than suitable for a spanking, her mother spanked her very hard and then scolded her for not obeying her orders to come downstairs.

Philis had become able to move by this time and quickly freed herself. Just after she explained to her mother that Kate had locked her legs so she couldn't move, the room filled with Kate's gleeful laughter and an ear-piercing exclamation, "That will teach you, you filthy little rascal. Don't be upstairs playing while you should be downstairs helping your mother. The both of you also need a bath. I despise how you slaves smell, especially you two and that smelly big sister of yours, Anky!" [m] Four years Philis' senior, Anky worked in the fields every day and was regarded by the Bells as one of their best field slaves.

"Kate" Finds Anky

It was a well-known fact that Kate never visited any of the slave cabins because she emphatically detested "that old smell," as she put it. Keeping this in mind, Lucy Bell decided to try to outwit Kate by using her aversion to the smell of the slaves against her.

She thought carefully and devised a plan that would possibly rid the Bell home of Kate once and for all. Fearing the possibility of Kate catching and punishing her, Mrs. Bell decided to keep her plan a secret from everyone, including the rest of her family.

One afternoon Mrs. Bell paid a visit to Anky and told her, "Anky, I think that you would make a wonderful house girl. Your mother and sister have all the chores they can handle, and your grandmother, Chloe, is almost sixty years old and can't get around like she used to. There is more and more work to be done in the house, and I want you to be my house girl. I will even let you sleep in the same room with me." "Do you reckon that old witch will pester me," asked Anky. Mrs. Bell replied, "Why no, Anky, I don't think she will be anywhere around; and if she is, it would be downstairs bothering our guests. I also want you to keep this a secret so she won't know in the first place that you are sleeping in the house."

That same evening, and before the usual deluge of visitors began to arrive, Anky went into the house and up the stairs to Mrs. Bell's room. After setting up and hiding her pallet underneath the bed, she lay down on it for a long nap knowing that nobody besides Mrs. Bell knew she was there.

The house later filled with visitors who were soon exposed to Kate's usual demonstrations. While giving the visitors a lecture about not speaking in John Bell's defense, Kate all of the sudden stopped and angrily exclaimed, "There is a bad smell in this house, and it's 'Ank;' I smell her under Old Luce's bed and she's got to get out!" A loud noise coming from upstairs was suddenly heard. Anky, with her head and face covered with white foam, ran down the stairs exclaiming, "Oh missus, missus, it's going to spit me to death. Let me out, let me out!" Mrs. Bell opened the door and Anky ran back to her cabin as fast as she could, crying and screaming all the way.

Kate then set her sights on Mrs. Bell, "Say Luce, did you bring her in here?" "Yes," replied Mrs. Bell; "I told Anky that she might go under my bed where she would be out of the way and still be able to hear you talk and sing with that ever-sweet voice of yours." Not phased by Mrs. Bell's seemingly good intentions, Kate responded, "Nobody but you, Luce, would have thought of such a smart trick as that; and if anyone else had done it, I would have killed 'Ank.' Lord, Jesus, I won't get over that smell in a month! The only thing I've smelled any worse than that was when I turned Old Dean into a mule one night and he got too scared."

CHAPTER FOURTEEN

Andrew Jackson Visits "Kate"

OF ALL THE VISITORS who came from around the world to investigate and witness Kate's demonstrations, perhaps the most prominent was Major General Andrew Jackson, who lived in nearby Nashville at the time.

Jackson was a military leader, lawyer, and statesman. After fighting in the Revolutionary War at a very young age, he studied law and became a lawyer. Joining the Tennessee Militia in 1801, he enjoyed a long and decorated military career that included the Battle of Horseshoe Bend in 1814 and the Battle of New Orleans in 1815.

Both Jesse Bell and John Jr. had fought under Jackson; Jesse at Horseshoe Bend and New Orleans, and John Jr. at New Orleans. Already aware of the Bell disturbances, Jackson, upon learning that Jesse and John Jr.'s family was the same Bell family that was being tormented, decided to pay a visit to the Bell farm to see for himself just what Kate was all about.

Jackson's Wagon is Stopped

General Jackson made his visit to the Bell farm in late 1819. As the Jackson entourage approached the Bell property line, the wagon came to a sudden and mysterious halt. The horses spooked and the wagon master repeatedly whipped them but to no avail. The whipping and cursing continued for several minutes before Jackson suddenly exclaimed, "By the eternal, boys, it must be the witch!" After Jackson made this statement, a feeble voice heard coming from the woods nearby said, "Alright General, let the wagon move on, I will see you again tonight." Baffled, Jackson's men checked up and down the road and in the woods, but found no sign of anyone having been there and spoken to them a moment earlier. The entourage then proceeded down the lane and to the Bell home.

Upon his arrival, Jackson had a long and pleasurable discussion with John Bell about the Indians, the Battle of New Orleans, and other topics as his men waited patiently in the family room for Kate to manifest herself.

Jackson's "Witch Tamer" Becomes a Believer

One of the men in Jackson's entourage claimed to be a "witch tamer," and, after several uneventful hours, decided to call upon Kate. He pulled a shiny pistol from his holster and boldly announced his intent to kill her. The man slumped over almost instantly and began moving his body in different directions around the room, screaming, "Oh...oh...oh...No! My God, help me! Oh...Oh...it hurts! I'm being beaten to death and stuck with pins all over! Somebody do something, darnit!" He quickly threw down his pistol and ran out the door, then Kate announced, "There is yet one more 'fraud' in this bunch, and I will identify and properly deal with him tomorrow evening!"

Perplexed and terrified, Jackson's men begged him to leave the place as soon as possible; however, Jackson insisted on staying so he could learn who the other "fraud" in his party was. After some tense discussion, Jackson and his men went outside to their tents to get some much-needed rest. Unable to sleep, and for obvious reason, the men continued begging Jackson to leave the Bell farm.

Jackson remained unmoved by his men's pleading and maintained his position of wanting to stay so he could find out who the other "fraud" in his party was. By noon the next day, however, Jackson and his men had already left the Bell farm and were seen going through Springfield as they headed back to Nashville. It is not known what caused Jackson to change his mind so abruptly and leave the following morning.

Jackson, a popular and well-liked military hero, was quoted as having later said, "I'd rather fight the entire British Army than deal with that thing they call the Bell Witch!"   Jackson later went on to become the President of the United States.

After Jackson and his entourage had left the Bell farm, Kate declared that it was time to finish her mission of "tormenting 'Ol Jack Bell' to his grave." She continued expressing her strong dislike for Bell, often reiterating her vow to make his death the slowest and most painful type possible.   Such remarks increased over time, and Bell's condition worsened all the while.   Kate's acts of violence and ridicule escalated, and John Bell was on the receiving end.

CHAPTER FIFTEEN

John Bell's Final Days

THE AFFLICTION that once affected only Bell's tongue and jaws now affected his entire body. He frequently encountered seizures and other violent episodes that often struck without warning and left him without strength for several days at a time. John Bell's episodes grew more intense and frequent as his health continued to deteriorate.

John Bell's Shoes Fly Off

Early one morning in October of 1820, John Bell and one of his younger sons, Richard, set out walking towards the hog pen to separate some hogs. Shortly after they began their walk, John Bell's shoe quickly flew off his foot. Richard helped him put the shoe back on, securing it with a double knot. After they resumed their walk, Bell's other shoe flew off as quickly as the first one did. Regardless of how tight his shoes were tied, they repeatedly flew off his feet as quickly as Richard could put them back on. This exercise lasted until they reached the hog pen, at which time Bell removed both of his shoes and relaxed his feet before tending to the hogs.

They began walking back to the house after they finished separating the hogs and John Bell's shoes began flying off his feet again, just as they did earlier. Bell suddenly felt a hard blow to his head as he stopped to retie his shoes. He described the blow as a hard, stinging slap in the face. Now very upset and beginning to feel light-headed, Bell sat down on a log beside the road to regain his composure. His body began trembling and his face twitched uncontrollably as he became overtaken by a seizure.

The seizure was not severe, and upon its passing, Bell looked up to the sky and said a long, fervent prayer asking again, "Why?" Feeling much better after having said the prayer and resting for a few minutes, Bell walked back to the house with his son. They encountered no more problems that day.

The Affliction Worsens

Upon returning, John Bell took to his bed for a long nap. Over the next several weeks, he lacked the strength and determination to go out into the fields and spent increasingly more time in bed as his health rapidly deteriorated. He never went outside the house again. What little that was heard from Kate during this time was a far cry from grapes and hazelnuts. She sang louder and more frequently during this period, as if she was celebrating Bell's demise.

Both Lucy and John Jr. stayed by John Bell's side day and night, comforting him and praying for the Almighty to release whatever curse had befell him so he could once again have a normal life. Unfortunately, this would never happen. Friends visited often, but at this late stage of Bell's life, there was nothing they could do but pray for John Bell's deliverance from the malevolent Spirit that had tormented him so long.

It was apparent to those who visited that Kate intended to torment Bell increasingly during his final and most painful days. While Kate refrained from speaking during Bell's last days, she made her presence known by singing hymns in multiple, simultaneous voices, and by covering the dell with flitting candles as she had several years earlier. On occasion, people who came to visit Bell reported hearing the voices of small children quoting scripture and singing hymns as they walked up the lane to the house, and a constant, cold drizzle falling over the dell outside the Bell home at night — all of this reported during John Bell's final days.

The Death of John Bell

One morning in December of 1820, John Bell did not awaken at daybreak as he normally did, so Lucy and John Jr. thought it best to let him sleep until after breakfast. Elizabeth went upstairs to awaken him shortly after breakfast, where she discovered that his breathing had become irregular and that he had apparently lost consciousness. Hearing Elizabeth's cries for help, both Lucy Bell and John Jr. rushed up the stairs to see what had happened.

John Jr. walked over to the cupboard where his father's medicine was stored and discovered that the medicine had been replaced by a smoky-looking vial that was one-third full of an unknown, dark liquid.

After checking with others who knew nothing about how the vial had gotten there, Lucy and John Jr. sent for the family doctor, George Hopson. Despite the seven-mile buggy ride from Port Royal,

Hopson arrived quickly as did Alex Gunn, Frank Miles, John Johnston, and Richard Powell. After carefully examining the vial and its contents, Dr. Hopson reported, "I have no idea what this liquid is or the purpose of it being here; however, I am absolutely sure it's the same odor I detected near Mr. Bell's face!"

After a short period of silence, a shrill voice filled the room and exclaimed, "It's useless for you to try to relieve Ol' Jack, I have got him this time; he will never get up from that bed again!" "No he will not, he is a bad rascal and will spend eternity in hell," exclaimed another voice. "For it is written that repentance is no recourse against the sins of the father," exclaimed the voice of a small child. "For this man dies and suffers the fruits of his evil forever just as other men shall in future generations," the first voice proclaimed. "And it shall be so, and it shall be so," all three voices said in unison.

"Listen! This liquid is something I have never seen before; it's not medicine, and I think it's in my patient's best interest that you tell me what it is and how much you gave him!" Dr. Hopson angrily exclaimed "Doctor, there is no use in trying to engage this worthless, demonic jackass in any type of intelligent conversation," John Jr. exclaimed. Kate then replied to Hopson, saying, "I put it there, and gave Ol' Jack a big dose of it last night while he was asleep, which fixed him!" "Yes, it fixed him," said a child's voice coming from the other side of the room. John Bell suddenly began jerking and turning his head from side to side, trying desperately to say something but to no avail. Bell's mysterious jerks continued for several minutes despite Dr. Hopson's best efforts to calm him. After vomiting several times, he quickly calmed and became unconscious once again. Everyone noticed what looked like whip marks all over his face, however no sounds were heard during Bell's episode.

The group decided to test the vial's contents on the family cat. Alex Gunn caught and held the cat as John Jr. poured some of the liquid into its mouth. The cat fell to its side, stretched and kicked for a short time, and then died. Everyone decided that the vial and its contents should be destroyed at once. Frank Miles volunteered to throw it into the fire. "No, don't do that," ordered Dr. Hopson; "I would like to take this strange vial with me and analyze its contents." "Yes, that is what needs to be done; I want to know what it was that Kate gave to John. If it can kill our cat that quickly, I am sorrowfully afraid that my husband's end is near," said Lucy Bell.

"Oh, this is absolute nonsense! Can you not see that it no longer matters? The man is dying, for God's sake! Can you not let him die in peace so as not to be clouded by the additional controversy of what might be in that bottle? The doctor has much better things to do than play games with this so-called "witch" by analyzing what is in the vial. John Bell is dying! It doesn't matter what is in the vial or how it got there!" Richard Powell angrily exclaimed as he jerked the vial away from Dr. Hopson and threw it into the fire. When the vial hit the fire, a popping sound was heard and it burst into a bright, blue flame that burned out quickly.

John Bell remained in a coma for the rest of the day and night, as Lucy Bell, John Jr. and John Johnston stayed by his side and comforted him. On the following morning, December 20th, John Bell breathed his final breath. Kate began singing hymns and laughing fervently upon his passing, not letting up until the end of the day. Nothing further was heard from Kate until Bell's funeral.

"Kate" Sings at John Bell's Funeral

John Bell was laid to rest in the Bell family cemetery, located on a cedar-covered knoll some 300 yards north of the Bell home. It was a bright winter day, and friends from all over the countryside came to pay their last respects. Bell's funeral, conducted by Reverend Sugg Fort and the Revs. Thomas and James Gunn, was one of the largest ever held in Robertson County. All three preachers were very close friends of the Bells despite John Bell's excommunication from the church two years earlier. As they promised, their respect for him remained until the very end.

As the large crowd of family and friends began to disperse after Bell's burial, Kate began laughing hysterically and sang, "Row me, O Row me, Row me up some brandy O," which continued until the last person had left the cemetery.

John Bell's Unanswered Request

In hopes of being reinstated into the fellowship of Red River Baptist Church, John Bell had in 1819 requested a review of the events that resulted in his excommunication the previous year. The matter was assigned to a committee representing the leadership of five different churches, which recommended Bell's reinstatement.

The matter of Bell's reinstatement frequently appeared on the church meeting agenda but was never taken up, always being "postponed till next conference." At the time of Bell's death, the matter still had not been taken up. The lone entry in the church minutes for the month of December 1820 stated, "No conference in December." [30]

---

[30] *Red River Baptist Church Minutes (1791-1826)*, p. 215.

CHAPTER SIXTEEN

Hearts are Broken

IN THE WEEKS THAT FOLLOWED John Bell's death, many friends and neighbors visited his family to comfort them and share in their grief. The reason or reasons why Kate tormented Bell to his death were no longer of concern, as there was now a great feeling of relief in knowing he was no longer suffering the pain he had been forced to endure in the last four years of his life. Kate's visits, now fewer and less frequent, centered more around Elizabeth than other members of the Bell family. It appeared that she was extending sympathy to Elizabeth by comforting her as she grieved the loss of her father.

Kate ceased abusing Elizabeth and speaking unfavorably of her courtship with Joshua Gardner, and Elizabeth's much-needed feelings of relief were obvious to those around her — her mischievous smile began to reappear, the circles below her eyes and the bruises on her arms went away, the paleness of her face was replaced with a rosy-red complexion, and her mood became very cheerful compared to what it had been the last four years.

Elizabeth's changes were due not only to having gotten over the death of her father, but also renewed optimism in her relationship with Joshua Gardner.

The Relationship Grows Stronger

While Elizabeth's renewed optimism was quite strong, there still existed the fear of the unknown. Did Kate's newly found silence about the relationship mean that she now approved of it? What if she disregarded Kate's earlier warnings about marrying Joshua Gardner if he proposed — would they suffer the same fate as her father? These and other questions often ran through Elizabeth's mind, fueling the constant struggle in her heart between love and fear.

The two lovers spent much time discussing their plans to possibly marry and move far away from the land that had brought them much fear and suffering for so long, sometimes nearly crushing their hearts in an inescapable vise. They were very eager to move away; however, they decided to give the matter more time to make sure Kate did not rescind her implied approval of their courtship.

Joshua Gardner continued his bold and relentless pursuit of Elizabeth, often telling her, "Nothing is stronger than love, and no love is stronger than my love for you; I love you even more than my own life, and no force, no matter how great, can come between us and destroy what we have endured so many hardships to build." The arrival of spring was much awaited, as the winter of 1820 and 1821 had been bitterly cold, gloomy, and tragic — a time that everyone wanted to forget.

Spring Arrives

The spring of 1821 came early and with all its beauty and splendor — the birds singing cheerful melodies in concert with the ripples of the Red River, wildflowers blooming in the meadow and along the river, and the sweet aroma of honeysuckle and budding trees filling the air around the countryside. Spring's arrival blew an uplifting breath of fresh air through the countryside, reviving the smiles and Spirits of those who lived there.

Easter soon came in all its glory, and it was on this day that Joshua Gardner and Elizabeth Bell sealed their mutual intention to spend the rest of their lives together.

A Proposal of Marriage

Joshua came to visit Elizabeth early that morning, and the two lovers took a pleasant stroll through the orchard before taking a seat under their favorite pear tree. After Elizabeth's fervent acceptance of his proposal, Joshua slipped an engagement ring onto her finger. They sat silent and motionless, looking into each other's eyes and embracing in a deep kiss as tears of happiness flowed freely down their cheeks. Smiles came to their faces as they began discussing their future together, and after a happy discussion, they returned to announce their engagement.

Joshua Gardner proposes to Elizabeth Bell under the pear tree. [31]

Visiting the Bell home that morning was John and Calvin Johnston, Reverend Thomas Gunn, Jesse Bell, and Frank Miles. As Joshua held the front door open for Elizabeth, a big smile came to her face, and her eyes began to sparkle as she entered the front room where everyone was sitting.

"Why Miss Betsy, I never seen ya' so happy an full of yourself before! What's goin' on in that purdy little head of yours!" inquired Frank Miles. Embarrassed, Elizabeth turned her head and rested it on Joshua's chest to conceal her blushing from the visitors. Joshua hugged her tightly, and then gave her a pat on the back as he looked in the direction of the others and displayed a bold and happy smile. "I believe there is something they want to tell us," an

---

[31] Engagement photo from *Authenticated History of the Bell Witch*, M.V. Ingram, 1894.

excited Lucy Bell told everyone. "It was your older sister first, then me," Jesse remarked, "and now it's you, little sister. Am I right?" "Oh Jesse, must you rub it in like that?" Elizabeth asked laughingly. "Oh, yes indeed!" replied Jesse.

Standing with his arm around Elizabeth, Joshua Gardner then proclaimed, "It is with the greatest of pleasure that Elizabeth and I inform you that we sealed our mutual and holy commitment to spend the rest of our lives together 'as one' earlier this morning." Smiles came to the faces of everyone in the room, and Elizabeth ran over to her mother and began hugging her. Lucy Bell whispered into her ear, "It is the will of God, it was the will of your father, and it is my will that you marry Joshua and live a lifetime of happiness. I am sure your father is very proud right now." "I know, mother," said Elizabeth, "but it deeply saddens me that he didn't live to see this day," said Elizabeth. "But he is here with us in Spirit, my dear child; and, he will continue to look down and rejoice over the happiness you have found," replied Lucy Bell

"Well, let's see your ring, Elizabeth," Calvin Johnston said, "I know that with all the love Joshua has for you, it must be a real beauty of a ring!" Elizabeth extended her arm, showed the beautiful emerald engagement ring to her mother, and then walked around the room to let the others see it. Following just behind her was Joshua, who after hugging Lucy Bell began receiving congratulatory handshakes and pats on the back from the others.

"Gardner, now you always know'd I think of Miss Betsy like my little sis; so you'd better treat er' rite or ya' know I'll come a lookin' fer' ya'," Frank Miles jokingly remarked. "And I will, too!" exclaimed a happy Reverend Thomas Gunn, "and I hate having to be selfish, but I must be honest and say that I would be most disappointed if I didn't receive the honor of joining your hands as 'one' in the sight of the Lord." "The feeling is mutual, Reverend Gunn," replied Joshua Gardner, "and we are hoping to be married very soon." "Have you lovebirds decided on the big day?" inquired Reverend Gunn.   Elizabeth replied, "No, Reverend; but we will tell you as soon as we decide. You need to be one of the first to know!"

"Well I know what the big news will be at tomorrow's festivities," remarked John Johnston; "many of us have wondered how long it would be until you two decided to take the big step, and the news that you have finally overcome the obstacles to your happiness and are forging ahead will be well-received by everyone; well, almost everyone." "Oh, I think Professor Powell will be most happy to hear the news; he has always cared a great deal about Elizabeth," Lucy Bell remarked. "We shall soon find out!" Johnston exclaimed.

Everyone continued happily discussing Elizabeth and Joshua's engagement, teasing Joshua about treating her well and teasing Elizabeth about how many children they planned to have and what their names would be.   Alex and Esther Porter soon stopped in for a visit and were delighted to hear the good news. After the initial excitement began to die down, discussion shifted to the events planned for the following day, Easter Monday — the day following Easter customarily set aside for picnics, games and fishing along the Red River.   Even the slaves were given the day off to enjoy the fun and festivities.

"What are your plans for tomorrow, Elizabeth?" inquired Esther.   "Joshua and I will be hunting wildflowers, picnicking and fishing with Theny, Alex, Rebecca and James.   We're going to meet out in the orchard first thing in the morning and then go to Brown's Ford together," replied Elizabeth.   "Do they know of the recent excitement in your life?" "No; I was thinking of telling Theny, but Joshua and I decided that we want it to be a surprise for everyone tomorrow!" Elizabeth exclaimed. Joshua then added, "And there's no better way to begin Easter Monday than by sharing our good news with everyone. It will set a nice, warm tone for the day; and who knows, it might just be what it takes to get Alex and James more interested in Theny and Rebecca!"

"Nothing would be more beautiful than you three couples marrying at the same time," Calvin Johnston chimed in. "That would be a most wonderful idea, Mr. Johnston," exclaimed Lucy Bell, "but I don't know that Theny and Rebecca are as close to their suitors as Elizabeth is to Joshua; however I could be wrong!"

Dinnertime was drawing near and the guests began dispersing. Elizabeth walked Joshua to the front door and hugged him goodbye, telling him she would be waiting for him bright and early the next morning.

Easter Monday on the Red River

A clear sky and the sweet scent of honeysuckle and wildflowers over the countryside greeted the dawn of Easter Monday. After an unusually cool night, the rising sun quickly began drying the dew and warming the cool, gentle breeze blowing through the orchard.

Joshua Gardner hurried to the Bell home and found Elizabeth waiting on the front porch. The two joined hands and made their way to the orchard, discussing their happy future as they strolled toward the place they were to meet the other couples. As they neared an opening in the trees, they spotted the other couples talking, laughing, and frolicking.

Theny Thorn was the first to spot Elizabeth and Joshua, and her first words were, "Oh! There you are! I am so happy for you, dear!" Elizabeth's plan to surprise her friends had apparently been foiled; the news of her and Joshua's engagement had already spread around the community. Everyone was happy to hear the good news; that is, with the possible exception of Professor Richard Powell.

"Do you see those beautiful pear trees, arrayed in white, representing the bride of the morning?" asked Elizabeth; "they bow to us a hearty welcome this lovely holiday." "Yes, I see," replied Theny, "they are lovely; but you overlook the peach trees on the other side of the path, dressed in pink. They represent the bridesmaids." "Then I should like to know what these pretty little violets represent which you all are unconsciously mashing under your big feet?" asked Rebecca Porter. "They're Cupid's arrows," answered Joshua; "they cannot be crushed by trampling; see how quickly they rise back up?" "Why yes," exclaimed Elizabeth, "that's why I love them so much; break or bruise one, and it comes out again as fresh as ever!" Alex Gooch then asked, "Please, Miss Elizabeth, what does this refreshing zephyr, which blows such a pleasant gale, represent in your beautiful Easter picture?" "Oh, that is the breath of the bridegroom!" Elizabeth exclaimed. [32]

Picnicking by the River

"Oh, poo!" exclaimed James Long, "please hold up a bit and find your equilibrium. We started out to go fishing, but you girls are about to turn to fairies and

---

[32] M.V. Ingram, *Authenticated History of the Bell Witch* (1894).

take wings on the morning air!" "Yes," agreed Joshua, "lets go fishing; why linger here?" The couples made their way through the orchard, across the meadow, and down to the bank of the Red River where they found many of their friends and neighbors already picnicking, playing, and fishing. After picking some wildflowers and frolicking a bit, the three couples treated themselves to a picnic at the edge of the river.

As they were finishing their food and beginning to clean up the area, they heard the sound of a horse approaching. Professor Powell soon appeared on his black horse, greeting the couples by name and expressing his joy about being there, and reminiscing about how close they all had been when he taught them in school. The couples were overjoyed to see Powell as he had been very popular among his students and they held a great deal of respect for him. After more than an hour of pleasant conversation, Professor Powell politely bade farewell to the couples and wished them good luck with their fishing trip.

Powell Speaks Privately to Elizabeth

After he had mounted his horse and proceeded several yards, Powell turned around and said to Elizabeth, "Miss Elizabeth, would you please join me for a moment over by the bluff? There is an important and rather private matter I wish to discuss with you if Mr. Gardner does not have any objections." Joshua Gardner indicated his approval in his usual pleasant and mannerly style. Elizabeth walked next to Powell's horse as they made their way to a nearby bluff and climbed up to a large rock guarding the mouth of a cave overlooking the river.

Powell then said, "I have heard the exciting news of

your recent engagement, and have been in awe of your beautiful ring for the past hour." "Thank you, Professor Powell!" exclaimed Elizabeth, who was growing uncomfortable because her suspicions of Powell's fondness for her were finally being confirmed. Powell continued, "Miss Elizabeth, I want you to know that you have grown up to be more beautiful and charming than I ever dreamed you could. I admired you very much back in the days when you were my student, but now you have blossomed into the most beautiful, witty and charming woman I have had the honor of knowing since my arrival here some five years ago. I most definitely envy Mr. Gardner's good fortune in having won your hand in marriage; he is such a lucky gentleman."

Despite Professor Powell's obvious attempts at flattery, Elizabeth was becoming uncomfortable and quite frustrated. The notion that Powell was trying to impose feelings of guilt upon her, or solicit her sympathy for his cause, worried Elizabeth because he was the man whom she had always looked up to as an authority figure who was such behavior. Nevertheless, she maintained her composure while he finished.

"Just as I always told your mother, you were the brightest and smartest girl in school, but then she declared that I would spoil you; but I did not, did I?" "I think not, Professor; I hope I don't act like a spoiled girl," Elizabeth responded. "No you do not, and Joshua will bear me out in that. By the way, he is a very fine fellow. That boy never could help loving you, and I never did blame him as you were my little pet also; and I have waited almost as patiently as did Jacob for Rachel, hoping that you and Joshua might forget that young 'school love.' Nevertheless, I have now been very disappointed, and my only wish at this point other than your future happiness is to be present when you wed. Goodbye, I wish you well." [33]

Shocked and at a loss for words, Elizabeth exclaimed, "Professor, I shall let you know when that happens; and I promise that you will be in attendance!" She then rejoined Joshua and her friends at the riverbank to prepare for the long-awaited fishing trip.

The Mysterious Fish

The group broke into couples, each surveying the riverbank for a good place to fish. They had planned on fishing between Brown's Ford and Gorham's Mill; however the good fishing spots along that section of the river had already been taken by the slaves who had arrived much earlier that morning. The couples soon found what looked like some promising fishing holes below Brown's Ford near Clark's Mill, then scattered out along the riverbank and baited their hooks. Joshua and Elizabeth settled farther down the riverbank than the other couples, baiting their hooks and securing their fishing tackle before climbing up on a large, moss-covered rock where the Enchanted Spring empties into the Red River.

Time passed quickly as they discussed the fun and events that had been happening throughout day, including Professor Powell's shocking behavior after having seen Elizabeth's engagement ring. Oblivious to their fishing tackle and the activities of the other couples nearby, Elizabeth and Joshua discussed their wedding day and the new life that their soon-to-be and far-away home would bring them.

Joshua had heard his family speak on many occasions of beautiful and fertile land to the west,

---

[33] M.V. Ingram, *Authenticated History of the Bell Witch* (1894).

near the Tennessee River in Henry County, Tennessee. Elizabeth was overjoyed by the thought of moving to this area and starting a family with Joshua. "Ka-whomp!" All of the sudden, their hearts stopped, and their attention turned to the sounds of a large fish jumping in the river below.

Looking towards the river, Joshua noticed that his float was completely under the water and his fishing pole had been jerked out of the ground and was sliding towards the river's edge. They quickly slid off the rock and dashed over to their fishing tackle, but by the time they got there it was too late. The giant fish had pulled Joshua's fishing pole into the water and was carrying it upstream, much to the amazement of those who had gathered at the riverbank after hearing the noises and seeing the pole being pulled from the ground.

The giant fish swam erratically around the river, darting back and forth between the north and south banks, and then taking an occasional plunge to the bottom before returning to the surface. After swimming about a quarter-mile upstream, the fish turned and swam back downstream in the same manner. As the crowd tried to catch the large fish, it jumped out of the water — shaking its head furiously and freeing itself from the hook.

Those who had seen the fish stood around for a while after the excitement to ponder what kind of fish it might have been. One person guessed it was an "eel," another guessed a large "catfish," and Frank Miles declared that it was a "shark" that had made its way from the sea to the Red River. Everyone returned to their places along the river and baited their hooks in anticipation of catching the large fish if it returned. Joshua and Elizabeth returned to the moss-covered rock and continued their discussion.

Joshua Senses a Problem

"The land to the west will give us a much-needed break from the events past, but is still close enough for us to visit our families each year and send them letters often," Joshua said. "Oh," responded Elizabeth. "And it's very close to the Tennessee River, too. Donelson and several families used that river when they settled at Nashville some years ago. They followed it up to the Ohio River, then crossed over to the Cumberland and went all the way down to Nashville. You know what? I've heard that the Tennessee River boasts some of the biggest catfish this country has ever seen, much bigger than the big fish we just saw!" "Oh," Elizabeth responded as she maintained her trance-like stare at the rock.

"You look as though something is terribly wrong, my dearest. What has happened?" asked Joshua. "Nothing," replied Elizabeth. She trembled and her face began to lose its color as if she had suddenly became ill or seen a ghost. "You can't tell me that. I know you, and I easily notice when something is bothering you. Will you please tell me what's wrong?" asked Joshua. "Ok," replied Elizabeth, "it's not that there is anything wrong, I just 'feel' wrong, like something bad is happening or about to happen. I was on top of the world just minutes ago, but now something is pulling me down and I can't seem to put my finger on what it is." "I offer you my condolences and concern, as I can see that you're not feeling well at all, my dearest," said Joshua; "but I also understand that you and your family have endured much hardship over the last four years, and that human nature doesn't always let us forget such things. It sometimes provides us with chilling reminders of things we would rather forget, and usually when we least expect or need them."

"Thank you for your concern and understanding, my dearest Joshua," Elizabeth said, "but why would such negative feelings manifest themselves while I am sitting here talking to the man I love most in this world?" Joshua replied, "My dearest, I think what you're experiencing is a form of reverse guilt. That is, you have been feeling on top of the world as of late, but because you lived for a period of years in a situation where pain and evil were the norm, your mind is conditioned to manifest feelings of guilt when you are in a loving and peaceful situation – because that is not the norm your mind has been accustomed to for the last four years." "You are so right, Joshua; and I love you with all my heart," replied Elizabeth.

All of the sudden, loud screams were heard echoing throughout the valley and along the riverbank, "Look out, look out! It's coming back!" The large fish was paying a return-visit. It wasn't long until the fish left and the excitement died down; however, the excitement about the fish was no match for what was about to befall the two lovers, an event that would change their lives forever in just a matter of seconds.

"Kate" Ends the Relationship

The gentle breeze suddenly stopped and the once animated valley fell under a grave, eerie silence. The birds stopped singing, the ripples in the river ceased playing their cheerful melody, and the air became so thick that neither Joshua nor Elizabeth could easily breathe.

A light but profound breeze blew through the tops of the trees, crying out in a soft, melancholy voice, "Please Betsy Bell, oh please; please Betsy Bell, don't marry Joshua Gardner. You will never find happiness with him, and by marrying him you will seal the same fate for future generations." These sad and desperate pleas repeated until the young lovers were totally consumed by dismay and trembling with fear. The voice became fainter as the wind from whence it came died down, eventually leaving in the same manner it came.

Brokenhearted, Joshua and Elizabeth sat speechless for some time after the voice had gradually faded away — looking into each other's eyes and knowing that their best days were behind them, and that the future they had often dreamt of was not meant to be. Despite the courageousness he was known for, Joshua Gardner knew he could no longer say or do anything to change the painful situation that had just revisited them and broke their hearts. Elizabeth looked down to the ground and shook her head as tears streamed down her cheeks. Joshua put his arms around her and gently rubbed her head as she rested it on his shoulder and wept uncontrollably.

After regaining some of her composure, Elizabeth told Joshua, "It is of no use, my dearest Joshua. I now know that regardless of the happiness we might someday find together, the evil force that tormented me and killed my father will undoubtedly follow us throughout our lives and to the ends of the earth, causing us much pain, sorrow and hardship." Joshua pleaded with her, "But I love you, Elizabeth, and that is all that matters. Our love is strong enough to endure the worst of the worst, and we shall boldly conquer all that which is evil and stands in the way of our happiness. Where there is a will, there is a way. Don't you know that?"

Elizabeth responded, "But even if that came to be, it would mean not only I, but you as well, would be tormented forever. It would be most selfish and unfair of me to subject you to that which you do not deserve, and it would be a wrong for which I could never expect forgiveness." She continued, "This is the saddest day of both our lives, and what I must now ask of you is the hardest thing I have ever asked anyone. I ask that you please release me from my promise to marry you, by removing the ring from my finger."

"Elizabeth, your love for me is so great that you are willing to sacrifice our future together to ensure that my own life is a happy one, and I respect and admire you for that more than you will ever know. I have not any choice but to accept the inevitable; however, I want you to keep the ring in my memory and as a token of my gratitude for giving me the happiest days of my life," Joshua responded.

"You will always have a place in my heart and I will always remember you, Joshua; but the ring is a seal to my solemn vow, and that vow cannot be broken in the sight of God unless you accept the ring's return. I could not retain it without retaining the thorn that now pierces my heart; and I know, Joshua, that you are too generous not to accede to my wish." Elizabeth extended her arm and Joshua slowly removed the ring from her finger as he tearfully exclaimed, "Elizabeth, my love, the adoration of my soul, the long hope of my life, this is the bitterest draught of all, but for your sake I drink to the dregs, releasing you from the promise which I know was earnest." [34]

Kate's voice blowing through the trees had also been heard by the other couples and cast a dark shadow over what had begun as a most enjoyable Easter Monday. Silent and downhearted, Elizabeth and Joshua made their way back to the field where the other couples had gathered in preparation of

---

[34] M.V. Ingram, *Authenticated History of the Bell Witch*, (1894).

leaving.   Given the terrifying and gut-wrenching event that had just occurred, fishing and frolicking was the last thing on everyone's mind.

As the three couples left and began their long stroll across the meadow, Elizabeth and Joshua's friends walked a fair distance behind them.   Knowing how badly their hearts had been broken, there was no sense in trying to console them — the damage had been done.

One by one, the young people broke away from the group and went home.   Because their farms were in the same direction from the river, Elizabeth and Joshua were the last ones to split from the group.   As they approached the Bell property line, Elizabeth and Joshua silently parted — never to see each other again.   Kate had now accomplished her second and final mission, which was to make sure that Elizabeth Bell and Joshua Gardner didn't marry.

In the months that followed Easter Monday of 1821, Theny Thorn married David Alex Gooch, and Rebecca Porter married James Long.   Joshua Gardner soon got his affairs in order and moved to Henry County in western Tennessee, where he remained for some time before moving to Weakley County, Tennessee in 1840. Twice married, Joshua Gardner had two sons and died at the age of 84 after a successful career as a magistrate and farmer.

CHAPTER SEVENTEEN

"Kate" Leaves for Seven Years

KATE'S VISITS BECAME FEWER after that fateful Easter Monday in 1821, and the power and intellect she once possessed rapidly diminished. What little Kate had to do with the Bells was in the form of an occasional conversation with Lucy Bell or mildly scolding the Bell children when they did not follow their mother's orders.

"Kate" Says Goodbye

Late one afternoon in May of 1821, Lucy Bell, Joel, Richard, and Elizabeth were talking in the hallway when it suddenly filled with smoke. The smoke cleared as quickly as it came, and a round object resembling a cannon ball rolled down the hallway, into the front room, and across the floor to the fireplace. Kate's voice was then heard, "Goodbye, Luce and the rest of you. I will be absent for a period of seven years. I will visit your home, as well as every other home in this area, upon my return. Farewell!" The mysterious ball then shot up the chimney in a fury of smoke and blue blazes.

While the Bells were happy to learn of Kate's departure, Elizabeth, still broken-hearted and grieving her loss of Joshua Gardner, did not seem phased. She often spent entire days laying in her bed crying, hoping, and praying that she would wake up any moment to discover that Kate was only a bad dream and that Joshua was waiting for her downstairs. Nevertheless, knowing the difference between fantasy and reality, Elizabeth was determined to deal with her anguish as best she could.

Elizabeth's New Suitor

Over time, Elizabeth Bell conquered much of her anguish and began casually associating with the man who many times came to comfort her by reciting poetry and witty sayings, that man being none other than Professor Richard R.P. Powell, her former schoolteacher and long-time admirer.

Powell called on Elizabeth more frequently as time went on, and they slowly grew closer together and began a courtship. Their courtship lasted two years, culminating in their marriage on March 21, 1824 at Red River Baptist Church. [35] Elizabeth had kept the promise she made three years earlier, that Professor Powell would be present at her wedding.

Richard Powell's marriage to Elizabeth Bell was not his first, however. On December 7, 1815, he married Esther Scott of Williamson County, Tennessee, and formerly of Dickson County, Tennessee. [36] Esther

---

[35] Richard Powell *Ciphering Book*, TN Manuscript Accession Number 75-260, p. 222.

[36] Richard Powell, *Ciphering Book*, TN Manuscript Accession Number 75-260, p. 179.

Scott is believed to have been eighteen years Powell's senior [n] and had been married previously. [37] Records indicate that Esther Powell died in 1821 of unspecified causes. [38]

Richard and Elizabeth Powell made their home on present-day Route 1012, between the towns of Cedar Hill and Springfield, Tennessee. Richard Powell became increasingly involved in the state's social and political circles, eventually giving up his job as schoolmaster to pursue a career in politics. [39]

---

[37]Williamson County TN Circuit Court, *Minute Book 1*, p. 504.
[38] Robertson County TN, *Will Book 3*, pp. 506-507; Robertson County TN, *County Court Minutes Book 6*, p. 392.
[39] A complete biographical sketch of Professor Powell is included in Appendix A.

CHAPTER EIGHTEEN

"Kate" Returns

THREE PEOPLE LIVED IN THE BELL HOME after Elizabeth married and moved away in 1824 — Lucy Bell, Richard, and Joel. The other Bell children made their homes elsewhere in the Red River community.

Esther Bell and Alex Porter settled on Sturgeon Creek, Drewry Bell settled across the Red River from the original Bell farm, John Bell, Jr. built a house on the Bell farm about a quarter-mile south of the original house, and Jesse Bell was living about one mile south of the Bell farm, near what is now Bellwood Cemetery. They visited Lucy, Richard, and Joel often, as did the Johnstons, Frank Miles, the Reverends Gunn and Fort, and other close friends.

The Bell farm was now seemingly back to normal — no more torment and demonstrations, no more unexpected visitors lined up outside the door, and no more "witch doctors" mixing strange concoctions in the family room. The Bells still had a few infrequent visitors, but nowhere near the number they had at the height of Kate's disturbances. Few visitors wanted to spend the night or sit and talk; instead, they usually just asked the question, "Has it come back yet?"

January of 1828 came without incident. While happy that Kate had yet to make her return-visit, her promised 1828 return loomed in the minds of the Bells still living in the Red River community. The subject of Kate's promised return was discussed but a few times since her 1821 departure, and Mrs. Bell took comfort in the notion that she might not return at all. All of this wishful thinking turned out to be for nothing, however. For in February of that year, Kate made good on her promise to revisit the Bells. Richard Williams Bell wrote of Kate's return-visit:

"The demonstrations announcing its return were precisely the same that characterized its first appearance. Joel occupied a bed in mother's room, and I slept in another apartment alone. After considerable scratching on the weatherboarding on the outside, it appeared in the same way on the inside, scratching on the bed post and pulling the cover from my bed as fast as I could replace it, keeping me up nearly all night. It went on in this way for several nights, and I spoke not a word about it, lest I should frighten mother.

However, one night later, after worrying me for some time, I heard a noise in mother's room, and knew at once what was to pay. Very soon, mother and Joel came rushing into my room, much frightened, telling me about the disturbance and something pulling the cover off.

We sat up until a late hour discussing the matter, satisfied that it was the same old Kate, and agreed not to talk to the witch, and that we would keep the matter a profound secret to ourselves, worrying with it the best we could, hoping that it would soon leave, as it did, after disturbing us in this way for two weeks." [40]

"Kate" Visits John Bell, Jr.

After spending some time at the Bell home with Lucy, Richard and Joel, Kate then paid a visit to the man who was undoubtedly her harshest critic and the mortal whom she feared the most: John Bell, Jr.

Late one night in March of 1828, John Jr. picked up a military book from his bureau and proceeded to his chair where he sat down to relax and read by candlelight.   A former soldier, John Jr. was very interested in military history and spent a good deal of time reading military books and battle maps.   He often told his friends the reasons why particular battles were lost and how they possibly could have been won.   He would later in life tell others about why the Confederacy would never be able to win the Civil War, although he only lived to see a short part of it.

As he thumbed through the book's pages and studied Napoleon's actions at Waterloo, Bell's eyes grew tired and he decided to read only one more page before retiring for the evening. Kate was the very last thing on his mind. As he read the last page and slowly began nodding off, an old and familiar voice began filled the room.

"John, I am in..." "Go straight to Hell!" John Jr. quickly interrupted as he sprung from his chair, "wherever you have been, or wherever you are, your proper place is in Hell, and the next visit you make

---

[40] Richard Williams Bell, *Our Family Trouble*, 1846 (Mini-Histories: Nashville, 1985).

you should go there and stay!" Kate responded, "Again, John, I am in hopes you will not be as angry at me on this visit as you were on my last. I shall do nothing to cause you offense; I have been in the West Indies for seven years, and..." "Oh shut your nasty mouth you old bitch from Hell; and stay away from me, my family, and everyone else!" John Jr. angrily interrupted.

Maintaining her composure, Kate responded, "John, I knew you would not understand why I came; but if you could, you would know that some of the things I have done will at last result in the best for succeeding generations." She continued, "You are telling me to go to Hell, John; such Spirits as I sometimes get a vacation, even banishment from their abode; but I will tell you there are thousands of human beings now living on this earth who are worse than I; they are only restrained by their fellow beings. If, after reaching their future abode, their Spirit could return to this earth, they would raise a thousand times more Hell than I have done." "I fail to recognize how that could be true!" replied John Jr.

The Past, Present, and Future

"Don't forget that each one of you will have a Spirit, and that men on earth are best controlled through Spiritual influence. If this influence is not recognized finally, the world will be lost. As you think of me now, you would add millions of others to your thoughts and think a thousand times worse of most of them, if their Spirits came back on earth," responded Kate; "there are Spirits millions of years old, John, that never have been connected with a body, but were created Spirits. Here on earth, only the physical part of man, under mental control, is visible to his fellows. What a difference, John, if you knew what they are thinking! I know what you are thinking now."

John Jr. responded, "I want you to know what I am thinking! It is that I would give my life freely if I could tangibly grasp your form in my arms and crush you slowly, giving you the pain you caused my father scores of times, and then throw you straight into the fires of Hell, if there be any such place!

"You would not be here if you did not know of your safety. I think you are thrice a demon Spirit; you belong to a world of demons; you come to this world where its inhabitants cannot harm you. You are now neither of this world nor your own — a wandering thing between this world and some other; you must be as unhappy as you admit. I feel as if you would like to get back to your home, if they would let you stay there. You are too mean for them to wish to exist in your presence. I have repeatedly told you that I don't believe what you say of the good that will come of my father's demise, and as often told you..."

Kate interrupted, saying, "I am leaving you for the night. Just think over the things I have told you and be assured that I am willing to give you all the information I may possess. Let me know of the things you believe might result in some good."

"Kate" Makes Predictions

Kate returned the next evening as John Jr. was reading some maps and literature that pertained to the Battle of New Orleans, a battle in which he had fought alongside his brother, Jesse, and was very familiar with. Immediately upon recognizing what Bell was reading, Kate remarked, "There will be another battle at New Orleans, which will be part of a bloody and intense war, the outcome of which will be the Negroes' freedom. The city will be captured and held by one of your fellow Tennesseans; he is an officer in the United States Navy right now, but he will be on the other side."

Kate continued, "This fight at New Orleans will determine you to go into the army against the north, but you will not realize your decision. You will depart from this world just after that battle at the city in which you have felt so interested." "I just might depart shortly if there is any prospect of your remaining here long," replied Bell.

Kate continued visiting John Jr. each night, engaging him in discussions about wars, civilizations and Christianity. These long and thought-provoking discussions amounted to a series of conferences regarding the past, the present, and the future.

In addition to predicting the Civil War, Kate spoke of another war that would be of major significance to Americans. This war would take place at a time when the United States had established itself as a strong, global power, and because of this, would be heavily involved in the war along with several other major countries.

The world would lose millions of men in what some people would call "the war to end all wars." This phrase, which Kate coined while making a prediction in 1828, ended up being the phrase used by many to describe World War I.

Kate also predicted what many believe to have been World War II. During one of their discussions, Kate said to John Bell, Jr., "There will be threats and signs of another great upheaval which, if it comes, will be far more devastating and fearful in character than the one the world thought too terrible for the mind to grasp."

"Kate" Bids Farewell

One evening after several months of these long discussions, Kate told John Jr. that she would make her final appearance the following evening. John Jr. then confided in his best friend, Frank Miles, that Kate had returned some months earlier and that they had discussed a great number of topics. He invited Miles to his home to witness Kate's final appearance.

At precisely eight o'clock that evening, Kate appeared to John Jr. and Frank Miles saying, "To you two, who are inseparable friends, I say that whether the world ever hears of what I have told John or not, as bad as you both think I have been, I hope it will be recognized that what I have said to John is for the best, and the world will so live. I shall be there; you two will know what I am doing; the world may not recognize Spirits, whether good or demon; both will be here; it will have many of each.

"Again, John, your descendants will not be worried by me, but I promise you now if it is for their good, and I am allowed, for once I will be helpful to them and their country. I am bidding you and Frank a last farewell. I will be here again in another seven years, to which one hundred will be added."

Some 34 years later, on April 25, 1862, New Orleans was captured by the Union Army under the leadership of Captain David Farragut of Knoxville, Tennessee, who had been a junior officer in the United States Navy at the time Kate predicted the capture of New Orleans. The Union Army took control of New Orleans on May 1, 1862 — nearly a month after Bell died of pneumonia on April 8, 1862. Kate apparently missed this prediction.

Life after "Kate's" Departure

In the final years of his life, John Bell, Jr. spent

three days describing in meticulous detail his private conversations with Kate as his son, Dr. Joel Thomas Bell, listened attentively and took notes. The younger Bell later passed this information to his son, Dr. Charles Bailey Bell, who included much of it in his book, "The Bell Witch: A Mysterious Spirit," published in 1934.

Lucy Bell remained in the old Bell home up until her death in January of 1837, after which it was used to store grain and other farming materials until about 1843. The house was then razed, and its stones and logs were used to construct other houses and farm buildings in the area. The families of Esther Porter and Jesse Bell had moved to Panola County, Mississippi by that time, also. Both families had discussed leaving Robertson County Tennessee to escape Kate; however, it was not until the 1837-1842 period that they moved — years after Kate's departure. [41]

In 1846, Richard Williams Bell, the second youngest child of John and Lucy Bell, wrote a comprehensive eyewitness account of Kate's disturbances. Known as "Our Family Trouble," Bell's manuscript was incorporated into a number of later publications and was published under its own name in 1985. [42]

In 1848, tragedy struck Elizabeth "Betsy" Powell when her husband, Professor Richard Powell, died after a slow decline in his health that followed a massive stroke he suffered in 1837. Powell's family suffered significant financial hardships because of his no longer being able to make a living.

In 1849, only one year after her husband's death, Elizabeth learned that a publication known as *The*

---

[41] Time frame arrived at by examining real estate, tax, and census records.
[42] Richard Williams Bell, *Our Family Trouble*, 1846 (Mini-Histories: Nashville, 1985).

Saturday Evening Post, which was circulated only in Pennsylvania at the time, had published a lengthy article about her family's experiences with Kate, or the "Bell Witch" as the Spirit was often called. Much to her chagrin, the entire article suggested that she was the culprit behind Kate's disturbances. She contacted an attorney and threatened legal action in the form of a libel suit if the publication did not retract the comments made in the article. In response, *The Saturday Evening Post* issued a public apology and retracted the comments made regarding Elizabeth's alleged involvement with the disturbances.

What was once a thriving plantation and the apparent center of Kate's disturbances, was divided into several tracts and became the property of not one, but many owners. The land was farmed just as it had been by John Bell some two decades earlier; however, there was no longer a maligned Spirit constantly torturing those who lived there and their visitors.

Did "Kate" Really Leave?

A quick look at the land records of Robertson County will substantiate the former; however, there is no evidence of any kind that suggests Kate *really* left the place after she bade farewell to John Bell, Jr. and Frank Miles on that summer night in 1828. To the contrary, many people claimed to have encountered mysterious apparitions and other phenomena on and around the old Bell farm long after Kate's alleged departure.

Reader's Notes:

CHAPTER NINETEEN

The Trouble Never Ended

JOEL BELL INHERITED A PORTION of the old Bell farm that bordered the Red River on its north side and roughly followed present-day Keysburg Road on its western side. The land also contained the cave from which Kate once rescued a young boy whose head became stuck in a crevice. On the hill directly above the cave, Joel Bell built a house using logs salvaged from the original Bell home when it was razed. At the time, this hill was known as Brown's Ford Bluff. °

On a winter day in 1852, Dr. Henry Sugg visited this house to tend to a sick child, presumably one of Joel Bell's children. With the air having been so cold outside, the doctor sat close to the fire to warm his hands when he arrived. While discussing the child's symptoms with Joel Bell, Dr. Sugg heard what sounded like glass breaking and corks popping off the vials in his medicine bag.

"Mr. Bell, did you hear that!" inquired the doctor.

"Yes, I did," replied Bell; "it is not uncommon to hear

strange noises or see strange things around here. I have not been able to determine the source, but I can assure you that no one here has ever been hurt because of these strange things." "Might this have something to do with the 'witch' that haunted these parts many years ago?" asked Dr. Sugg. "I don't really know," replied Bell, "but it would not surprise me at all."

Dr. Sugg then fetched his medicine bag and checked its contents for damage. "Mr. Bell!" exclaimed Dr. Sugg, "I am astonished. I cannot believe this! Every vial in my bag is intact, just as I arranged them earlier this morning. How do you live day in and day out with such mind-boggling events occurring right here in your home?" "I suppose it's because I grew up with such things and they don't bother me much anymore," Joel Bell replied, "but one thing I've learned to do when these things happen is to ignore them. They usually stop, and very quickly."

Dr. Sugg's strange encounter was not the last to be experienced in the house atop Brown's Ford Bluff. Another strange event occurred at the same house in early 1861, six years after Joel Bell had sold it to his brother, Richard, who died two years later and left it to his son, Allen Bell.

Reynolds Powell's Encounter

Allen Bell and Reynolds Powell, son of Richard and Elizabeth Powell, served together in Company F of the Eleventh Tennessee Regiment of the Confederate Army. Powell was a private and Bell was fourth sergeant, both ultimately taking orders from Captain James Long, husband of Elizabeth's childhood friend, Rebecca Porter. [43] Bell had been discharged from the Confederate Army because of health problems, and was at home recuperating when Powell came to visit and spend the night with him. [p]

The men sat up until late in the evening, talking about many things and occasionally playing with Bell's dog. It had gotten somewhat stuffy inside, so before retiring for the evening they opened the doors to allow some fresh air to circulate in the house. Shortly after they fell asleep, the dog began fiercely barking and ran into the house with its tail tucked as if it had been frightened.

Both men awoke to strange noises outside their windows. These noises were later described as sounding like animals fighting in a strong wind; however, the wind had been calm that evening. Despite being inside the house, the dog continued barking, snarling and growling as if it was fighting with some invisible entity. After investigating and finding nothing, Bell and Powell put the dog outside and closed the door in hopes of being able to sleep again.

They once again fell asleep but were awakened later on by an invisible force that jerked the pillows from behind their heads and pulled the covers off their beds. They could neither see nor hear anything, and the activity continued off and on until daylight. [q]

Five years later, another remarkable event took place on the old Bell farm at the Enchanted Spring, the same landmark the Spirit said contained buried money some 50 years earlier, and the site where Joshua Gardner and Elizabeth Bell said their final farewell on Easter Monday of 1821. However, this

---

[43] Albert Virgil Goodpasture, *Goodspeed History of Tennessee – Robertson County*, 1886, p. 856.

time it was the sound of beautiful music, and not the melancholy voice blowing through the trees.

Beautiful Music at the Enchanted Spring

One day in the spring of 1866, John Gunn and A.L. Bartlett crossed the Red River near the Enchanted Spring on their way home to Adams Station after having spent the day with their lady friends in nearby Guthrie, Kentucky. Hot and exhausted from the trip, they partook of the Enchanted Spring's cool and flowing water once they crossed the river.

As they finished guzzling the refreshing water, they began climbing the long and gradual slope next to the spring where they would soon reach Johnston Springs Road. Having gotten no more than a few yards, they began hearing loud, ear-piercing tones that evolved into a musical score they later described as being the sweetest music they had ever heard.

The music filled the entire forest with a loud and sweet melody like none ever heard before. Neither of the men could move while they listened to the music; the loud tones and sweet melody had a paralyzing effect on them. They listened to this beautiful music until it stopped some thirty minutes later. The men tried desperately to find the source of the music but found nothing. Neither man crossed the Red River in this area again, nor married on the north side of the river. ʳ

One of the more frequent happenings in the Nineteenth Century was the machinery's mysteriously running at Clark's Mill, just down the Red River from the Bell farm. Many times, someone could go by there at night and either see mysterious lights glowing or hear the sound of the machinery grinding.

CHAPTER TWENTY

Early Published Accounts

THE THREE NINETEENTH CENTURY accounts published above are but a few of many reported encounters with Kate after her supposed departure. Such accounts were even taken under oath on some occasions. The following are among the earliest published accounts of the "Bell Witch."

The Goodpasture Account

One of the earliest published accounts of Kate was a paragraph written in a history book by Tennessee Historian Albert Virgil Goodpasture, in 1886:

"A remarkable occurrence, which attracted wide-spread interest, was connected with the family of John Bell, who settled near what is now Adams Station about 1804. So great was the excitement that people came from hundreds of miles around to witness the manifestations of what was popularly known as the 'Bell Witch.'

This witch was supposed to be some Spiritual being having the voice and attributes of a woman. It was invisible to the eye, yet it would hold conversation and even shake hands with certain individuals.   The freaks it performed were wonderful, and seemingly designed to annoy the family.   It would take the sugar from the bowls, spill the milk, take the quilts from the beds, slap and pinch the children, and then laugh at the discomfiture of its victims.

At first it was supposed to be a good Spirit, but its subsequent acts, together with the curses with which it supplemented its remarks, proved the contrary.   A volume might be written concerning the performances of this wonderful being, as they are now described by contemporaries and their descendants.

That all this actually occurred will not be disputed, nor will a rational explanation be attempted.   It is merely introduced as an example of superstition, strong in the minds of all but a few in those times, and not yet wholly extinct." [44]

The Ingram Account

Few encounters with Kate were reported in the late 1880s and early 1890s, partially because of the long-awaited publication, "Authenticated History of the Bell Witch," by Martin V. Ingram of Clarksville, Tennessee.   Ingram's efforts in researching the legend over a period of many years and publishing a comprehensive account of it were well-known, and many people kept silent about any encounters they

---

[44] Albert Virgil Goodpasture, *Goodspeed History of Tennessee – Robertson County*, 1886, p. 833.

experienced which might have been the work of Kate so as to avoid being labeled as "fools" by those who would read Ingram's book. They expected Ingram to solve the mystery of the "Bell Witch" using conclusive evidence.

Published in 1894, Ingram's work was the first book written exclusively about Kate and was the culmination of his efforts over several years to obtain eyewitness interviews and testimonial letters, collect stories passed down from eyewitnesses to their descendants, and to publish Richard Williams Bell's manuscript, *Our Family Trouble.*

One of Ingram's closest friends was Joel Egbert Bell. Although very young at the time of Kate's apparitions and demonstrations, he remembered a great deal and shared lots of this information with Ingram. Ingram had discussed the idea of a book with both Joel Bell and Allen Bell, who discussed the matter with their relatives and decided it best for Ingram not to publish his book until all of John Bell's immediate family had died. Joel Egbert Bell, who was the last surviving child of John Bell, died in 1890.

At that time, Ingram obtained Richard Williams Bell's manuscript from Allen Bell and resumed his work, finishing it in late 1893 and publishing in 1894. Originally published with a white cover and gold lettering, the book was printed by Donnelly Printing in Chicago, and Sanders Engraving Company in St. Louis the picture plates. A small number of copies were printed, and most were sold by mail order.

This abandoned building near McCormick Place in Chicago, Illinois was the site of Donnelly's printing operations during the 1890's when Ingram's book was printed. It was replaced by a parking lot shortly after this picture was taken.

The "Red Book"

Charles Elder of Nashville first reprinted Ingram's book in 1961; and then later, in 1971, a company in east Tennessee also made reprints. The first few reprints featured a white cover and gold lettering just as the original copies did, but were later replaced by a red cover and black lettering — thereby earning the book its popular name, "The Red Book."

Because Ingram's book was written a relatively short time after Kate's disturbances, and contains Richard Williams Bell's 1846 manuscript and other eyewitness accounts, it serves as the basis of most later publications that pertain to the "Bell Witch."

Despite the small number of copies printed, 2,000 or so, Ingram's book did a lot to increase public interest in the legend of the "Bell Witch." By 1909, postcards were printed showing the cave and other parts of the old Bell farm.

The FGWPA Account

Several years later, in 1933, the Federal Government's Works Project Administration published the following paragraph:

"Sure enough, tradition says, the Bells were tormented for years by the malicious Spirit of Old Kate Batts. John Bell and his favorite daughter Betsy were the principal targets. Toward the other members of the family the witch was either indifferent or, as in the case of Mrs. Bell, friendly. No one ever saw her, but every visitor to the Bell home heard her all too well. Her voice, according to one person who heard it, 'spoke at a nerve-racking pitch when displeased, while at other times it sang and spoke in low musical tones.' The Spirit of Old Kate led John and Betsy Bell a merry chase. She threw furniture and dishes at them. She pulled their noses, yanked their hair, and poked needles into them. She yelled all night to keep them from sleeping, and snatched food from their mouths at mealtime." [45]

Encounters with Kate have been reported in the Twentieth Century just as they were in the Nineteenth Century. Most Twentieth Century encounters with Kate were reported after 1935, the year in which she promised John Bell, Jr. and Frank Miles that she would return to visit John Bell's closest direct descendant.

---

[45] Federal Government Works Project Administration, *Guidebook for Tennessee*, 1933.

The Charles Bailey Bell Account

John Bell's most direct descendant in 1935 was Dr. Charles Bailey Bell, a neurologist in Nashville, Tennessee. He was the son of Dr. Joel Thomas Bell, son of John Bell, Jr. and grandson of John Bell. Dr. Bell wrote his own book about Kate, "The Bell Witch – A Mysterious Spirit," in 1934 — one year before Kate's promised return.

In addition to many of the same stories published in Martin Ingram's earlier book, Bell's book presents a comprehensive account of several private conversations that allegedly took place between John Bell, Jr. and Kate during her 1828 visit. It is said that many members of the Bell family were outraged when Dr. Bell's book was published.

Even to this day, some people believe that Dr. Bell or his father fabricated the story of conversations between John Jr. and Kate as a means of expressing their own religious and philosophical views — essentially, using Kate as their mouthpiece. Whether the conversations between John Bell, Jr. and Kate really took place, nobody knows. The notes allegedly taken by Dr. Bell's father, Dr. Joel Thomas Bell, under the direction of his father, John Bell, Jr., have never been found. Even if such notes were found and proved to be the handwriting of Dr. Joel Thomas Bell, there remains no way to prove that he penned them under the direction of his father, John Bell, Jr.

The "Black Book"

Originally red in color, Dr. Charles Bailey Bell's book was first reprinted by Charles Elder, Bookseller, of Nashville in 1972 under the title, "The Bell Witch of Tennessee." [46] The reprints feature a black cover with white lettering, which earned the book its popular name, "The Black Book." The "Black Book" contains not only Dr. Charles Bailey Bell's original book, "The Bell Witch – A Mysterious Spirit," but also a book written by Harriet Parks Miller, a Montgomery County school teacher, which is entitled, "The Bell Witch of Middle Tennessee." [47]

Dr. Bell never published a follow-up to his 1934 book, and there are no documented reports of Kate's visiting any of John Bell's direct descendants in 1935 as she had promised. However, if Kate did in fact revisit any of John Bell's descendants, the likelihood of such a visit being made publicly known is slim to none. Dr. Charles Bailey Bell died in 1945, and is buried in Bellwood Cemetery on Highway 41 just east of Adams, Tennessee.

---

[46] Charles Bailey Bell, M.D., Harriet Parks Miller, *The Bell Witch of Tennessee* (n.p., 1930, 1934; facsimile reproduction by Charles Elder, Bookseller: Nashville, 1972).
[47] Harriet Parks Miller, *The Bell Witch of Middle Tennessee*, Leaf-Chronicle Publishing Co., Clarksville, 1930.

The grave of Dr. Charles Bailey Bell at Bellwood Cemetery in Adams, Tennessee.

The releases of Miller and Bell's books in 1930 and 1934, respectively, when combined with existing interest in the "Bell Witch" due largely in part to Ingram's earlier book, generated considerably more interest during the 1930's than in previous years. Each year, more people visit Adams, Tennessee hoping to have an encounter with Kate.

CHAPTER TWENTY-ONE

"Kate" in the Twentieth Century

THE FACT THAT THE OLD BELL FARM is private property kept many people away from the original Bell home site and cemetery; however there were always some who managed to get in. By the early 1940's, the family who owned the tract of land with the cave that the Bells used for storage and where Elizabeth Bell and her friends once played began allowing select visitors to picnic near the cave's entrance and explore the first two rooms on occasion.

Choking Sensation on the Porch

On one occasion in the late 1940's, the author's uncle visited some friends who owned the cave tract at the time. Several old outbuildings stood on the property, some of which are believed be built by John Bell's immediate family or close-generation descendants. One of these buildings had been the home of Joel Egbert Bell, and later his nephew,

James Allen Bell. Built in the late 1840s, the house was constructed partially of logs and stones salvaged from John Bell's house when it was razed in 1843.

Located on what was known by previous generations as, "Brown's Ford Bluff," this house was where Dr. Henry Sugg, Joel Bell, Allen Bell, and Reynolds Powell experienced several mysterious encounters during the Nineteenth Century. The house was used as a storage building during the period the author's uncle visited the place, and the family who owned the land lived in another old house nearby.

After visiting the family for the better part of a spring afternoon, the author's uncle graciously accepted their invitation to stay for dinner that evening. After finishing dinner, he and the man who lived there decided to go outside for a walk around the farm to get some fresh air and burn some calories before night set in.

After walking for some time, they made their way to the front porch of the old house where they lit their cigarettes and sat down in two big rocking chairs. After several minutes of conversation, an unusually strong gust of wind consumed the porch and, in the words of the author's uncle, "All of a sudden, something just didn't seem right about that front porch. I wanted to get my tail out of there in a hurry!"

As the men continued talking, they began developing what they later described as a strange, "choking sensation." The longer they sat on the front porch of the old house, the tighter their throats became – reaching a point where if felt as if a noose had been placed around each of their necks and was being slowly tightened.

The strange tightness in their throats subsided after a short time, giving them a much-needed chance to return to the main family house. "We got back a helluva' lot faster than walked up there, that's for sure!" the author's uncle later said. The author's uncle spoke on many occasions of Kate and his personal experience at the farm that spring afternoon. In addition to the many stories about Kate that he shared with the author shortly before his death in 1984, he also passed his original copy of Martin Ingram's book, "Authenticated History of the Bell Witch," to the author.

Tragedy after Theft of John Bell's Gravestone

Several years after the incident on the front porch of the old house, three boys from Nashville, Tennessee went joy riding one night and ended up in Adams, some 50 miles away, to see what all the talk about the "Bell Witch" was about. The year was 1951. They had heard many stories of people experiencing strange encounters while visiting the cave and the old Bell farm, so they were eager to see how much "trouble" they could encounter.

Arriving in Adams at around 9:30 P.M., the boys stopped by several service stations and stores to talk with local residents with hopes of finding out where to begin their ghostly adventure. After a bit of small talk and discussing the "Bell Witch" with several of the locals, the boys gassed up their car and headed east on Highway 41 until they reached a dirt road that turned off the highway.

They slowly drove down the road, observing the eerie surroundings as they proceeded through the darkness looking for the land that was, almost a century and a half earlier, the thriving yet haunted plantation owned by John Bell. After traveling about a mile, they noticed the old, brick house on the right-hand side of the road that a man back at the service station had spoken of. This house, according to the man, was "right in the middle of 'Bell Witch' country."

The boys stopped the car, turned off the lights and motor, then put the gearshift in neutral and began coasting quietly down the hill past the brick house. They had been told the land across the road and down the hill from the old house was at one time John Bell's largest field, and that the old Bell home stood about 400 yards back in the field from the road's edge. Atop the hill on the right-hand side of this large field is the old Bell cemetery, where John Bell, his wife, and several of their children are buried.

Tall and dense thickets consumed what was once John Bell's front yard and largest field. Even with the flashlights they had brought along, there was no way the boys could find their way through the many acres of thickets to where the Bell home once stood or up the thorny hill to the cemetery. They discussed their options as they continued looking into the thickets in hopes of finding an opening. As the boys were about to start the car and leave, they noticed what looked to be an old road off in the thicket to their left. What was left of the old road led through the thicket for a good distance before curving and going up a hill. Curious as to where the road would take them, the boys started the car and maneuvered through several yards of dense brush to the old road.

They followed the road up a hill and across a flat for about a quarter-mile before reaching the end and getting out of the car. There weren't nearly as many thickets on this part of the property as there were nearer to the main road, so they turned on their flashlights and began hiking off into the darkness across a small, sloped hill and then up another hill.

After having made it half way up the second hill,

the boys shined their flashlights in directions to get a good sense of their surroundings and what lay ahead. They were shocked to find that, within fifteen feet of where they were standing, several gravestones sat in what looked to be a very old, neglected and forgotten cemetery nestled among the towering cedar trees and underneath some brush.

When the boys moved closer to investigate, they saw the words, "Richard Williams Bell 1811-1857" inscribed on the largest gravestone. The boys were astonished – they thought they had already passed where the old Bell cemetery was, but knew then that they were actually right on it because of the name, "Bell" inscribed on one of the stones. They moved to a smaller stone, about fifteen feet in front of the one they had just read, and it read, "John Bell 1750-1820, and his Wife Lucy Bell 1770-1837."

They sat down to celebrate their prized finding as they discussed what to do next and how long they could remain there before having to return to Nashville. Without a word, two of the boys got up and began pushing John Bell's gravestone back and forth until it became loose to the point they could pull it from the ground. Each of the two boys carried one end of the gravestone and the third boy shined the flashlight as they made their way down the hill, across the field, and back to their car. Upon arriving back at their car, they placed John Bell's gravestone in the trunk.

They backed down the old road, then turned onto the main road and followed it to Highway 41 where they headed towards Nashville. After reaching nearby Springfield a few minutes later, they took a shortcut to the Joelton community in northern Davidson County because one of the boys lived just south of there. Frightened by what they had done earlier and the possibility of being followed by

Robertson County law enforcement officials, the boys continued towards Nashville at a high rate of speed.

Just as they flew past Joelton and headed south toward where one of them lived, they reached the infamous, "Devil's Elbow" curve. The boy who was driving immediately lost control of the vehicle, sending it sideways for several hundred feet before topping an embankment and plunging more than 100 feet into a deep ravine.

They boy driving the car was killed instantly, and the other two boys suffered only minor injuries. Several days after the boy's funeral, the car was brought to his family's home so his belongings could be retrieved before it was scrapped. Upon opening the car's trunk, the boy's mother discovered, in clear sight, John Bell's gravestone.

Being familiar with and believing in the "Bell Witch" legend herself, the boy's mother jerked and tugged on the stone until she got it out and into her own trunk. She then drove to the area near Adams, Tennessee where she thought the Bell farm once was and unloaded the stone, placing it next to the road and covering it with some brush. She was too late, however – for just hours earlier, both boys who had been with her son the night of the gravestone's theft were involved in separate, freak-accidents. One was killed, and the other lost his hand. s

Later in the 1950s, Boston contractor and John Bell descendant Leslie Covington created a cemetery in Adams, Tennessee to honor of the family of John Bell family and their descendants. Known as "Bellwood," the cemetery is located on Highway 41 about one mile east of Adams and is easily identified by its marble front gates and a large monument that Covington erected at the back of the cemetery. [48]

---

[48] Bellwood Cemetery is also discussed in Appendix E.

Adjacent to several shady oak trees and surrounded by a marble fence, lies a small plot of land reserved for the graves of John Bell's direct descendants. Each lot within this small area has its own headstone, precisely aligned with the so that all graves can be viewed without having to walk over them.

The plot reserved for John Bell descendants at Bellwood Cemetery in Adams, Tennessee.

Several of John Bell's direct descendants are buried in this special plot, including surnames such as Bell, Winters, Turner, Covington, and Abshire, to name just a few. At the time this plot at Bellwood was completed, the graves of several John Bell descendants were exhumed and taken to the plot from such distant places as Texas and Oklahoma. This bizarre action explains why the deaths of some people buried at Bellwood predate the cemetery itself.

In 1957, six years after John Bell's gravestone was stolen from the old Bell cemetery, Covington replaced it and put additional stones on the old farm property, about one mile from Bellwood, denoting the location of the Bell family's well and where the homes of John Bell and John Bell, Jr. once stood. All of these stones remain intact today.

This gravestone, placed in 1957, replaces the original gravestone that was taken in 1951.

The Eden Family Buys the Cave

In 1964, the 105-acre tract of land encompassing the cave, Brown's Ford Bluff, and many acres of prime tobacco farmland was purchased by William "Bims" Eden, a local farmer who had always lived near the old Bell farm and been fascinated by the legend since he was a boy. [49]   Although he had already experienced several first-hand encounters with Kate over the years, the things he experienced after purchasing the land were nothing like he had experienced before. They were far more frequent and bizarre.

Just after purchasing the farm, Eden razed the old house that sat on the spot he intended to build a new house for himself and his family. Built partially with logs and stones from the original John Bell house by Joel Bell in the late 1840's, this house was the site of several strange happenings in the mid to late Nineteenth Century. [t] The house had been used

---

[49] H.C Brehm, *Echoes of the Bell Witch in the Twentieth Century*, 1979.

only as a storage room in the fifty years leading up to when Bims bought the property. After the old house was razed, Bims built a brick home in its place.

Bims' house was situated along what was once known as the "Nashville-Clarksville Road," a pioneer trail connecting Nashville and Clarksville in the days of John Bell and for several decades afterward.

The driveway, which turns off Keysburg Road about a mile north of Adams, roughly follows the old Nashville-Clarksville roadbed for some distance to a large sinkhole formed above the cave many years ago. At this point, the driveway picks up the old road's direct path and makes a right turn before continuing up Brown's Ford Bluff and through several fields, eventually intersecting with the old bed of Brown's Ford and Springfield Road," which was the main thoroughfare during the John Bell era. A long stretch of the old Nashville-Clarksville roadbed is now used for farm traffic and hayrides at Halloween.

"Bell Witch" Cave

Nestled below a steep limestone bluff overlooking the Red River is the entrance to "Bell Witch Cave." During the months of winter and spring, and following periods of heavy rain, a crystal-clear spring flows along the cave's floor and out its entrance before falling some 75 feet to the Red River.

The cave has two main rooms, the first of which can be found down a straight, narrow passageway about 125 feet from the entrance. Near the back of the first room is an opening where one can look up and see overhead passages on the cave's second and third levels. Because of the vast deposits of mud that collect on the upper levels, they are generally not accessible. The cave's second, or "back" room, is located down a very narrow passageway about 200 feet beyond the first room.

The cave maintains a comfortable temperature of 57 degrees Fahrenheit, year-round, and was often used as a storage area by John Bell's family. It was also in this cave where one of Elizabeth Bell's young friends got his head stuck in a crevice and was pulled completely out of the cave by Kate. Although more than fifteen miles long, the cave can be explored safely only to the back room. Beyond the back room, the passageways become so narrow that one must crawl through loose rocks, mud, and knee-deep water to explore the cave.

Once his new house had been completed and his family settled in, Bims began equipping the cave with lighting so that he could take visitors on tours of the two rooms. Aside from a handful of cave explorers and archaeologists, very few people had been inside the cave since the Nineteenth Century; and as a result, neither Bims nor his sons knew what to expect when they began stringing the wires and lights. As it turned out, they experienced strange events that, unbeknownst to them, marked the beginning of a series of events that would haunt them until they left the property many years later.

Towering some 40 feet above the Red River, this bluff marks the location of "Bell Witch" cave.

A Wire Disappears

Early one morning, one of Bims' sons and a friend followed the narrow path down the hill to the cave and began stringing wire for the lights. Starting at the entrance, they slowly worked their way back through the cave as they installed clamps, taped connections together, and made sure that all wiring was tucked neatly and out of the path of future visitors to the cave.

After reaching a point about halfway to the first room, Bims' son turned on his flashlight because there was very little light left from the entrance. He watched his friend, who was blind in both eyes, with amazement as he effortlessly routed wires through the cave and taped their connections tightly. After they had been working for some time, Eden's flashlight began to dim. In an effort to conserve what little battery power that remained, Eden turned off his flashlight and sat it down.

As the men continued working, Eden's eyes adjusted to the darkness. Eden felt a sudden jerk as the strand of wire he was holding for his friend completely left his hands. Each man thought the other had accidentally jerked the wire, but after some brief discussion, they realized that someone or something else had jerked it.

Both on their hands and knees, they felt around the cave's floor in search of the missing strand of wire. They began feeling up and down the cave's walls after their search of the floor turned up nothing. Still unable to find the wire, Eden traced the men's footsteps back to where he had put the flashlight.

As his friend sat and waited, Eden began carefully scanning the cave's floor, walls, and ceiling with his flashlight. The wire was still not seen. Then out of anger and desperation, Eden walked in the direction opposite the area where they had been running the wire – knowing the wire wouldn't be there but not wanting to leave any unturned stones, either. As he shined his flashlight up at the ceiling, the misplaced strand of wire came into clear view — lodged between two rocks in an area of the cave they had not yet reached.

The wire finally came loose after several minutes of frantic tugging and jerking. The men eventually got all of the lights installed in the cave after several days of hard work and tricks being played on them.

A Distorted Picture

Several weeks after the lights had been installed, a man and several young boys from nearby Guthrie, Kentucky visited the cave for a tour with Bims. After finishing the tour, the man asked one of the boys to pose for a picture with his dog in front of the cave's entrance. The man then made what he thought would turn out to be a normal picture, but soon learned that it was far from normal.

As the picture began to develop, Bims and the man who took the picture noticed that while the dog and the boy's lower body appeared normally, his shoulders and head were covered by what appeared to be a "white sheet" stretched across the cave's entrance. Aside from the fact that no sheet had been around at the time it was taken, the picture showed distinctive bulges in the "sheet" where the boy's head and shoulders should have been.

Human Mist Figure in the Cave

On another afternoon, Bims and several teenagers were talking in the cave's back room when one of the group suddenly yelled, "Hey, look at that! What is it? It's right there! See it?" "Yeah!" replied the other members in the group.

What they saw was a misty, human-like figure facing in the opposite direction of where they were standing. They could clearly see the body from its head down to its knees; however there was nothing but air below the knees. As the mysterious entity seemed to float through the passageway toward the cave's first room, the group cautiously followed behind it in amazement. The entity became more transparent as it got closer to the first room and eventually disappeared.

This was one of the very few occasions when everyone present saw an apparition. In most cases, only one or two people in a group will encounter something strange if it happens. On one such occasion, Bims took a man, his wife, and their son for a tour of the cave where the wife saw something but the others did not.

A Woman's Figure in the Upper Passage

As Bims pointed out the various flowstones, crystal-clear pools of water and rock formations that line the cave, he noticed that the woman was staring in the direction of an overhead passage that led to the cave's second level. She appeared to be either very scared or in some kind of trance. Soon, the woman screamed, "There she is! It must be the 'Bell Witch!' She is so young looking, and her long black hair is the most beautiful I've ever seen. She isn't walking, either. She seems to be floating through the air! Look up into the hole and you'll see her!"

Curious, Bims and the woman's husband and son rushed over and looked up into the passageway where they saw nothing out of the ordinary. The woman kept her eye on the passageway and insisted once again that the entity was present and floating through the air. The group continued looking through the passageway and watching the second level, but it appeared that the only person able to see this terrifying apparition was the woman. After a short time, she indicated that the entity was still lurking in one of the cave's upper levels but had floated out of her sight.

The people quickly made their way towards the front of the cave; however, they did not make it far past the first room before something else happened – and this time, everyone experienced it. As they were passing through the first room and into the passageway leading to the entrance, they began hearing what sounded like faint breathing coming from a large stone that juts out from the cave's wall.

Although terrified, the group remained calm as they listened to the breathing sound become more intense and labored as it continued. After about a minute had passed, the breathing evolved into gasps that sounded as if the entity was fighting and struggling for each breath it took.

After the noise stopped several minutes later and the group had gotten outside the cave, the only explanation that could be thought of was that both the apparition seen by the woman and the breathing sounds heard by the group were Kate, and, that the breathing sounds were her way of showing them that she had died a slow and miserable death. In addition to her rare apparitions and frequent rumblings in the cave, Kate has also been known to touch people on occasion.

Known as "Eagle Rock," this large flowstone sits in the back room of the cave where many unexplained things have been encountered over the years.

A Girl is Pushed by an Invisible Force

One summer evening, Bims took a group of teenagers into the cave for a tour. After they had been there about an hour looking at rock formations and talking in the back room, they began walking back toward the entrance when one of the girls in the group began making sarcastic remarks about Kate. She cursed and said many nasty things about Kate, most likely because she was disappointed that she did not see or hear anything strange.

Groups must walk in single-file between the cave's back and first rooms because the passageway is so narrow. As the group of teenagers made their way between the rooms, the girl who had been cursing and making sarcastic remarks about Kate suddenly began to fall backwards as if she had been pushed. Landing on the cave's floor, she angrily exclaimed, "I was just slapped!" Because the ceiling is very low in the back passageway, Bims and the others suggested that she had probably just bumped her head and would be fine.

"No!" exclaimed the girl, "something hit me in the jaw, and damned hard! It felt soft like velvet, but the blow was solid." After the girl got up and the group reached a better-lit area, Bims and the others looked at her face and found welts and fingerprints where she claimed she was slapped. The whole group, Bims included, hightailed it out of the cave — leaving several shoes behind in the process. At least the only footsteps in the cave that evening were those of the group and not like the invisible ones Bims encountered several weeks later.

Mysterious Footsteps in the Cave

One morning after a storm, Bims was in the cave straightening out rocks that had been either dislodged or dislocated by the water flowing through the cave because of the recent storm. While sifting the rocks with his shovel and hoe, he began hearing a noise that was much different from the sounds coming from his tools. It sounded as if someone was walking towards him from the cave's back room. This sound of what he thought to be approaching footsteps compelled him to ask who was there and what they needed. There was no answer, so he asked again; and again – still no answer.

Bims gathered his tools and moved closer to the cave's entrance where began working again. After a few minutes passed, he once again heard the sound of approaching footsteps. Frightened, his german shepherd stood motionless and stared in the direction the sounds were coming from. The invisible footsteps progressed down the front passageway and past Bims – leaving behind what he later described as "an eerie set of human footprints." Bims' dog never entered the cave again.

Singing Heard Near the Red River

One Saturday afternoon in the late 1970s, a group of people from Nashville visited the cave in hopes of seeing Kate; however, upon their arrival they learned that Bims was not there to give them a tour. Knowing they wouldn't be able to get past the cave's entrance, they decided to walk down the path and at least get a look at the entrance and the Red River below.

After talking and joking around several minutes near the steel entrance gate, everyone began to feel a very strange feeling they later described as like they were being watched and were unwelcome. While hurriedly walking up the path to their vehicles, they began hearing what sounded like an old woman's voice somewhere near the cave's entrance — singing religious hymns in what was later described as a beautiful, high-pitched voice but not understandable. The singing faded away, as did the visitors.

What makes the account of the visitors from Nashville so significant is that noises were heard coming from the cave by people who were some distance away at the time. Unlike most noises, which faded as soon as visitors left the cave, the singing was heard all the way up the path and in Bims' back yard. Nevertheless, as time went on, more events of this nature occurred — sometimes inside or right outside of Bims' house.

Sounds of Glass Breaking

One evening, a friend of the Eden family came to visit and spend the night. Everyone decided to retire after talking for a good portion of the evening. As the woman entered the guest bedroom, she heard what sounded like someone dropping and breaking a glass of water on the floor in front of her. She yelled, "Hey, something dropped right in front of me and broke all over the floor! I didn't even have time to turn on the light, but I know that nobody else was in here. What's going on!"

Having also heard the sound, Bims and his wife went to the room to see what happened and clean up any broken glass. However, to their amazement, they found no broken glass and the floor was in the same, clean shape as it had always been. Notwithstanding, the noise was easily recognizable and heard by everyone in the house. No glass or scrapes were ever found on the floor of the guest bedroom.

In the days of John Bell, animals, dogs especially, became agitated when Kate came around – usually growling, tucking their tails, and letting the fur on their backs stand straight up. Even almost two centuries later, dogs still occasionally act this way on and near the old Bell farm. While it is common for dogs to bark and chase other animals, it is very much out of the ordinary for two dogs to suddenly awaken in the middle of the night and begin fighting with something "invisible."

Dogs Attack an Invisible Entity

One of Bims' sons was sleeping peacefully when he was awakened by the sound of their dogs growling, snapping, and making other vicious noises. He sprang quickly from his bed and looked out the window. He saw the dogs running around in circles under one of the outside lights, trying to fight with something that was seemingly invisible.

Because of another outside light, Bims' son could clearly see the front yard as well, and there did not appear to be any other animals present. The fight eventually died down but nothing in the form of an animal was ever seen. The dogs remained in a frightened, trance-like state for the next several days.

Human Figure Leaves No Tracks in the Snow

Another strange happening at Bims' house occurred around 4 A.M. one morning in the dead of winter after several inches of show had fallen. After having slept several hours, Bims was suddenly awakened by what sounded like knocks at his front door.

He slowly got out of bed and proceeded to the living room where he looked out the window to see who was knocking. It was too late — the person had left. After giving some thought to the bitter-cold temperature and snow that covered many roads in the area, Bims concluded that the person would most likely return to his front door in the next hour or two.

After staying awake and puffing on a cigar for

about an hour, Bims once again heard knocks at his front door. By the time he opened the door a few seconds later, he noticed that the person was already walking away. He could not identify the person because they were wearing a long, black coat with a high collar and were walking in the opposite direction. One strange thing Bims did notice was that this person was wearing very wide boots, similar to those made from partially treated leather back in the early 1800s.

After watching the person walk toward the nearby sinkhole and stop behind a tree, Bims yelled for his wife to wake up. She came into the living room and he asked her to watch the tree. They thought the person was knocking to see if anyone was at home, and if there was not an answer, planned on breaking in.

Bims quickly got dressed and fetched his shotgun, and then slowly proceeded out a door and through the back yard to an area away from his security light. He quietly inched his way around the yard until he reached a place where he could see behind the tree where the person was hiding. He found nothing behind the tree and no sign of footprints other than his own anywhere in the yard, even where he had seen the person walking just minutes earlier. There was more than four inches of snow on the ground at the time.

Flickering Lights on the Bell Farm

On many occasions, even years earlier when Bims was living on other parts of the old Bell farm, he has seen flickering lights float across the fields and above the trees that dot the banks of the Red River. On many occasions the lights moved in the direction of the old Bell cemetery and came to a stop, sometimes hovering for more than thirty minutes before disappearing. The lights always began very faint and seemed to pick up energy as they moved closer to the Bell cemetery. Once the lights appeared to be in the cemetery, they remained bright for some time before instantaneously disappearing.

Others have reported flickering lights on and near the old Bell farm as well. Even John Bell's family and their slaves reported this phenomenon in their era. These lights typically resemble candles and flicker as they move across the fields toward the old Bell home site or the Bell cemetery atop the hill next to it. It has been said that the best time to see these lights is on cold, winter nights with a strong wind and constant drizzle.

Unidentified Male Figure in Cemetery

One evening, a man was driving his family along what was once known as Brown's Ford and Springfield Road when he saw what looked like more than a hundred candles floating in different directions across the field that was once John Bell's front yard. Being curious more so than frightened, he stopped his car and began walking across the field – eventually ending up near the old Bell cemetery where the candles had seemingly led him.

Although the candles were no longer visible, the area seemed very well lit considering it was a moonless night. As the man looked around in several directions, more or less just to "get his bearings," he noticed a male figure walking just beyond the Bell cemetery and down the slope on the opposite side of the hill.

He called out but received no answer, and the figure soon disappeared over the horizon. The man later described the figure as being about six feet tall and having a receding hairline, a short beard, and a somewhat "long" face. Some say that the ghost of John Bell himself haunts the old Bell cemetery, and the description given by the man in the previous account would have fit John Bell to a tee.

The Old Steel Bridge

For many years, the road between Adams, Tennessee and Keysburg, Kentucky crossed the Red River on an old, steel bridge that was removed in the mid 1970s and replaced by the concrete span that is used today, some 100 feet down the river.

Many people have reported seeing strange things on and around the old bridge at night, such as a light, human-shaped mist floating just above the bridge's surface. The mist usually began to fade away or drift down into the Red River within a few minutes of initially seeing it. No explanation has been given to this phenomenon, and it has been seen many times when the weather was such that no fog could have possibly formed.

Another anomaly encountered on the old bridge was car motors mysteriously dying and not starting for several minutes, then finally restarting and moving on. This phenomenon was also experienced by earlier generations, long before the automobile was invented, when horses mysteriously stopped in the middle of the bridge and refused to move for several minutes. The horses eventually started moving again as though nothing had happened.

Double Shadows on Brown's Ford Bluff

There is a particular spot along the old Nashville-Clarksville roadbed on Brown's Ford Bluff where it is said that a person can stand and cast a double shadow on certain nights.

A clear, moonlit night obviously accounts for one shadow; however, it is unknown what causes the second shadow to be cast at times. In addition, one only needs to walk a foot in any direction to "lose" the second shadow. This spot is also a good distance away from the glare of any nearby lights.

Like all other reported encounters with Kate, the double shadows cast along the old roadbed is not a consistent thing; i.e., some people experience it and some don't, standing in the same spot at the same time. For example, two people walked up to this spot late one night and only one could cast a double shadow, despite the fact that both were wearing the same color of clothing and stood on the same spot.

Also consistent with other reported encounters with Kate is that there is no predictability of when this phenomenon will occur. It could happen two or three nights in a row, then not reoccur until several months later and only on one night. To those who are scientifically inclined, there obviously exists no less than twenty different variables pertaining to this scenario; however, to the author's knowledge, a correlation among those variables has yet to be made by anyone in the scientific field.

The Kirby Family Buys the Cave

Bill "Bims" Eden died in the 1980s, and the Kirby family purchased the farm in the spring of 1993 after it had stood vacant for several years. The Kirbys have experienced a number of strange occurrences in and around the cave. One of the first such experiences for the Kirbys took place around 1994, when their daughter, Candy, was photographed sitting on a rock outside the cave's entrance.

Strange Figure Appears in Photo

After the picture was developed, it was noted that some "thing" that was not present when it was taken appeared to be standing behind Candy. The entity appeared as a human-like figure, resembling a man in his mid-twenties with a dark, thick mustache and very large muscles in his upper body.

The picture has been analyzed on different occasions and it has been confirmed that the human-like figure is not a "double," but an entirely separate entity. The shoes worn by this entity do not match those worn by Candy, and part of the entity's body was actually in front of her at one place in the picture.

A Serpent Crawls Up a Girl's Leg

At the same rock on another occasion, a picture was taken of two Girl Scouts. After being developed, the picture no longer showed one of the girls and showed a two-headed serpent crawling up the other girl's leg. Other strange pictures have been taken near this rock, and for reasons unknown, getting a good picture of the cave's entrance is almost unheard-of.

Another picture, taken in the 1970s when Bims Eden lived at the farm, shows a group of people standing in front of an old outbuilding that was still on the property at the time near the top of Brown's Ford Bluff, where many strange things have happened over the years. In this picture, a lady casts a shadow different from what her own would look like. Instead of a side-profile of her head and body, the side-profile of a woman dressed in pioneer clothing and holding a baby appears in the picture.

Orbs and Mists Appear in Pictures

The three pictures mentioned above, in addition to many other pictures that show mists, orbs and other strange phenomena in and around the cave, are owned by the Kirbys and shown to visitors who tour the cave.

Many pictures that show unexplainable things consistently reveal orbs in certain areas of the cave. [u] The most common places where orbs are captured on camera are at the cave's entrance and inside a small, dark hole in the back room. Whether digital media or regular film is used, the pictures always turn out the same.

One must be careful when analyzing pictures of orbs, as the light from a flashbulb can reflect off a falling drop of water and produce an image almost identical to an orb. Generally, if an image is not a complete circle, it is most likely not an orb. Most orbs are circular whereas drops of water lose their circular shape while falling through the air.

Many people with video cameras have captured orbs moving randomly in and out of scenes. These scenes must be analyzed in slow motion to determine whether they contain real orbs or only drops of water falling from the cave's ceiling. If the image moves across the scene in a horizontal pattern, it is not a falling drop of water — this would defy the law of gravity, and there is no wind inside the cave.

A picture that Chris Kirby took of the sinkhole near her home one winter revealed a light mist rising from the depths of the sinkhole. This is normal in that the temperature outside was very cold and the sinkhole's base is in the cave, which is 57 degrees year-round. It is the equivalent of warm water being poured onto a cold surface — steam rises. What makes this particular picture stand out is that the mist forms the image of an evil-looking face with perfectly placed attributes — eyes, nose, and mouth.

In addition to pictures like those described above, investigators have taken samples of unrecognizable footprints and made tape recordings of sounds such as children playing, women screaming, dogs growling, and labored breathing at different places in both the cave and around the old Bell farm in general.

Technology has made it possible to digitally photograph and electronically document unusual occurrences that could not have been communicated previously without aid of a pen and word-of-mouth, as was the case in the days John Bell and his family walked this land. Today, many of the unusual occurrences on the old Bell farm are captured not only in still picture and book form, but on videotapes and audio recorders as well.

Some anomalies believed to be manifestations of Kate are permanent in nature and can be seen at any time. Perhaps the most astonishing of such permanent manifestations is a rock formation near the back of the cave that closely resembles the left side of a "witch" head. [v]

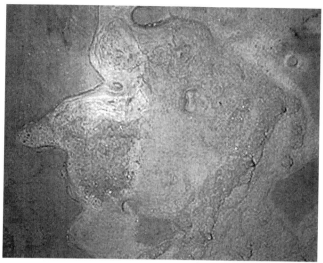

This natural rock formation on the ceiling of "Bell Witch" Cave is known as the "Witch Head."

The "witch head" formation clearly shows a forehead, eye, ear, nose, mouth, and chin that were forged by nature onto the cave's ceiling. In all likelihood, this natural formation evolved over thousands, and perhaps millions of years. Many believe this eerie rock formation to be a manifestation of Kate; however, many modern-day stories suggest that she still manifests herself in what was unmistakably her favorite form during the days of John Bell – that being none other than the form of a rabbit.

A Rabbit Leads to an Ancestor's Grave

One morning several years ago, one of John Bell's direct descendants was rabbit hunting a few miles from Springfield when he came upon a rabbit and tried to shoot it. Unscathed, the rabbit quickly darted across an old road and hopped into a patch of deep undergrowth. As the man walked through the undergrowth trying to flush out the rabbit, he found a lone, pointed rock near the center and decided to investigate.

Upon removing the undergrowth from around the rock, he discovered that it was the gravestone of Joel Egbert Bell, one of his ancestors and the youngest child of John and Lucy Bell. The rabbit was never seen again; but because Kate often manifested herself in the form of a rabbit, it was decided that this incident was her doing. Despite Kate's seemingly bad reputation, this particular descendant of John Bell was most likely glad to have found the grave of his ancestor.

It has been the author's experience on occasion to jump large rabbits in the weeds near the old well on the Bell property, about one hundred yards from where the old house stood. The same can be said for the Batts cemetery that is located about a mile south of the old Bell farm.

When rabbits on the old Bell farm hop out of the weeds adjacent to the old well and into the tobacco field, they seemingly vanish. It should not have been difficult to see a rabbit hopping across the field because most of these incidents happened after the tobacco harvest and when the field was clear. One experience with the "rabbit phenomenon" took place on a fall afternoon in 1999, when the author and several others were on the farm (with permission, of course) taking photographs for a book.

A Rabbit Throws Dirt Fifteen Feet

One of the people in the group, who was standing some fifteen feet from the well, saw a large rabbit spring out of the weeds and begin hopping in the direction of an open field. In the process, the person was hit in the face by several large chunks of dirt that flew through the air as the rabbit jumped.

The rabbit all of the sudden vanished and was never seen again. The notion that a rabbit can kick chunks of dirt fifteen feet at a 45-degree angle and hit someone in the face is unheard of. What exactly caused the dirt to fly so far remains a mystery; however, the author and several other people witnessed this remarkable occurrence with their own eyes.

Rabbits Disappear from a Video Tape

In early June of 2000, the author was in Robertson County making pictures for the book you are now reading, when he was suddenly forced to take cover from an approaching storm that consisted of lightening, hail and funnel clouds. As his car shook violently from the force of the high winds, he made his way down an old road between two fields where he came upon a shady, secluded area next to a sharp curve in the road.

He pulled into a small opening in the weeds and sat until the storm blew over. As the fog began clearing from his windows, the author noticed several very old gravestones under the large trees just beyond the weeds. This was apparently one of several forgotten cemeteries in the northwestern end of Robertson County. Glancing out his window at the gravestones, he recognized the names of people who lived in an era now long forgotten. Many of the names were those who had figured prominently into the early growth of Robertson County and, in several cases, the legend of the "Bell Witch." One name in particular stood out – Batts.

After getting his raincoat from his trunk and

assembling his photography and video equipment, the author made his way through the weeds and undergrowth to get a closer look at the graves. Two rabbits suddenly jumped out of the nearby weeds. This seemed very natural at the time and only served to spawn visions of rabbit stew and a fried rabbit dinner in the author's mind.

The rabbits began darting in and out of the weeds around several of the graves, and then hopped playfully in wide circles around the author as if trying to surround him. A third rabbit had joined the others by this time and the author began filming just for fun. The three rabbits continued their playful antics for some time before hopping into the deep undergrowth and not returning. The author spent the next two hours filming the Batts cemetery, transcribing names and dates to compile what might be referred to as a "video genealogical report." After returning home late that evening, the author reviewed the images he captured of the Batts cemetery on both cameras. While the entire cemetery and gravestones appeared as was expected, the rabbits were nowhere to be seen in the picture.

Baby Cries Heard from a Gravestone

Another incident, which took place on this same day, happened at the present-day location of Red River Baptist Church in Adams, Tennessee. While walking the massive graveyard behind the church, the author saw a small rabbit standing between two gravestones several yards in front of him. The rabbit quickly darted behind a large gravestone in hopes of hiding.

A little background information is necessary at this point. The author spent most of his childhood and formative years in the country, and as such, developed a strong passion for the taste of fried rabbit. After having hunted rabbits for most of his life, he knows that if you "startle" a rabbit, it will go into cardiac arrest and die on the spot.

After thinking about the situation for a short time, and without taking his eyes off the gravestone that the rabbit ran behind, the author decided to sneak up to the gravestone in hopes of startling the rabbit hiding on the other side. Fortunately, for the rabbit, the author made too much noise and it hopped several yards before hiding behind a different gravestone.

The author walked over to the second gravestone in a normal fashion, no longer wanting to startle the rabbit. When he got there and looked, the rabbit was nowhere to be found. This particular gravestone was very tall and had no inscription on its sides; but instead, had an inscription on the top. The author, who is well over six feet tall, stretched upward to read the inscription. It turned out to be the grave of an infant who had died many years before.

Thinking the rabbit might have crawled under the exposed bottom corner of the gravestone, the author slapped one of its sides in hopes of flushing out the rabbit. The author began walking away when he realized that the rabbit was not going to come out. After taking about four steps, he heard the very distinct sound of a baby crying. It was impossible to tell from where this sound was coming; it seemed to be coming from "everywhere." After looking towards several houses, learning that no windows were open, and no babies were outside, he looked back at the gravestone. The crying immediately stopped.

CHAPTER TWENTY-TWO

Letters Describing Encounters

THE FOLLOWING WRITTEN ACCOUNTS are but a few of the many received by the author, which he feels are indicative of Kate's characteristics for the most part. The author personally observed the encounters described in the last of the following accounts and has every reason to believe the first two as well.

Orbs, Moaning and Mist at the Cave

"I first came up with the idea of going to the Bell Witch Cave back in June of 1999, when my mother was down visiting and brought a newspaper article about the cave. At that point in time, I had made up my mind to go, and we were low on money so I was glad to have an affordable outing I could do with my teenage son, Rick. He is into folklore, Spirits, etc., plus was always in a cave whenever possible with his Aunt Toni when we lived in middle Tennessee.

We arrived in Lebanon, TN the last week of June. We had family to visit first, but going to the cave was high on both our lists of things to do. During this time, I found my Mom's copy of the Red Book (too bad the cover has fallen off) and decided to go ahead and read it again (I had read it several times in my life). It would make me too nervous to read it at night, though.

Every day for about 5 days, that we had planned to go to Adams, it would rain; so we would have to change our plans, knowing we could not go into the cave if the water was too high.

Our chance finally arrived on July 3rd, but our plans were almost changed at the last minute. My 3-year-old son, Gordon, and I were playing and he scratched the inside of my eye. It immediately started watering, and I couldn't keep it open without terrible pain. I was determined to get to the cave, as it was almost an obsession by this point. My son, Rick, stated, 'Maybe something doesn't want you at the cave.'

When the continuous watering had stopped, I decided to try to drive to Adams. The pain was VERY uncomfortable, though. Rick needed to stop off at Rivergate Mall while on the way, and while he was inside the continuous watering started again. When he came back out, he suggested that I go to the doctor instead of driving on to the cave. I wasn't about to lose my last chance to go to the cave so on we went.

As we exited off the interstate and began the 10-mile journey to Adams, we became more and more anxious. Of course not knowing where we were going at first got us slightly lost. We eventually found the Post Office, received directions, and finished out the short drive to the cave.

As we drove down the gravel driveway, the anxiety between us grew. We weren't nervous or scared, but very excited. With my eye still hurting badly, we went up to the house where Lisa took our admission fee and started us down the path leading to the cave.

I had a 35mm camera, and Rick had a Camcorder with night vision. Our first stop was in the front room of the cave, where an Indian grave is located. As Lisa was giving the tour speech, Rick was recording. He did not see it as he was recording, but during this time an orb very quickly entered the frame on the right in the middle and exited the bottom on the right side.

We next went to the back room where we sat on a rock, talked a little and listened a lot. At the same time, my son and I heard a slapping sound. We know we both heard it because we looked at each other with an excited look. We heard the slapping once again. Rick also said he heard a moaning sound, but I did not hear this. I have no reason to think he would make this up. At that time though, my eye all of a sudden stopped hurting. I could still feel where it had been scratched, but the pain had totally disappeared.

As we were leaving the cave, I decided to pick up a rock out of the cave to take with me, and I still have that rock sitting in my kitchen. Lisa then showed us the photos they had in their albums, and those kind of gave me the creeps, but we never were scared. We never had bad luck since picking up the rock. My mother did not want it in her house though, so it sat out in my rental car.

About 1 1/2 weeks after our return home, I did dream, twice, of the Bell Witch Cave. There not anything bad in the dream, however I did not feel comfortable, but I was never scared. I have never dreamt of it since. Upon watching the video of our trip, we discovered the orb and it did give me the chills at first, but now it just excites me. I had a picture from the 35mm of a mist along the driveway leaving the Bell farm, and a picture that has something that resembles a face with eyes and nose. Rick and I have decided this would be a yearly trip for us, and we have even kicked around the idea of relocating to that area in a couple of years once he graduates high school. ᵂ

Lisa Edgeworth
Boca Raton, Florida
September 1999

A Bad Day in Adams, A Terrible Night in Los Angeles – Kate Follows a Family

On August 21, 1999, my wife and our oldest granddaughter visited the Bellwood cemetery in Adams. We had no intentions of going to the cave until we noticed some really strange things about some of the gravestones of the descendents of John Bell.

On the east side of the cemetery there are several graves of Bells. In each case, the males died at about 20 years old but their wives lived long lives; kill the males and you kill the namesake. There is one male buried there that lived to be 30. He had been studying to be a lawyer at some highly rated law school and, after returning home from law school, died shortly thereafter.

On the west side there was one grave that really blew us away, and was probably what made us to decide to go on over to the cave for a visit.

However, at this time I in all honesty was still quite doubtful of such things, although I have had several odd things happen to me. The grave is resting place of a male child who was born around the turn of the century on Aug. 21. He died two years later, on Jul. 21. As I mentioned earlier, the day's date that we were there was Aug. 21.

Well let me tell you, and believe me please, I under no circumstances would dare tell things concerning Spiritual matters if I didn't at least believe what I am saying. I have at least some respect for my soul, although I don't walk in the presence of the Holy Spirit. At one time, I did live that life every waking moment but somehow have let myself stray from the narrow path. [x]

The moment that we entered the cave, I was overcome with a sense of being watched, or at least aware of some unseen presence, although I never thought of myself as a person with that gift.

In the room where the Indian grave is, I felt as if something was looking at me from the small tunnel that is just behind it. The lady that was escorting us had not even mentioned anything about it, and I actually thought I was letting my imagination run wild. Then she started to tell us that things had been seen and photographed in that tunnel, and shortly thereafter, two guys with video cams were picking up a sphere of light that was separating into two spheres and then joining back together into one. They were so carried away that they did not continue back into the cave with the rest of us.

Then, as we stood in the larger part of that same room, I was overcome by the feeling of rushing wind that sent a chilling feeling through me as I was staring at the tunnel that leads back into the cave. But, there was no air stirring in the cave!

Still, I was telling myself that I was just being too imaginative.   As we went back though that opening and deeper into the cave, a guy behind, who also had brought his video cam suddenly, said, 'my camera just went dead,' just a few steps past the spot I had been staring at earlier. Then, as he stepped a few feet farther, it suddenly came back on by itself. At this point, my doubts began to get replaced by astonishment.

A little later, he was showing me some tape he had shot where the camera was picking up something just before it went dead. There was nothing but static. After we had got back outside, he showed me some tape he had shot the day before that had captured a small ball of light in that same little opening behind the Indian grave. It was amazing.

My wife and I took sick after we left and stayed that way for weeks. This I cannot actually blame on the cave because we were told of a similar virus that was going around at the time. However, the symptoms were really a little odd for what I generally have when suffering from a virus. We are team drivers of an 18-wheeler, and are in Los Angeles every Monday evening, and have been for the last 3.5 years. We have a dedicated run, and deliver Saturn auto parts to the same Ryder warehouse every week. It is protected by a state-of-the-art burglar alarm, which I have to shut off when we arrive there after business hours.

As I was returning from the keypad to drive the truck though the gate after disabling the alarm, I heard my wife beating on the windshield of the freightliner we drive. When I climbed back in, I asked why she was beating on the glass, and she said she wasn't as she looked at me like she thought I was goofy. I asked her again, and she again said she didn't and thought there must have been someone close-by that was hitting on something and it was echoing between the concrete buildings, which is quite common.

When we stopped at the back of the lot, my wife was letting our Yorky Terriers relieve themselves as I parked the truck. I heard what I thought was some goofy truck driver making a ridiculous sound on the C.B., but when I reached up to turn it off I discovered that it wasn't even on. At that point, I began to feel very worried.

I returned to the keypad and reactivated the alarm as my wife put the dogs back in the truck. That keypad has never made but one sound, and that is a little beep as the buttons are pushed to enter the code and to turn it on and off. As I pushed the final button to turn it back on, it made a sound like either a bunch of children laughing, or a sound like an old woman laughing wickedly; but I can't say for sure which. I jumped back about three feet and looked all around in panic. Of course there wasn't anything around me that wasn't supposed to be. I reached and shut the box that houses the keypad, and then took off running like a madman.

Halfway across the lot, I stopped dead in my tracks and realized that if something had followed me all the way from Tennessee to L.A., I had no place to run and that there was no sense in acting like a childish fool. I have not been scared or panicked since, but there is something with me. I can sense its presence all the time, and in fact know that it's with me now.

I had planned on going back to Adams the following week with my video cam after the first visit, but have been putting it off not only because of being sick, but also I am just now getting back the nerve to return. I have been having nightmares and have been hearing voices, the last of which was last Wednesday night as I was drifting into the drowsy state just before falling asleep. I have thought for years that I could hear voices at that point. I think of that point between sleep and consciousness as 'twilight,' but it always sounded like many people at one time and could never understand what was being said. Last Wednesday, I distinctly heard a woman's voice say, in a low-pitched tone, 'come with me.'

Things have happened here at our home from time to time, but until we went to the cave in August, I was telling myself it was just our imaginations. I have since begun to believe we have been victims of some type of paranormal events in our own home, but are just now beginning to face the truth of it all.

Don Hampton
Robertson County, Tennessee
September 1999

Miscellaneous Happenings in the Cave

With this letter, I wish to share with you just a few of the things I have either witnessed or been told about by people I've run across when visiting the Bell Witch Cave in Adams, Tennessee.

While I don't doubt that these encounters involved a supernatural entity of some type, only the first strikes me as being characteristic of Kate, the so-called 'Bell Witch.' As you will learn later, there is a strong possibility that hundreds — and possibly thousands — of Spirits roam the area.

One afternoon in the summer of 1995, I was near Adams and decided to stop by the cave. As I waited for a guide to return, I noticed a very frightened young couple standing in the owners' front yard. I pretended to ignore them, but I was closely watching their facial expressions and listening to them.

They had apparently been on a tour of the cave an hour or so earlier and encountered something that terrified them to the point that their teeth were still chattering as they spoke. After about five minutes, the guide came up the hill with some other visitors and then took me down to the cave. I found out that the young couple, while standing near the cave's back room, heard the sounds of children playing and an old woman talking behind the large flowstone at the end of the passageway. The others didn't hear anything.

On another occasion, I was standing in the cave's first room talking with some friends when one of the group began complaining of "growling" sounds coming from the cave's upper-level. No one present, myself included, heard these "growling" sounds, but the person said it had been going on since we first got there. Most of the group, including myself, thought the person was joking; however, after about five minutes, his face had become white as a sheet and sweat was pouring from his head.

One afternoon in the summer of 1999, I was walking along with a group and taking pictures of the cave for a book when one man began complaining of an ice-cold 'sticking' sensation in his neck. He said it felt as if he was being stuck in the neck with a cold needle. As the tour continued, he kept his right hand over his neck but said nothing more of the incident.

After the tour concluded, everyone walked back up the hill and began talking and looking at some pictures that the cave's owner had on display. Convinced that the man's earlier neck problem was either a circulatory or nervous system anomaly, I inquired, "Hey man, how's your neck doing; any better now?" "Yes, much better!" replied the man, "but it's still very cold."

At this point, I began trying to think up an acceptable reason to feel of this man's neck, which was of course to no avail. I decided to turn the tables a bit. "Wow! That must be a strange feeling – I mean, after all, we've been standing out here for over an hour in ninety-degree heat and you say your neck is still cold. If you neck's still cold, I bet Kate really has it in for you!" I exclaimed. As my calculated logic would have it, he responded, "Well here, reach over and feel it for yourself!"

Several of us felt his neck and agreed that one spot was ice-cold despite the hot weather! I gave the man my card, and he called the following day saying that the cold sensation in his neck went away as soon as he left the property.

Pat Fitzhugh
Nashville, Tennessee
July 2000

CHAPTER TWENTY-THREE

The Bell Farm Today

TODAY, ONLY SMALL TRACES REMAIN of the once-thriving Bell plantation where cotton, corn and tobacco were grown, children strolled merrily through large pear orchards, slaves worked in the fields from dawn until dusk, and where the most terrifying and baffling phenomenon ever known to humankind took place.

The land that was once John Bell's front yard, covered by an orchard of towering pear trees and having a small, fenced-in lane leading through it from the main road, is now a tobacco field. There are no signs suggesting that pear orchards and a pretty lane existed on that location during the Tennessee's early frontier days, an era that has long been forgotten and about which very little is known today. The last of the original Bell pear trees deteriorated more than a century ago, the land has been cleared

and tilled many times over since then.   The only
structure on this land today is a tobacco barn that
was built in the Twentieth Century.

**This is what remains of the Bell farm today. It
was John Bell, his sons, and their slaves, who
first cleared the fields in the foreground. The
field in the left background was a pear orchard
among which the Bell home was situated**

All that remains of what was once home to John
Bell and his family is a long, narrow hole surrounded
by trees and filled with runoff dirt, stones from the
house's   foundation,   and   thorny   undergrowth.
Almost 200 years ago, this "hole" was the cellar
underneath the Bell homestead. It is located on the
back side of the tobacco field and barely visible from
any road.

The trees in the foreground are leaning because the cellar of the old Bell home is filling in.

Amidst a large clump of weeds and undergrowth some 100 yards due north of the old Bell home site, and guarded by a lone tree in the middle of the tobacco field, is the well that was once used by John Bell and his family. An inscribed stone stating that Bells once used the well marks this site. The well has filled in considerably over the years and is now completely dry and less than eight feet deep.

This is the old well used by John Bell and his family. The concrete square is a modern addition.

Located on a cedar-covered knoll about 300 yards due north of the old Bell home is the final resting place of John and Lucy Bell, Richard Williams Bell, and a number of the slaves who worked on the Bell farm during its heyday. [y] Despite the many graves in the old Bell cemetery, the only one remaining with an inscription is that of John and Lucy Bell, placed in 1957, six years after the original was taken. Other headstones in the old Bell cemetery were either never inscribed to begin with or have since become worn or stolen. [z]

The thicket in the picture above is all that remains of the old Bell cemetery. The only gravestone in the cemetery is the replacement stone for John Bell.

As a result of John Bell's estate settlement, John Jr. inherited the tract of land adjoining the homestead tract. [50] About a half mile due south of the old Bell cemetery, at the edge of a large cornfield, is a small cemetery that contains the graves of John Bell, Jr., his wife Elizabeth Gunn Bell, and several of their children. [aa] Across a dirt road from this cemetery is an inscribed stone that marks where John Bell, Jr's house stood. The house burned sometime after his death. [bb]

John Bell, Jr's house stood where the clump of trees is. A marker placed by descendants is all that remains.

A lot has changed since the days Kate terrorized the western end of Robertson County, torturing John Bell to his death and breaking the hearts of his daughter and the young man she loved so dearly. While some land has been cleared, the forests have reclaimed much of the land that was farmed during the days of John Bell.

Let us put all of this into perspective. One hundred and ten years, including the sinking of the Titanic, World Wars I and II, The Great Depression, the Holocaust, the Korean and Vietnam Wars, and scandals at the highest levels of government, have elapsed since the death of the *last* eyewitness to Kate's disturbances. 180 years, inclusive of the events listed above and in addition to the Civil War, the Industrial Revolution, and the first American railroad, have elapsed since John Bell breathed his final breath.

In the John Bell era, a horse was the only mode of transportation other than the foot. Now, we fly thousands of feet above the ground at speeds greater than 700 miles per hour, and have sent people on expeditions through space and to the moon. When a person misbehaved in the days of John Bell, they were tied to a tree, stripped, and beaten. Doors remained unlocked, people went wherever they chose, and people worked together for the common good.

Today, we have a judicial system that declares the misbehaved among us as the victims, and the more behaved and protection-conscious among us, the enemy. In the John Bell era, one human being could "own" another human being. Today, we are all of one people and everyone receives compensation for his or her work.

The graves of many of those who were very educated, wise and prominent during the John Bell era, and whose social etiquette far surpassed that which is commonplace today, lie beneath the earth unmarked and forgotten in fields of tobacco and corn, the forest, highways, and fenced-in areas on private property. cc

The way of life in the days of John Bell was much different than it is today, as incomprehensible to us today as life today was to those who lived then. The future always has the advantage of hindsight by its very nature, that being in the form of history; however, history provides us with little more than legal documents from the past and scattered patches of undergrowth upon which me can base our perception life in that long-past era. The rest is entirely up to our own, unique imaginations.

Aside from the Red River, the Red River Baptist Church, and the dirt that John Bell's family and slaves once farmed, the only remnant we have from that forgotten era is the Spirit that drove John Bell to his grave.

CHAPTER TWENTY-FOUR

Is Kate Always to Blame?

EACH WEEK, THE AUTHOR RECEIVES many written accounts of purported encounters with Kate in and around Adams, Tennessee. He also receives a number of letters from people who became disappointed because they did not experience anything unusual while visiting Adams.

While the notion that one will experience an encounter with the supernatural just by visiting Adams, the old Bell farm, or Bell Witch Cave is an easy one to accept, it must be understood that non-eventful visits far outnumber those in which something unexplainable and possibly of the supernatural occurs. There is no guarantee that one will experience a supernatural encounter just by visiting Adams, Tennessee.

One must take into consideration that many people have lived near the old Bell farm all their lives and never experienced anything unusual. Moreover, these same people pass the old Bell farm twice a day on their way to and from work. On the other hand, however, one might visit the old Bell farm on several different occasions and experience something unusual during each visit.

While the written accounts of supernatural encounters the author has received have been believable for the most part, he feels that only a small number of these encounters –might- the work of Kate. As was mentioned earlier, there are many supernatural entities, and Kate is not the only supernatural entity in Adams, Tennessee – there are probably thousands, as is the case with any other place. Although many of the entities encountered have reportedly possessed some of Kate's characteristics, conclusive evidence supporting claims that these encounters were in fact the work of Kate is lacking – mainly because human nature forces us to hasty conclusions when we are frightened.

The Power of Suggestion

To illustrate this point, let us return to the early Nineteenth Century in Robertson County and review the observations of one person who figured prominently into the legend.

John Johnston, who was one of the Bell family's neighbors and closest friends, saw the shadow of what looked like a long, sharp knife behind him while walking home from the Bell farm one morning.

He thought to himself, "If the Lord wants me to die, then I will die; I will not run." He stood still in his tracks to see what fate would deal him. The "knife" never disappeared, and after taking the time to analyze his surroundings, Johnston finally realized that the "knife" was actually the shadow of a cornstalk blade blowing in the wind.

After this incident, Johnston concluded that many

alleged encounters with "Kate" were most likely manifestations material things such as the cornstalk, but people jumped to hasty conclusions and ran for their lives without taking the time to adequately observe their surroundings.

Because stories of Kate's disturbances were so prevalent during that era, it was easy for a person to succumb to "the power of suggestion." This is not to say that Kate never existed or still doesn't exist; but only that the human mind is highly vulnerable to the power of suggestion, which can get the best of us if we don't stop for a reality check. When analyzing an experience believed to have been a manifestation of Kate, one must show that no logical basis and explanation for the encounter exists, and that based upon Kate's known characteristics, the entity encountered was in fact Kate.

Can the Encounter be Validated?

Any suspected encounter with the supernatural begins with an unexplainable incident, one for which no logical explanation exists after a reasonable effort has been made to analyze one's surroundings when the incident took place. What John Johnston did nearly two centuries ago is one of the most reasonable efforts one can put forth. Stop, look, and think before you decide to run. What you really see might be the shadow of a leaf blowing in the wind; or, it might be a Spiritual entity sapping away your energy until you faint helplessly.

Mechanics of Argument and Persuasion

Let us suppose that you have experienced an incident and found it "unexplainable." At this point, there is a subtle hint that you had an encounter with the supernatural. Although you have succeeded in establishing *possibility*, your case will remain weak until you establish *probability,* at which time your case will strengthen somewhat.

Establishing *probability* with regard to suspected supernatural encounters requires successfully matching the details of the incident to known characteristics of supernatural entities after making a detailed comparison between the two. One must understand not only the characteristics of the many different supernatural entities, but also which entities possess the powers to do certain things.

The differences among various supernatural entities are more than subtle, and a comprehensive discussion of the most significant differences is presented in a later chapter. For the purpose of our discussion, the important thing to understand at this point is that an incident's being deemed "unexplainable" does not, in and of itself, mean that an encounter with the supernatural has taken place.

For now, let us suppose that the details of the incident you experienced match closely with the characteristics of some supernatural entity. Congratulations are now in order: you have successfully established a *compelling* argument based on *probability*, which carries more weight than *possibility.*

While the author now feels *compelled* to accept your argument, you have yet to *persuade* him to accept it. A *persuasive* argument is based upon *reasonable certainty*; i.e., information that would lead a reasonable person to believe, with a high level of confidence, that something is certain – no questions about it.

Building a persuasive argument with regard to a suspected supernatural encounter entails evaluating many general theories about the supernatural world, and using those theories to link the elements of *cause, medium,* and *effect* to the incident you experienced. Without delving into supernatural theories, some of which will be examined in a later chapter, let us instead identify the hypothetical incident we have been discussing, its matching supernatural characteristics, and a generally-accepted supernatural theory that will link the elements of *cause, medium* and *effect* to the incident and formulate a persuasive argument.

The hypothetical incident you experienced on many occasions was the repeated slamming of your 12-year-old daughter's bedroom door in the middle of the night while she was fast asleep. You checked to make sure all doors and windows were shut and not creating a draft, you made sure the dog was outside and not rubbing up against her door, you made sure her ceiling fan was not causing a draft, and you locked her door.

Despite of all this, her door continued to slam open and shut, repeatedly. You have established a good reason why this incident is unexplainable, which in turn suggests that it is *possibly* the manifestation of some supernatural entity.

The details of the incident are specific in nature – a door is moving on its own and is making a lot of noise. After reading up on various supernatural entities and their characteristics, you are satisfied that a "poltergeist" is responsible for your daughter's door being slammed. Objects moving by themselves and spontaneous loud noises are indicative of the presence of a poltergeist.

Based on your description of the incident and the known characteristics of poltergeists, which are in fact supernatural entities, it is now *probable* that you are experiencing encounters with the supernatural. The author feels *compelled* to believe you; however, you have yet to *persuade* him.

After conducting further research on the attributes and characteristics of poltergeists, you learn that many (but not all) poltergeists are evoked by brainwaves emitted from the subconscious mind of adolescent or pre-adolescent people, usually because of severe emotional or physical trauma. Things now begin to come together – your daughter was involved in a near-fatal accident several months ago, her boyfriend left her, and she has been treated for severe depression for the past several months. You have now established probability that a poltergeist is responsible for the incidents you have been experiencing.

Thus far, you have established a likely *cause* (your daughter's miscellaneous trauma), an *effect* (her door being repeatedly slammed without explanation), and a suspected *medium* (a poltergeist). In an attempt to link these elements together and persuade the author to believe that a poltergeist is what you are experiencing, you research several paranormal encyclopedias and other resources, eventually locating an interesting topic, "Recurrent Spontaneous Psychokinesis."

As you read about the topic, you learn that the moving of the door is the result of psychokinesis; i.e., mind over matter. In this case, as is the case with most poltergeist cases, it is not the conscious, but the subconscious mind that moves inanimate objects. It is recurrent because it happens more than once, and spontaneity means that these occurrences happen suddenly and without warning, following no schedule or pattern.

Congratulations! You have *persuaded* the author to believe that a poltergeist is disturbing your household. Your finding the term, "Recurrent Spontaneous Psychokinesis," which is the correct term in this case, links the elements of *cause*, *medium,* and *effect.* However, what if you later tell the author that you occasionally hear voices when the door is slamming? At this point, the author rejects your entire poltergeist argument – because poltergeists do not speak. Point: Understanding the characteristics of supernatural entities is essential to furthering your argument beyond the point of *possibility.*

While a person might experience and report what they truly believe to be a manifestation of Kate, it could have been some other supernatural entity, or perhaps just an encounter with their own imagination; i.e., the power of suggestion.

We have just discussed the building blocks of a persuasive argument that should make one feel reasonably certain that an encounter with the supernatural has taken place, if the requirements are met. Let the author note that he used an oversimplified example in the previous discussion. Real-life situations involve more variables and conflicting theories, but the same analytical thought processes are required nevertheless.

CHAPTER TWENTY-FIVE

Supernatural Concepts

WHERE DOES KATE FIT IN? What was or is the entity that held an entire community captive in a malevolent reign of terror during the early 1800s, and which became the only documented case in history where a man was killed by a supernatural entity? Numerous researchers, historians, and authors have attempted to answer this question for nearly two centuries; and while having posed many thought-provoking theories, they still cannot provide an accurate explanation of this complex entity. The many personalities manifested and various disturbances created by the "Bell Witch" have made the legend not only the most terrifying legend known to humankind, but also the most perplexing.

In addition, unlike most legends and stories of the supernatural, the legend of the "Bell Witch" involves real people who actually lived at the places and during the times mentioned in the legend. This has already been proved by trips to the Tennessee State

Archives in Nashville and the Robertson County Archives in Springfield. Everything is there – official records pertaining to every character, place, time, and social event mentioned in the legend of the "Bell Witch."

It would seem that with all the factual information pertaining to the characters, places and times, believing Kate really existed would be easy. However, the issue of "believing versus not believing" is not what has kept the legend of the "Bell Witch" alive for almost two centuries and compelled no fewer than ten authors to publish extensive works pertaining to it; nor is it why the Bell Witch Cave was recently identified as, "The Most Haunted Place in America" by a well-known paranormal organization. The legend of the "Bell Witch" is gaining in popularity all the time; however, if "believing versus not believing" is not the reason for its popularity, then what is?

Almost everyone the author has discussed the legend of the "Bell Witch" with, both locally and on the other side of the world, agrees that the legend is not a product of fabrication — there was in fact "something" wrong on the Bell farm in the early nineteenth century. A second point of consensus is that there still appears to be "something" wrong, although not nearly of the sinister forces it once carried.

What has made the legend of the "Bell Witch" the most perplexing paranormal mystery ever known to humankind is not the question of whether something was or is "wrong," but instead, the question "What was or is that 'something,' and why did it terrorize Robertson County and torment one of its most prominent citizens to his death?"

The basic attributes of any incident are: Who, what, where, when, how and why. The legend of the "Bell Witch" is more complex – the "what" attribute carries two, logically opposing connotations. Instead of only asking, "What happened?" (the normal connotation), we must also ask, "What was or is 'it'?" (the paranormal connotation). "What" is the most perplexing of all the legend's elements; however, we must still take into consideration the "who" attribute until we can prove that Kate was (or is) a supernatural entity – at which time the paranormal connotation of the "What" element will take center stage.

Proving whether the Bell disturbances were the acts of a supernatural entity or the product of a hoax requires two persuasive arguments — one that supports a particular theory and one that debunks the other theory. Can we do this? No. However, what we can do is build a persuasive argument supporting one theory and a compelling argument to debunk the other theory.

Even if we arrive at a conclusive answer as to "What" was and is still "wrong" at the Bell farm, there still remains another important attribute to consider: "Why?" Since attempting to explain the "Why" attribute would require considerable speculation, we will discuss possible "Why" scenarios later and without going to great lengths in trying to prove them.

Is the Incident Really Unexplainable?

The legend of the "Bell Witch" is the story of not one, but many unexplainable incidents that allegedly happened to a family. The story has been told here in such a way that the lack of any logical explanation should be self-evident; hence, we will not examine each incident from the standpoint of explainability. Our approach includes looking at several different entities and concepts, matching "Bell Witch" incidents to these entities and concepts, and then applying a theory that links the elements of *cause*, *medium*, and *effect*.

While reading the following discussions about supernatural entities and concepts, it is the reader's responsibility to keep an open mind and form his or her own conclusions as to *what* the "Bell Witch" was or is, and from there decide *why* the disturbances occurred. The reader may wish to form his or her own theory as to *why*, or adopt the author's theory – it is up to the reader.

Ghosts and Poltergeists

Many publications and researchers over the years have referred to the "Bell Witch" as either a *ghost* or *poltergeist*. The author has found no evidence that clearly suggests Kate was or is a *ghost*; however, her character and the nature of her disturbances closely align with the attributes and characteristics of a *poltergeist*.

The term *poltergeist* comes from the German words, *polter* and *geist*, which literally mean "noisy Spirit." Poltergeists cause physical disturbances ranging from rapping on walls to moving inanimate objects and physically abusing people. In addition to their propensity for noisy disturbances of a physical nature, poltergeists have been known to whisper on occasion.

A widely held misconception about these entities is that the terms, *poltergeist* and *ghost*, are synonymous. Although some similarity exists, there are differences that set the two entities apart. *Figure 1* on the following page illustrates the five major differences between ghosts and poltergeists.

Ghosts vs. Poltergeists

Attribute	Ghost	Poltergeist
Origin	Spirits of deceased beings, usually human, appearing frequently in certain places. They can appear in forms such as transparent entities, complete bodies, foggy mists, and smells (usually associated with the deceased while still living).	Theories suggest that poltergeists are mass forms of energy that a living person unknowingly controls, usually through a form of passive psychokinesis resulting from severe physical or psychic trauma. In some extreme cases, poltergeists have been linked to demons.
Association	Usually linked to a specific place or violent death. For example, the house the deceased lived in or the place where the deceased died.	Linked to a specific person or object. Some theories suggest that poltergeists can be linked to multiple objects and multiple people, taking a fraction of their energy from each person or object.
Apparitions	Appearance areas known to the deceased before their death. Unable leave those areas.	Can be triggered by a living person's trauma in any area at any time. Can travel.
Energy	Continuous over time.	Built up over time, then goes dormant and starts over again. Energy climaxes just before dormancy.
Danger	Not violent in a physical sense. Its appearance can cause severe mental terror, however.	At level-five (climax of energy), can become dangerous to the living – inflicting both mental and physical terror.

Figure 1: The major differences between ghosts and poltergeists.

Poltergeist activity is known as a *disturbance*, whereas ghost activity (fog, mist, transparent figures, etc.) is known as a *haunting*. The reasoning behind this distinction is that poltergeists are heard but not seen, and ghosts are seen but seldom heard.

Fewer than one thousand poltergeist cases have been documented over the years. A surprising number of those cases were the result of a prepubescent or teenage person's unknowingly evoking (bringing into existence) a poltergeist through psychokinetic energy generated by the subconscious mind, usually because of severe physical or emotional trauma. This energy process, commonly known as *Psychokinesis,* is the psychic ability to move or change the composition of inanimate objects; i.e., mind over matter.

Psychokinesis can be broken down into two major types: *Voluntary Psychokinesis* and *Recurrent Spontaneous Psychokinesis.* The former type is based on the power of concentration, whereas the latter type is completely independent of the conscious mind and is responsible for the spontaneous evocation of poltergeists. Despite psychokinesis playing a major role in many poltergeist cases, it should be noted that poltergeists can be evoked by other means as well. A poltergeist obtains its energy from the attention and fear paid to it by other beings, both human and animal.

The poltergeist is a progressive entity in that it passes through five, cumulative stages of power before reaching a period of dormancy and restarting at the first stage. Each stage in the progression compounds additional energy with the energy acquired at previous stages. The duration of each stage can vary from days to years, depending on the poltergeist's origin, initial type of power, and external influences. *Figure 2* on the following page illustrates the five stages of poltergeist progression. It can be seen clearly that Kate possessed a number of poltergeist-like characteristics.

Poltergeist Progression Stages

Stage	Description	Characteristics
1: Senses	The activity mainly revolves around the five senses of the human body.	Cold spots, strange noises, hearing footsteps, pets running from rooms, feeling of being watched.
2: Communication	Strange noises and smells are more easily discernable and direct.	Whispers, moans, animated shadows, breezes in closed areas, marks on floors or walls.
3: Physical	The poltergeist clearly makes its presence known. What could have been previously dismissed is now a real entity.	Appliances turning on/off, invisible hands touching people, doors opening and closing by themselves, strange knocks at doors and windows.
4: Trick	It might seem like a harmless and playful entity, but it is really gathering knowledge of what people consider frightening, which it will use to inflict terror in the next stage and derive its energy from the fright.	Flying and moving objects, objects disappearing and reappearing elsewhere, shaking furniture, appearing as frightening entities, creating visions or illusions, speaking in ordering tones; windows, mirrors or other objects breaking for no reason.
5: Danger	The poltergeist has reached its highest energy point, and should be considered dangerous. Violent and threatening actions begin. After this stage, the poltergeist will go dormant and then begin the cycle again at the first stage.	Biting, slapping or punching people; animating objects; blood on walls, floors and ceilings, attacks by unseen forces, flying knives or sharp objects, heavy objects falling. Threatening writings or visual signs of danger; onset of unknown medical illness.

Figure 2: The five stages of a poltergeist.

As you will recall, the first known way in which Kate manifested herself was by appearing to John Bell in the form of a creature resembling a dog and a rabbit. Shortly after this incident, Kate manifested herself to Drewry Bell in the form of a large bird sitting on the fence by the lane. These apparitions are consistent with the fourth stage of poltergeist progression, the *Trick* stage. [dd]

To manifest in these forms, Kate must have at some point passed through the three previous levels of poltergeist progression; however, no earlier accounts of strange incidents on the Bell farm were reported.

Another way in which Kate manifested herself early in the legend was by rapping on the outside walls of the house and making "gnawing" sounds at the foot of the children's bedposts. These disturbances are characteristic of the third stage of poltergeist progression, the *Physical* stage. The timing of these disturbances relative to the earlier apparitions suggests that Kate had once reached the *Trick* stage, but was unable to fully function there and reverted to the *Physical* stage as a result.

The Bells began hearing faint whispers after the rapping and other sounds had continued for some time, which suggests that Kate failed at the *Physical* stage and returned to the second, or *Communication* stage. A number of other incidents characteristic of the *Communication* stage occurred during this period, also. This would lead one to believe that Kate remained at this stage for some time, apparently long enough quickly pass back to the *Trick* stage because more apparitions and pranks occurred over time.

The incident that most clearly identifies with the *Trick* stage was when Kate began speaking in varying tones, similar to those of a low-pitched musical instrument. This was also during the period when she kicked a chair out from under John Bell and pushed the bureau that Drewry Bell was leaning against, making him fall to the floor, which is a classic example of the *Trick* stage.

Not long after this period, John Bell developed a mysterious affliction and Elizabeth was often slapped and pinched. Kate also physically abused guests such as Frank Miles, Andrew Jackson's "witch tamer," and Mr. Williams during this time. Kate later claimed to have been responsible for John Bell's death. These incidents are consistent with the fifth stage of poltergeist progression, the *Danger* stage.

Although Kate possessed many poltergeist-like characteristics, dismissing the legend of the "Bell Witch" as a poltergeist case would be presumptuous and premature. A poltergeist's regressing from the fourth to the second stage, then progressing back up to the fourth and fifth stages is not likely. In addition, Kate's speech was not limited to the low melodic tones associated with poltergeists. She possessed a number of different voices and characteristics of other supernatural entities as well. One such entity to which Kate has often been referred is the *demon*.

Demons

A demon is, in conventional thought, a being of pure malevolence; essentially, an element of evil consisting of the Devil and his many minions. Demons not in the underworld are either free on Earth or living temporarily in the *abyss* before going back to *Gehenna,* the "lake of fire," to join Satan, other demons, and the unsaved. ee

One similarity in demons among several cultures that embrace Christianity is the origin of the "head demon." It is frequently believed that the head demon started out as an angel in good standing with God, then after quarreling with God and being defeated, was condemned to rule the underworld. In the Bible, *Lucifer* begins as an angel, battles God, and is sent to rule the underworld after his defeat.

In most cultures, demons personify evil, pain, and suffering. A demon exploits a specific weakness in man, creates a certain suffering for man, or wants some special thing from man. Demons are said to have many powers, such as prophecy, that are alluring to men. One significant finding in the study of demons is that multiple demons exist in most documented cases, and frequently in a hierarchy where each has its own name and unique characteristics.

To the Ancient Greeks, *daimons* were minor deities that were not necessarily good or evil. The good demons were called *Eudemons*, and evil demons were called *Cacodemons*. Many Eastern religions recognize a number of different demons. For example, ancient Buddhists had the *Mira*, which embodied all that was evil; and the Indian demons are lead by the powerful *Ravana*, believed by that group of people to change shape and remain invulnerable to all Spirits. ff

Only in its modern connotation does the word *demon* evoke the idea of evil Spirits. The Greek word *daemon*, from which the words *daimon* and *demon* are ultimately derived, means "genius and intelligence," and is applied indiscriminately to all Spiritual beings whether good or evil. [51]

People have done about demons what they have done to angels. Just as they have imagined that there are beings created perfectly from all eternity, they have also imagined that beings created of lower

---

[51] Shipley, Joseph T., *Dictionary of Word Origins*.

degrees are eternally evil.

The most prominent example of demons in the legend of the "Bell Witch" is the "witch family" that put on a series of demonstrations for the Bells and their guests over a short period at the height of the disturbances.   Led by "Blackdog," the family consisted of "Cypocryphy," "Mathematics" and "Jerusalem." Each character had its own name and unique set of characteristics.   "Blackdog" spoke in the tone of a woman, "Cypocryphy" and "Mathematics" both spoke in the tone of little girls, and "Jerusalem" spoke in the tone of a little boy. As is the case with many demons, the "witch family" not only spoke, but also appeared.

The lone "witch family" appearance took place at the Porter farm on Sturgeon Creek, and was witnessed by Elizabeth Bell and her older sister, Esther Porter. A woman, two little girls, and one little boy appeared in the field across the road from the Porters' house and played by bouncing up and down on some bent saplings. Esther's husband, who could not see the figures themselves, fired a shot in the direction of where the saplings were bouncing and made the figures disappear. Later that evening at the Bell home, "Blackdog" made a comment to the effect that Alex Porter was a good shot and had broken the arm of "Jerusalem." Another of Kate's demon-like characteristics was her ability to tell of the past and the future.

When a visitor entered the Bell home, Kate often spoke up and told everyone about the person's past, especially if it was of an embarrassing nature. Kate was also able to predict the effects of an approaching storm in enough time to lead Elizabeth Bell and her friends to safety while horseback riding near the Red River. During her return-visit of 1828, she predicted the Civil War and other major events as she engaged

John Bell, Jr. in a series of long conversations.

It would be easy to conclude that Kate was part poltergeist and part demon; however, such a conclusion would be unfounded because many of Kate's demonstrations fell outside the realm of poltergeist and demonic activity. In addition to her ability to be at two places simultaneously, Kate possessed considerable intelligence and the ability to speak of civilizations that existed millions of years ago. In addition, she would on occasion aid the sick.

These characteristics transcend those of poltergeist and demonic entities, and give us a solid reason to explore the most elite, remarkable, and difficult to comprehend supernatural entity of all: the *Spirit*.

Spirits

The term *Spirit* is very difficult to comprehend because it carries many different and often conflicting connotations. For the purpose of this book, a *Spirit* is a self-aware being, good, or evil, which lacks a physical body.

The premise from which much spiritual theory is derived suggests that there are two general elements in the universe – the *intelligent* element and the *material* element, and that Spirits are the individualization of the intelligent element and bodies are the individualization of the material element.

This premise can be taken further in that the universe is widely believed to possess three modes of substantiality – soul, force, and matter. While the two former modes are non-material substances, the term *matter* is restricted to the element from which bodies are formed; i.e., the material element.

Although Spirit and matter are distinct entities, the <u>union</u> of Spirit and matter is necessary to give intelligent activity to matter. The Spirit and material worlds are independent; however, they continually react upon each other.

A Spirit can assume any form it chooses, manifesting itself in dreams and/or a state of consciousness, and can even assimilate a tangible form. Spirits are everywhere and can move at the speed of thought. The soul thinks; and as such, wherever thought is, so is the soul.

Spirits progress and mature over time, just as beings in the material world do. Unlike the material world, where such things as physical stature, intelligence, and attitude measure maturity, spiritual maturity is based on *purity*.

The purity levels of Spirits can be unscientifically reduced to three, principal orders. These orders are indicative of the Spirit's purity based upon an imaginary "ladder of progression" that takes into account the qualities that Spirits have acquired over time and the imperfections from which they must free themselves.

The levels of Spiritual progression are broadly classified as *orders*. Each *order* is further broken down into *subclasses*. *Subclasses* are continuous in that their numbering is independent from the numbering of *orders*. With regard to numbering the Spiritual orders and subclasses, low numbers represent high orders, and high numbers represent low orders. The number "one" denotes absolute perfection, whereas the number "ten" denotes absolute imperfection.

Figure 3 on the following page illustrates the orders of Spiritual progression and the subclasses that comprise them.

Order	Characteristics
Third Order	Imperfection. Propensity for evil, ignorance, pride, and selfishness. Intelligence is often married with malice, and sentiments are, for the most part, abject.
Subclass 10	Spirit besets those whose characters are weak enough to lead them to yield to their lure, and whom they draw away from the path of progress to impede their advancement.
Subclass 9	Reply to every question without paying any attention to truth; delight in causing annoyances, raise false hopes of joy, and mislead people by mystification and trickery. Typically servants under the orders of Spirits of a higher category.
Subclass 8	Statements contain a mixture of truths and falsehoods. The Spirit feels smarter than it really is.
Subclass 7	Spirit is in a state of confusion between good and evil; strongly attached to the material world.
Subclass 6	Spirit often manifests its presence by raps, the movement of solid bodies, loud noises, agitation of the air, etc., much like a poltergeist. This is the transitional stage between the third and second orders.
Second Order	Good Spirit. More attuned to the incorporeal (Spirit) world; desire to further journey to excellence. Sometimes bad; however characteristics of this order are positive in general.
Subclass 5	Spirit enjoys rendering services for and protecting people. Actions based more so on morality than intelligence.
Subclass 4	Spirit is interested in learning; less attuned to the emotional passions of Spirits at lower ranks.
Subclass 3	Spirit has developed an intellectual capacity that enables it to judge correctly; possess elevated moral qualities.
Subclass 2	Superiority in knowledge renders the Spirit more apt than any others to impart to us ideas pertaining to the incorporeal (Spirit) world, within the limits of the knowledge permitted to humankind. The Spirit willingly enters into communication with those who seek truth in simplicity and sincerity.

First Order	Perfection. The Spirit enters a life of eternity in the presence of the Holy Creator.

Figure 3: The Orders of Spiritual Progression

One can easily see by looking at Figure 3 that Kate possessed a number of Spiritual characteristics covering both the Third and Second Orders. One will also notice that poltergeist-like activity matches almost identically to subclass 6, which is the transition between the Third and Second Orders.

While this suggests that poltergeists are actually Spirits of the 6th subclass by virtue of being the subset of a Spiritual order, one must still keep in mind that not all Spirits are poltergeists, however. Many of Kate's characteristics fall within other Spiritual orders.

Another popular term used to describe Kate, and how the legend got its popular name, is the word, "witch." When Reverend James Gunn asked her who she was and what she wanted, she replied, "I am nothing more than old Kate Batts' witch..." hence the nickname, "Kate," and the description, "witch." The author does not believe that Kate was a "witch." To understand why, a discussion of magic and witchcraft is in order.

Magic and Witchcraft

The roots of magic come from the Celts, a people living between 700 BC and 100 AD. Believed to be descendants of Indo-Europeans, the Celts were a brilliant and dynamic people – gifted artists, musicians, storytellers, metalworkers, expert farmers, and fierce warriors. They were much feared by their adversaries, the Romans, who eventually adopted a number of their customs and traditions.

The Celts were a deeply Spiritual people who

worshiped both a god and goddess. Their religion was *pantheistic,* meaning they worshiped many aspects of the "One Creative Life Source" and honored the presence of the "Divine Creator" in all of nature. Like many tribes the world over, they believed in reincarnation. After death, they went to the *Summerland* for rest and renewal while awaiting rebirth.

The months of the Celtic year were named after trees. The Celtic New Year began at *Samhain,* which means "summers end," and was the final harvest of the year. This was also their "Festival of the Dead," where they honored their ancestors and deceased loved ones. Many contemporary Halloween customs come from Samhain.

Next on the wheel of the Celtic year was the *Winter Solstice,* celebrating the annual rebirth of the Sun. Our Christmas customs today are similar to this ancient celebration. Around the beginning of February came *Imbolg,* a time when domesticated animals began to give birth.

The *Spring Equinox* and *Beltaine,* sometimes called "May Day," were fertility festivals. The *Summer Solstice,* known as *Lughnassa,* celebrated the glory of the Sun and the powers of nature. Lughnassa, the Fall Equinox, and Samhain, were considered as Celtic harvest festivals.

The Druids were the priests of the Celtic religion. They remained in power through the fourth century AD, three centuries after the Celts' defeat at the hands of the Romans. The Druids were priests, teachers, judges, astrologers, healers, and bards. They became indispensable to the political leaders, giving them considerable power and influence. They were peacemakers, and were able to pass from one warring tribe to another unharmed. It took twenty years of intense study to become a Druid.

Translated, the word *Druid* means, "knowing the oak tree." Trees, the oaks in particular, were held as being sacred by the Celts. Mistletoe, which grows as a parasite on oak trees, was a powerful herb used in their ceremonies and for healing. It was ritually harvested at the Summer Solstice by cutting it with a golden sickle and catching it with a white cloth while never letting it fall to the ground.

The religious beliefs and practices of the Celts grew into what later became known as *Paganism*, not to be confused with the term *Neo-Paganism*, which is beyond the scope of this writing. The word *Pagan* is derived from the Latin word *Paganus*, meaning "country dweller." This outgrowth was consistent with the Celts' love for the land and their holding such things as the oak tree and mistletoe sacred.

Pagan beliefs and rituals blended with those of other Indo-European descended groups, and over several centuries spawned such practices as concocting potions and ointments, casting spells, and performing works of magic. These practices, along with many of the nature-based beliefs held by the Celts and other groups, became collectively known *witchcraft.*

The word *witch*, which means to "twist or bend," has its origin in the ancient, Anglo-Saxon word *Wicca*, which is derived from the word *wicce*, which means, "wise." The word *witch* is also related to the German word, *weihen*, which means, "to consecrate or bless." [52]

Some say that the origins of the *witch* date back thousands of years, to the days when the goddess was worshiped and humanity had great reverence for the powers of nature and for women as creators of new life. In the "New Age" philosophy, this relates to

---

[52] Shipley, Joseph T., *Dictionary of Word Origins.*

the concept of *Gaia*, or "Mother Earth," which views planet earth as essentially a living being.

Prior to the 14th Century, witchcraft came to mean a collection of beliefs and practices including healing through spells, mixing ointments or concoctions, dabbling in the supernatural (doing magic), divining or forecasting the future, and engaging in clairvoyance. Groups holding to other beliefs and rituals often branded witchcraft incorrectly as "demon-worship."

After North America was discovered and Europeans began migrating to the new land, witchcraft came into practice by some of the early colonial settlers. Since it had previously been branded as "demon-worship," witchcraft was forbidden throughout the North American colonies. Despite this decree by the powers of the day, some colonists secretly practiced witchcraft knowing they would be hanged or burnt if caught. It has been said that certain rituals performed by the early-American witches helped shield their settlements from attacks by Native Americans.

Allegedly, magic can affect many outcomes both good and evil, depending on the type of magic and the intentions of the practitioner. The better-known types of magic are denoted by colors.

Black magic is performed with the intention of harming another being, either as a means of building the practitioner's power or as the goal itself. The underlying ideology upon which Black magic is based states that the practitioner and his or her pursuit of knowledge and/or physical well-being are more important than other concerns, theological or ethical.

Green magic involves the practitioner's attuning himself or herself to nature and the world around him or her. *White magic* is where the practitioner attempts to attune him or herself to the needs of human society and attempts to meet those needs. This is a form of "personal betterment" magic, and does not entail harming other beings.

Grey magic is magic that is neither green, nor black, nor white, and which usually replaces the absolute stand of these realms with an ethical code that is particular to the practitioner. It is a type of magic all its own, and may be used for many different purposes.

Folk magic is an eclectic collection of herbalism, faith healing, curses and hexes, candle magic, and other workings that have thrived in rural areas for centuries. There is also the term *hedge wizard*, which refers to an individual who attempts to practice magic with little or no formal training.

The notion that Kate was a "witch" makes very little sense, if any. One might argue that the "Bell Witch" was the product of Black magic being practiced by Kate Batts or others in the Red River community; however, such an argument lacks compelling evidence and credibility. The terms, *witch* and *Black magic*, have been associated with the legend of the "Bell Witch" for many years. Another term has been associated with the legend in more recent years: *sorcery*.

Sorcery

Sorcery is the magical practice involving the summoning, binding, and commanding of multiple entities to impose altered perceptions of reality upon others, a condition known as *ensorcellment*. Sorcery does not identify with any specific color of magic, but can instead encompass any type of magic – even that which is unknown to all but a select few. The sorcerer or sorceress uses a philosophical approach to magic as opposed to a theosophical approach.

CHAPTER TWENTY-SIX

What Was "Kate?"

WE HAVE EXAMINED AND COMPARED the characteristics of several supernatural entities and learned that Kate, at one point or another, possessed characteristics associated with all of these entities. Who or *what* was Kate? What intelligent being could have inflicted such torment on an entire community and one of its most prominent families, escaping detection and baffling researchers for nearly two centuries?

For the purposes of the following discussion, the author uses the term, "Kate" in reference to the entity that disturbed the Bell family from 1817 to 1821, and again in 1828. We shall further assume that "Kate" is not the cause of unexplainable incidents on the old Bell farm today, for reasons that we will address later. Where did Kate fit in the plethora of supernatural entities and concepts we discussed in the previous chapter?

One Entity or Many?

Were John Bell's family and the small pioneer community along the Red River terrorized by just one supernatural entity, or by multiple supernatural entities acting in concert? To put pose this question another way, was Kate a lone entity or an entire conglomeration of entities?

While it would seem that Kate was composed of multiple entities because of the different characteristics she displayed, it is interesting to note that those characteristics all fall within the orders of Spiritual progression at some point or another. Let us examine this more closely.

We saw where John and Elizabeth Bell bore the brunt of the physical disturbances and how they subsided so quickly after John Bell's death. The physical torture indicates a low level of Spiritual purity, the Third Order, and "maps" to poltergeist activity at the 5th, or "danger" stage.

Because the early stages of poltergeist activity are consistent with the 6th Spiritual subclass (the transitional subclass between the Third and Second Orders), and the later stages of poltergeist activity are consistent with the 10th Spiritual subclass, it can be hypothesized that a poltergeist is a Spirit unable to attain purity beyond the Third Order (beginning at the 5th Spiritual subclass).

Not coincidentally, there are five stages of poltergeist activity and five Spiritual subclasses between the Third and Second Spiritual orders.

Was She Really a Poltergeist?

One could argue that if John and Elizabeth Bell's physical torture was indeed the work of a poltergeist, it drew its "power" either directly from John and Elizabeth's pain, or indirectly from the fear and

emotions of those who witnessed these physical acts
– thereby fueling a vicious cycle of fear and physical
torture (characteristic of a low Spiritual order and
the highest level of poltergeist activity). In other
words, one (fear) fuels the other (torment), which
fuels the first again (fear) – keeping the poltergeist
active at this level until some stronger power forces it
back to the first level to start over again (remember
that poltergeists recycle at some point after reaching
the fifth stage).

In opposition to this theory, one might argue that
the acts of physical torment were not the doings of a
poltergeist at all, but those specifically associated
with a low-order Spirit attempting to effect a "rite of
passage" to a higher Spiritual order or subclass.

To affect a rite of passage to a higher Spiritual
order or subclass, the Spirit must remove all
obstacles along its path – even if it meant, in this
case, John Bell's life. This is characteristic of the
10th Spiritual subclass, which is part of the third and
lowest spiritual order. The acts performed to achieve
this rite of passage to a higher order fall into the
category of self-serving benevolence – the promotion
of benevolence for the Spirit's own sake, as opposed
to the sake of humankind.

How could the life of one man and the engagement
of his daughter to a boy she loved very much, have
impeded a Spirit's progression to a higher order?
And, assuming that the "rite of passage" argument is
valid, was Kate's intention to effect benevolence for
the goodness of humankind or to fulfill a self-serving
desire to advance to higher Spiritual orders?

There was more to Kate's activities than just
physically torturing people; and as such, our
attention needs to be focused on areas beyond
poltergeist-like activity and Spiritual rites of passage.

Spiritual Aspects

Many of Kate's acts were completely spiritual in nature, exhibiting characteristics that only a Spirit can exhibit. Kate's continued evasion of the question, "Who are you and what do you want?" was clearly Spiritual in nature, and characteristic of the Third Order (lowest), and the 8th and 9th subclasses in particular.

When she attempted to answer this question during the early and middle parts of her visit, as was the case when she persuaded three men to dig for treasure by the Enchanted Spring, her contentions fell within the 9th subclass – mystification, trickery, and falsehood.

During the latter part of her visit, however, Kate utilized both fact and fiction when declaring an identity. This in effect "promoted" her from the 9th to the 8th subclass. One such example of Kate's mixing fact and fiction was when she claimed to have been the Spirit of someone buried in the woods nearby and whose bones had been disturbed, and was searching for a lost tooth.

While it was true that Drewry Bell and Corban Hall had disinterred a Native American grave and accidentally dropped a tooth under the Bells' front porch, Kate told everyone who had searched for the tooth (at her insistence) that her claim of having been that Spirit was nothing more than a joke for "Ol' Jack Bell."

Another of Kate's acts that was entirely spiritual in nature was her singing hymns and bringing hazelnuts and grapes to Lucy Bell during her illness. These benevolent acts towards Mrs. Bell, along with her bringing fruit to Elizabeth and her friends on occasion, placed Kate in the 5th Spiritual subclass during the 1819 period. gg

If Kate was a Spirit in the strictest sense of the word, her activities outlined in the preceding discussion suggest that she progressed five Spiritual subclasses, spanning two Spiritual orders, over the two-year period from 1817 to 1819. Her Spiritual progression continued beyond this period, however. It continued up until 1828, but at a much slower rate than in earlier years.

The highest Spiritual subclass to which Kate progressed was the 2nd subclass, one step below the First Order — perfection. Kate's most notable act that was consistent with the 2nd subclass was her relaying detailed information about the Spirit world to John Bell, Jr. on her return-visit in 1828. He asked many questions and gained a remarkable knowledge of the Spirit world. She refused to answer some questions, stating that she was "not permitted to share" certain things, which is another characteristic of the 2nd subclass. This suggests Kate progressed three Spiritual subclasses, from the 5th to the 2nd, during the nine-year period between 1819 and 1828.

The correlation between Kate's activities and the different levels of Spiritual progression suggests to some degree that Spiritual influence was present whether she was a Spirit or merely the "product" of a Spirit. Given our discussions about various supernatural entities and how Kate personified each of them on different occasions, it becomes obvious that Kate was not a single entity at all, but many different entities acting in concert.

An Answer

The author believes that Kate was the product of *sorcery*; that is, "the magical practice involving the summoning, binding, and commanding of multiple, supernatural entities to impose altered perceptions and/or interpretations of reality upon others."

An Explanation

While Kate personified different supernatural entities at different times, all of her demonstrations shared a common thread in that her aversion to Elizabeth's engagement and insistence upon killing John Bell remained constant throughout her visit. Demonstrations and statements made by Kate concerning Elizabeth's engagement and the demise of John Bell varied with the type of entity present at any given time, but were constant nevertheless.

Taking all of this into consideration, we can easily see where the entities who plagued the Bell family were summoned, bound and commanded by some "higher power" with an agenda all its own. Who, or "what," was the sorcerer or sorceress responsible for these poltergeists, demons, and Spirits who terrorized the family of John Bell and wreaked havoc throughout the western end of Robertson County during the early Nineteenth Century? The author feels that the sorcerer or sorceress was itself a Spirit.

Of all the supernatural entities discussed, only a Spirit possesses intelligence and has the ability to summon, bind, and command entities to act on its behalf. The Spirit behind the Bell disturbances manifested its "high-ordered" characteristics on its own and directed entities such as poltergeists and demons to manifest its "low-ordered" characteristics.

When looking at the Bell disturbances from a chronological perspective, one should be able to infer that the Spirit itself did not visit the Bells until about the time of John Bell's death, which was about the same time it progressed to the Second Order. The author feels that before John Bell's death, the Bells were terrorized by entities acting on behalf of the Spirit; and when the Spirit reached a higher level of purity and stability (around 1820 — the year of Bell's death), it commenced terrorizing the Bells directly.

The Spirit's order and subclass at a given time determined which entities were enlisted to do its "dirty work," and in what manner. This can easily be seen by comparing the aspects of any particular disturbance to the characteristics of one or more supernatural entities, and then "mapping" those characteristics to the orders and subclasses of Spiritual progression. Along the same lines, one must also remember that sorcery is a philosophical type of magic; and as such, enabled the Spirit to direct the different entities to act according to its philosophy at any point in time. A Spirit's philosophy changes as its order and subclasses change – from impurity to purity. Before discussing the Spirit's possible agenda and what "triggered" its manifestation at that point in history, let us first answer the question, "Where did the Spirit come from?"

Where Did "Kate" Come From?

A Spirit can attach itself to a person, place, or object. Because of continued reports of unexplainable incidents in the area, and the existence of certain factors to be discussed shortly, the author feels that the Spirit was not attached to any particular member of the Bell family, but to the land upon which they lived. Let us discuss the interesting history of this land.

History of the Land

The land that comprised the Bell farm is the final resting-place of hundreds and possibly thousands of

Native Americans. Archaeologists from the State of Tennessee have estimated that most Native American graves on this land are between 500 and 3,000 years old. Many years after these early Native Americans were buried in Robertson County, the Cherokees and Choctaws made their permanent homes in east Tennessee and Mississippi, respectively. These two Nations used Robertson County and other areas of middle Tennessee as a hunting ground, but buried their dead in the same regions they lived in.

The ancestors of the Cherokees and Choctaws were the Woodland and Mississippian tribes, both of which buried their dead throughout middle Tennessee, including the land that would later became the Bell farm. Even those who came before the Woodlands and Mississippians, thousands of years before Christ, buried their dead on the land that later became the Bell farm. This was determined by archaeologists who examined the different types of Native American graves and artifacts found in the area of the old Bell farm.

The most recent Native Americans to bury their dead on this land were the Mound Builders, a branch of the Mississippian culture that existed between 950 and 1650 AD. Spanish explorer Hernando de Soto encountered and wrote about the Mound Builders during his early expeditions through the area in 1540-1541 period.

Ancient Native Americans did not choose their burial grounds arbitrarily. The land had to be considered sacred and possess strong Spiritual qualities to become a burial ground. The land that comprised the Bell farm was used not by one, but several Native American cultures over thousands of years because of its perceived sacredness. Add to this perceived sacredness the hundreds and possibly thousands of souls that are buried beneath the old

Bell farm. It should not be difficult to conclude that this land was, and still is, a "hotbed" of Spiritual activity.

A Vortex on the Bell Farm

Paranormal investigators have detected unusual electromagnetic and other energy fields on and near the old Bell farm, especially in the cave and where the Bell home stood. The consensus among many of these investigators is that there exists a vortex on the old Bell farm. A scientific discussion of vortexes and related topics such as Einstein's theory of relativity, the Philadelphia experiment, Project Magnet, and the Temporal Transmission Research Project, is important but beyond the scope of this book. The important thing to understand about vortexes is that they are considered essentially as "doorways" between the material and Spiritual worlds. Such places usually possess one or more scientific attributes that bring two or more planes of existence together at a single point.

Spirits are everywhere; however, because the Bells lived on a Spiritual hotbed and near a vortex, the concentration of Spiritual and other supernatural activity on and near where their farm was is much greater than in most other places. The most logical question one could ask at this point is "If that land is still such a Spiritual 'hotbed,' then why are the supernatural encounters reported there today less frightening and intense than those which took place there nearly 200 years ago?"

Think about a vortex the same way you would think about a volcano. A volcano can be inactive, active, or erupting and sending hot lava everywhere. Volcanoes erupt because seismological conditions become such that an eruption is the only natural outcome. The supernatural encounters on the Bell farm nearly 200 years ago were more frightening and intense than those today because Spiritual conditions were right at the time. Dead souls remain buried in this sacred land, and a vortex still exists there; so, what happened during the time of John Bell that made the Spiritual conditions different than they are now?

The Spirit Was "Called"

The Spirit world was "called," thereby bringing the already-Spiritual activity at the vortex into full force. At first take, one might assume that some action or inaction on the part of the Bells "called" the Spirit world; however, many things happened in the Red River area at the time that brought Spiritual discontentment and emotional turmoil to its citizens, including the Bells.

The author feels that it was the community's emotional turmoil and Spiritual discontentment as a whole that "called" the Spirit world. What happened in the early Nineteenth Century that caused the otherwise happy and God-fearing citizens of the Red River community so much emotional and Spiritual grief?

Turmoil in the Early Nineteenth Century

This was at a time in history when revivals were everyday occurrences, evenings were spent praying and singing hymns, revival camps were the only vacation retreats, and the church took an aggressive interest in the business and personal lives of its members. In addition, the Red River area was considered by many to have been one of the most religious places in the country at the time.

A number of theological differences existed at the

time, which caused church congregations to split, people to be excommunicated from churches, and people to question their own religious beliefs and convictions. Sermons within the same religious faith but delivered by different preachers were often contradictory, prayer meetings were often disturbed by the emotional outbursts of those who questioned their own faith, and many friendships were ended because of religious differences.

The Cumberland Presbyterian Church was formed as a result of the "Second Great Awakening," or "The Great Revival," which began about 1798 in Logan County, Kentucky near the present-day town of Adairville and only a few miles from the Red River. In its infancy, this revival was known as "The Red River Revival," and later became known as "The Cane Ridge Revival." Although the entire country was affected by this revival, its impact was felt most heavily in Tennessee and Kentucky, where it was estimated that over 12,000 people attended one outdoor service at a time in history when the area was being settled and boasted only a sparse population.

During this period, the "Old Sides" dominated the Presbyterian Church. One of the revival's most significant effects was that the Presbyterians living in the west began to reject the Old Sides view and became known as New Sides, or "New Light" Presbyterians. Many people withdrew from the traditional Presbyterian Church and formed the Cumberland Presbyterian Church, which was so named because most of their churches were located in the region drained by the Cumberland River in Tennessee and Kentucky.

The "Second Great Awakening" was the first revival in which a noticeable number of people spoke in tongues. James Johnston, John Bell's closest friend and neighbor, was a strong supporter of this movement and founded a campground for prayer meetings and revivals on his property at the confluence of Johnston Spring and Sturgeon Creek. Within all likelihood, it was from the meetings at Johnston's Campground that the reference to, "Sturgeon Creek, where all the speaking in tongues went on," originated.   Johnston's Campground remained an active place of worship as late as 1854.[53]

This area at the confluence of Johnston Spring and Sturgeon Creek was once the site of Johnston's Campground.

Aside from the "Second Great Awakening" and its implications to the Presbyterian Church, another theological difference was inherent in the Baptist faith at the time.   The beliefs and teachings of Red River Baptist Church during the John Bell era were consistent with those of the Primitive Baptist faith, most notably the church's strict adherence to the doctrine of Predestination. [54]

---

[53] Correspondence with Mr. Jim Brooks, a direct descendant of James Johnston.
[54] A discussion of the Primitive Baptist faith is included in Appendix F.

Pioneered by the sixteenth century theologian, John Calvin (1509-1564), *Predestination* is the Christian theological doctrine that teaches that a person's eternal destiny has been predetermined by God's unchangeable decree, and is based on an understanding that the gift of God's presence is an act of sheer grace. To emphasize that God wills the gift independently, some asserted that their relation to God depended only on God and His eternal decree established before the beginning of civilization. [55]

There was considerable dissention among members of the Baptist faith regarding the intent and interpretation of scripture used by Calvin to justify his doctrine. At issue was whether the Bible intended Predestination (Calvinism), or Salvation (Arminianism).

Pioneered in Amsterdam about 1591 by James Harmens, which in Latin means *Jacobes Arminius, Arminianism* is based upon scripture which holds that, "He that believeth shall be saved: He that believeth not, shall be condemned," and that "Christ died for all, all that were dead in trespasses and sins."

Reuben Ross, an elder of Red River Baptist Church, was a leader in the movement toward Arminianism. Ross' long-awaited opportunity to preach his views came in July of 1817 when he was asked to preach a funeral sermon. The following account of Ross' sermon appears in a local history book:

"After years of careful study, Reuben Ross became thoroughly satisfied in his own mind that salvation is for 'Whosoever will,' and not for a

---

[55] Calvin's doctrine of Predestination is included in Appendix H.

select few. He determined to preach his views regardless of what the consequences might be.

An opportunity presented itself for him to express his views in the month of July of 1817. He was requested to preach the funeral sermon of Miss Eliza Norfleet, who had died some time previously near Port Royal. She had been buried in the Fort burying ground on the home site of Elias Fort.

This young lady had been greatly esteemed and beloved in the community where she had lived. It was reported that she was of a gentle manner and had a very loving character. There were a large number of people who wished to pay their last respects to the memory of the dearly beloved young lady, and also to hear a beloved preacher on this occasion.

On the day of the funeral, there was a large gathering at the graveyard. A rude platform had been built for the occasion. Reuben Ross, at the appointed time, mounted this platform without fear in his heart and expressed boldly, views that were contrary to those holding to the doctrine of salvation for the elect. He told his hearers that those who would yield to the influence of the Holy Spirit and become followers of Christ would be saved and pardoned; that none, unless he personally surrendered his heart and life to Jesus, could be saved and that anyone who is lost is lost because, it is his own fault.

As surprising as it may seem, the crowd gathered around the grave seemed to accept with favor the views expressed. As soon as the sermon had been concluded, Elder Ross descended from the platform looking straight ahead, walked to the place where his horse was tied, mounted him and rode home, a distance of twenty miles.

Apparently, he was not ready to meet, face to face, the kind old brothers that he had labored with for the past ten years. No doubt, he knew that many friendships would be ruptured because of the stand that he had taken." [56]

Divisiveness in the Baptist Church grew over time with many people, including Reverend Sugg Fort, acknowledging the Arminian doctrine. Many church congregations split, and additional churches came into existence as a result. Also during this period, an event of major religious significance took place along the New Madrid fault line in Missouri and west Tennessee, some 175 miles west of Robertson County.

During the winter of 1811-1812, the New Madrid area was plagued by a series of earthquakes of the highest magnitude ever recorded in American history. Both the loss of life and eyewitness accounts were minimal, however, due to the area's sparse population at the time.

These earthquakes caused the Mississippi River to run backwards, creating Reelfoot Lake in northwest Tennessee, and reportedly rang the Liberty Bell in Philadelphia. The quakes were felt strongly in the settlements along the Red River, where along with many other areas it became a popular belief that the Almighty was expressing His unhappiness with the sins of the world. What logically followed was the Spiritual "awakening" of many people and a major influx of new members into the church – most of whom were overcome by fear of the Almighty's wrath.

The author feels that the events described in the preceding pages brought about a collective state of emotional discontentment, which "called" the Spirit

---

[56] John M. Goodman, Jr., *Red River Baptist Church – A History*, pp. 40-41.

world into an intense and prolonged fury that triggered the vortex on the Bell farm to "erupt" – opening the "door" between the Spirit and material worlds. The author also feels that one of the many Spirits attached to the land became entwined in the vortex and suspended between the Spirit and material worlds.

This Spirit was probably of a very low order, and lacked the ability to free itself and return back to the Spirit world at its own choosing; hence, it spent a number of years progressing through the orders of Spiritual progression to the point it was able to free itself. The Bell family owned the farm, and because of this, it was they who the Spirit used as its stepping-stone through the Spiritual orders – enlisting other supernatural entities as necessary to help pave the way during the earlier years of its visit. On two separate occasions, Kate remarked that she was not happy and did not want to be at the Bell farm. [57]

---

[57] The first occasion was documented in Richard Williams Bell's manuscript, *Our Family Trouble*, and the second occasion was documented in Dr. Charles Bailey Bell's book, *The Bell Witch: A Mysterious Spirit*.

CHAPTER TWENTY-SEVEN

The Sprit's Agenda

U P TO THIS POINT, we have yet to discuss the possible reasons behind the Spirit's four-fold agenda, that being the killing of John Bell, preventing Elizabeth Bell and Joshua Gardner from marrying, taking a seven-year absence, and then taking a 107-year absence. One cannot help but question why a Spirit would have such an agenda and what benevolence, if any, could be attained by its execution. Let us look at Kate's agenda, some possible reasons behind it, and who or what stood to gain by its execution.

To Kill John Bell

John Bell died in 1820, the period in which Kate progressed to the 5th Spiritual subclass. This is the transitional point between the third and second Spiritual orders, and far superior to the lower, "impure" Spiritual orders. What act of benevolence (needed to progress to the Second Order) could have offset the vicious act of killing a man? John Bell's death must have been the lesser of two evils, for otherwise the Spirit would not have progressed to a higher Spiritual order around the time of his death.

What was this "greater evil," which was preventable only by John Bell's death? Since Bell's death prevented this "greater evil" from taking place, there is no evidence from which to devise an answer. As mortal beings, we cannot travel back in time and then speculate about a "future event" that current research suggests never took place. When asked essentially the same question by John Bell, Jr. in 1828, Kate replied that the Spirit world is not at liberty to share certain information with the material world. The author does not know what this "greater evil" would have been had John Bell had lived, and neither does anyone else. [hh]

The author does feel, however, that Kate's intentions of promoting benevolence were not for the sake of goodness to humankind, but to fulfill her own, self-serving desire to progress through the Spiritual orders to the point that she could freely return to the Spirit world.

To Break Elizabeth's Engagement

Although Elizabeth Bell and Joshua Gardner did not end their engagement until April of 1821, Kate had warned Elizabeth about marrying Joshua since her "arrival" on the Bell farm in 1817. This would indicate that her aversion to their engagement was not specific to any particular Spiritual order, but very general in nature. It was not until after Elizabeth and Joshua broke off their engagement that Kate progressed beyond the 5th Spiritual subclass.

As it has already been stated, Kate never gave a specific reason for her disapproval of their engagement. She would only say that Elizabeth would never be happy if she married Joshua, and that future generations would see it true. Her remarks about their engagement made it clear that some form of benevolence would, in the future, offset the agony and heartbreak felt by the two lovers and work to the good of all concerned. This reasoning falls in direct line with John Stuart Mill's concept of *utilitarianism*, which loosely states that the act that produces the highest ratio of good to evil for all concerned is the *right* act.

Given that Kate was averse to Elizabeth and Joshua's engagement for the entire duration of her "visit" (which spanned many Spiritual orders and subclasses over a period of time), never gave a clear reason as to why, and progressed to higher Spiritual orders and subclasses after their engagement was broken, it becomes apparent that the achievement of some perceived future benevolence at the cost of Elizabeth and Joshua's engagement was a long-term plot to effect a rite of passage to higher Spiritual orders. Moreover, as was the case with John Bell's death, the author feels that Kate's sole intent in promoting future benevolence was to fulfill her own, self-serving desire to progress through the Spiritual orders.

And, once again, the Spirit world knew that something of a benevolent nature would happen in the future – but only if Elizabeth and Joshua did not marry. Both Joshua Gardner and Richard Powell (the man Elizabeth finally married) enjoyed great success in their respective careers during the years that followed; however, Powell's success was short-lived. He became an invalid, passed away, and left his family in a state of poverty.

Gardner's success, on the other hand, continued until the day he died, some 63 years after their engagement had ended. Despite all of her family's hardships after Powell became ill and passed away, Elizabeth insisted that her relationship with her husband (Powell) was a very happy one. Why? The author does not know; however, he will state that Elizabeth Powell was not the only woman in the community with an invalid husband.

To Leave for Seven Years

Kate attained the ability to return to the Spirit world in April of 1821 with the breakup of Elizabeth Bell and Joshua Gardner, and left the Bell home a short time later, promising to return in seven years. The author feels that when Kate promised to return in seven years, she knew she would be of a higher Spiritual order at that time and possess the ability to make amends for some of the harm she inflicted during her first visit. As promised, Kate returned seven years later to check on Lucy Bell and relay as much information about the Spirit world as possible to John Bell, Jr. These acts were characteristic of the 2nd Spiritual subclass, to which Kate had progressed during her seven-year absence from the Bell farm – just as she had planned.

To Return in One Hundred Seven Years

Kate's promise to return in 107 years (1935) was most likely in anticipation of the emotional tensions that would follow the Great Depression and problems mounting in other nations at the time that would ultimately lead to World War II. Kate alluded to these events in her conversations with John Bell, Jr. in 1828. Emotional tensions were what "called" the

Spirit to the Bell farm to begin with; hence, Kate anticipated a return-visit, or "re-calling" in 1935. It is not known whether Kate actually returned in 1935, as no credible stories from that period exist.

Despite Kate's notion that emotional tensions would warrant her return-visit in 1935, which presumably never materialized, it is most certain that conditions on the Bell farm during the early Nineteenth Century were "right" for a visit from the Spirit world. The *cause* was the emotional tension that "called" the Spirit world. The *medium* that the Spirit world used to connect with the material world was the vortex. The *effect* was torment to the John Bell family and a general sense of terror throughout the Red River community. The *link* was a Spirit trapped between in the Spirit and material worlds, who by summoning, binding and commanding other supernatural entities, used the John Bell family and the fear of others as a catalyst to progress to a higher Spiritual order so it could free itself.

While this would seemingly explain what happened to the John Bell family in the early Nineteenth Century, it does not provide any explanation for the unexplainable incidents that occur on and near the old Bell farm today. Today, we don't have the elements of *cause, medium, effect* and *link* to produce a Spiritual phenomenon like what was witnessed by the John Bell family and others in the Red River community nearly two centuries ago.

What About Present-Day Encounters?

The only element that remains today is the *medium,* the vortex. The fact that many Native Americans are buried on the land is also important. Moreover, the Native American graves on the land are most likely the original source of the Spirits themselves.

The author feels that the existence of the vortex is the catalyst for present-day supernatural encounters reported on and near the old Bell farm. Aside from the vortex, or *medium*, conditions are much different today than they were when John Bell and his family tilled and walked this land. A visit from the Spirit world such as that which John Bell and his family experienced is not likely today. However, because of the vortex and passive acts of "calling" the Spirit world, minor encounters with the Spirit world will always take place on the old Bell farm.

Where is the Vortex?

Where on the old Bell farm is the vortex? Nobody knows the exact size and location of the vortex, however several factors suggest that its center is near the back room of the cave at the bottom of the nearby sinkhole. The easiest way to determine the location of the vortex is by comparing past and present-day supernatural encounters and taking into consideration the locations where they occurred. While it almost goes without saying that most supernatural encounters on this land in the Nineteenth Century occurred in the Bell home, one must remember that a vortex encompasses more than just an area the size of a house. While most of the supernatural encounters in the days of John Bell occurred in the Bell home, some did not; and, any supernatural encounters that occurred after the house was razed in 1843 certainly did not.

What we will discuss here is not the vortex in general, but the *center* of the vortex – the area from whence the Spirit world came in the early Nineteenth Century, and which is likely to be the source of present-day encounters with the supernatural.

Despite a large number of strange apparitions in the area, including the "little boy in overalls," only twice in modern times has anyone described seeing what might have actually been Kate. Both apparitions took place inside the cave and were witnessed by two or more people. Although they took place at different times, both apparitions were described as being the figure of a slender, young woman with dark hair and a pale facial complexion.

In both cases, the apparition first appeared to have been a woman taking a tour of the cave and keeping a small distance from the tour group; but after closer observation, appeared to have no feet. Holding a candle in front of her, the figure seemed to "float" through the cave just above the floor between the first and second rooms before slowly disappearing. In neither case did the figure acknowledge the presence of visitors in the cave. Both apparitions of this woman-like figure were visually consistent with an apparition encountered by Elizabeth Bell and her two younger brothers some 180 years ago.

As told about earlier in this book, Kate once appeared to Elizabeth and her younger brothers in the form of a young, dark-haired woman with a pale complexion and hanging from a tree. Aside from the visual similarities, another and perhaps more haunting similarity is that both Elizabeth's encounter 180 years ago and the modern-day apparitions took place in roughly the same location.

Elizabeth and her brothers encountered the woman-like figure hanging from a small oak tree at the crest of a large sinkhole. The small oak tree still stands today – old, towering over all other trees, and only a very short distance from the back room of the cave where both modern-day apparitions of the woman-like figure were encountered. The oak tree is located on property now owned by the Kirbys and only a short distance from their home, which was where Bims Eden lived when he once spotted a stranger walking through the snow without leaving tracks.

The oak tree at the crest of the sinkhole as it appears today. The tree is estimated to be several hundred years old. The horizontal lines are fencing.

Joel Bell's house, where Allen Bell and Reynolds Powell encountered Kate, and where Dr. Henry Sugg's medicine bag rumbled mysteriously, was located on the hill above the cave only a few yards from the oak tree and sinkhole. This is the same place where "double shadows" are sometimes cast when a person stands at a particular spot along the old road.

This hill also holds what is believed to be the largest concentration of Native American graves on the old Bell farm, and legend says that it was on this hill where Drewry Bell and Corban Hall unearthed the Native American grave that Kate alluded to when trying to convince the Bells that she was a Spirit looking for a lost tooth.

The author believes that the center of the vortex is the sinkhole, not because of its place in the legend, but because of the similarities between past and present-day encounters with the supernatural that have occurred in roughly the same location. Before closing this chapter, the author wishes to describe yet another stunning similarity between past and present-day encounters with the supernatural around the old Bell farm.

What Role Does the "Witch Family" Play?

Both modern-day apparitions of the woman-like figure discussed earlier are also visually consistent with the apparition encountered by Esther Porter and Elizabeth Bell when they saw a strange-looking woman and three children bouncing on some saplings across the road from the Porter home, as described earlier in this book. Esther's husband, Alex, fired his gun in the direction of where a little boy's head was seen behind a knot in a log, grazing the log and breaking the little boy's arm.

This encounter took place during the same period that Kate's "witch family" regularly visited the Bells over the period of several months and conducted many baffling and terrifying demonstrations. It was during one of these demonstrations that "Blackdog," the self-proclaimed leader of the "witch family," remarked that Alex Porter shot at "Jerusalem" and broke his arm.

Being familiar with the four characters that comprised the "witch family," one should be able to deduce that the woman who appeared to Esther Porter and Elizabeth Bell was "Blackdog," and that the small children who appeared with her were "Mathematics" and "Cypocryphy," the two girls, and "Jerusalem," the little boy who "Blackdog" said had been shot at by Alex Porter.

For several reasons, credibility is given to the notion that the "witch family" might still be present in the area today. Modern-day descriptions of the woman-like figure seen in the cave are consistent with those given of "Blackdog" almost two centuries earlier. The sounds of children playing near the back of the cave can often be heard when no children are present, and the figure of a little boy has been seen in pictures taken near the mouth of the cave and at Bellwood Cemetery.

No conclusive evidence exists to prove the present-day existence of the "witch family," however, the author feels that the resemblance between the two modern-day apparitions just discussed and those documented many years ago by Richard Williams Bell and others is more than just a coincidence – something was wrong on the Bell farm almost two centuries ago, and there is still something wrong on the Bell farm today.

EPILOGUE

"Well, it was a tough campaign, but I must say that I will do it again if the opportunity avails itself. It paid off, and I've finally been elected to the most prestigious office this wonderful nation has to offer." "Yes," his wife replied, "I am so very thankful for this day; I knew you would win, and I have all the confidence in the world that you'll be the best president this country has ever seen." "I'll do my absolute best, my dear. I will not fail you or my country. Now if only I could decipher what the mirror on my bureau is telling me," he responded.

"Why, what do you mean? Is something wrong?" "I don't know, Mary, but I see my face as it looks today in one side of the mirror, and in the other side I see a pale and sad-looking face. Can you make anything of that?" "Oh God, I can. It means that you will enjoy a successful first term in office and be re-elected, but you will die during your second term," his wife replied. Abraham Lincoln was assassinated during his second term of office. Was Lincoln's premonition nothing more than mere coincidence?

An elderly woman in a nursing home dies at 5:15. Upon arriving at her house several days later to go through her belongings, her family discovers that the clock is stopped precisely at 5:15. The house had been locked for weeks. In another instance, a man dies in his home and the clock beside his bed stops instantaneously. Are these cases of mere coincidence, or is there more to it?

On a cool April morning in the year 1900, Mrs. Jones awakened to the eerie feeling that her husband, out of town, was dead. She lay there almost an hour thinking this morbid thought before finally deciding to get up and start her morning. Her mind continued dwelling on this horrible thought as she made coffee, ate a light breakfast, and went to check the front porch for a package she was expecting.

As she opened the door, she noticed one of her neighbors walking up the steps toward the porch. The neighbor embraced her and delivered the terrible news that her husband, Luther "Casey" Jones, had lost his life in a train derailment the prior evening near Vaughan, Mississippi. Was Mrs. Jones' premonition a mere coincidence?

Is there really anything to the legend of the "Bell Witch?" Although the people, places and dates were real, what about "Kate?" Was she real? Theories that purport to logically explain the mystery behind the "Bell Witch" are abundant in large bookstores and on the Internet; however, the unrelated scenarios we discussed above clearly illustrate that some events stretch and sometimes exceed the bounds of reality and defy all logic. This leaves the human mind with much to process.

It would be a mistake to think nothing at all happened in Robertson County back in the 1800's – too many people have written about it (and under oath, I might add), and the legend has endured too long for there not to be anything to it. As is the case in a court of law, one is presented with evidence and must draw conclusions of fact. The evidence in the case of the "Bell Witch" is overwhelming.

Something out of the ordinary did happen in northwestern Robertson County during the early Nineteenth Century, and it terrified everyone who experienced it. I feel that it happened to the Bell family for the reasons I discussed earlier. Who knows — if something so incredibly sinister ever happens again, it just might be your family caught in the middle of it. Good night, watch those covers, and pleasant dreams.

APPENDICES

Appendix A:

Biographical Sketches of Those who Figured Prominently Into the Legend

MANY PEOPLE FIGURED INTO THE LEGEND of the "Bell Witch." Because these people actually lived and led very interesting lives, the author has provided biographical sketches of those he feels played the most prominent roles in the legend.

John Bell (1750-1820)

Often called "Ol' Jack Bell" by Kate, John Bell is the only person in history whose death was attributed to the doings of a Spirit. In 1817, Bell contracted a mysterious affliction that worsened over the next three years, ultimately leading to his death. Kate took pleasure in tormenting him during his affliction, finally poisoning him one December morning while he lay unconscious after suffering a number of violent seizures.

Born in Edgecombe County, North Carolina, John Bell apprenticed as a barrel maker during his formative years and later pursued a career in farming. He married Lucy Williams in 1782 and settled on a farm he had bought earlier. The Bells prospered over the next eight years and were among the most successful planters in the Tar River area of North Carolina.

With the birth of their first child, Jesse, they began a family. In the years that followed, John and Lucy Bell had three more sons, John Jr., Drewry, and Benjamin. All went well with the Bells until the 1801 and 1803 crop seasons when their crops failed and they decided to move westward and join their friends who had started successful farms there.

In the winter of 1803-1804, John Bell and his family embarked on a journey over the treacherous mountains of North Carolina and east Tennessee to an area known as "The Barren Plains," settling in the northwest section of present-day Robertson County, Tennessee. Bell became a successful farmer and gained considerable respect in his new abode. He later became an Elder of Red River Baptist Church.

The affliction that John Bell was stricken with in 1817 was most likely a neurological disorder. Very little was known about such disorders during the early Nineteenth Century, thus few treatment options were available.

It is interesting to note that Sir Charles Bell, a Nineteenth Century anatomy professor, discovered a neurological disorder that yielded symptoms almost identical to those John Bell suffered at the onset of his affliction.

This usually non-fatal disorder is known as "Bell's Palsy," and was discovered several years after John Bell's death. The fact that John Bell's earliest symptoms mimicked those of Bell's Palsy, a disorder named for the Bell surname, is coincidental.

John Bell died on December 20, 1820, and is buried in the old Bell Cemetery near Adams, Tennessee along with his wife and some of their children.

Lucy Bell (1770-1837)

Born in Edgecombe County, North Carolina to a family of wealthy planters, Lucy Bell was a pleasant and mild-mannered woman who was nearly always on Kate's good side.

All throughout her reign of terror over the Bell family, Kate pretended to treat Mrs. Bell nicely – singing to her, bringing her food when she was sick, and comforting her in other times of need. The emotional damage suffered by Mrs. Bell because of having to see and hear Kate's acts of physical abuse towards her husband and daughter offset any good deeds that Kate performed for her.

After John Bell's death and estate settlement, Lucy Bell inherited one slave, Dean, and a 106-acre tract of land that included the Bell home and cemetery. She remained at the old homestead up until her death in 1837. Lucy Bell is buried in the old Bell Cemetery near Adams, Tennessee along with her husband and some of their children.

Elizabeth "Betsy" Bell (1806-1888)

Like her father, Elizabeth Bell suffered a great deal from Kate's acts of physical abuse by having her hair pulled and getting slapped and pinched to the point that her face and arms covered with welts and bruises. [58] Kate never gave a reason for her relentless abuse of Elizabeth, but she emphatically disapproved of her engagement to Joshua Gardner.

[58] Elizabeth Bell's photo from *Authenticated History of the Bell Witch*, M.V. Ingram, 1894.

Elizabeth broke off her engagement to Joshua in the spring of 1821 after enduring several years of ridicule about her decision to marry him.

Elizabeth Bell married her former schoolteacher, Professor Richard Powell, in March of 1824, settling a few miles from the Bell farm and near a community that later became known as "Cedar Hill." Elizabeth Powell became a homemaker and the mother of eight children. Only four of Elizabeth and Richard Powell's children reached adulthood, one of which was Leftrick Reynolds Powell. He died in the Civil War Battle of Franklin, Tennessee in November of 1864 at the age of 23.

Elizabeth was very supportive of her husband's political career and stayed by his side during his many bouts with misfortune, including a debilitating stroke in 1837 and his ensuing loss of $10,000 in a steamboat accident while attempting to raise money for their family's financial well-being. Elizabeth insisted that her marriage to Richard Powell was a very happy and fulfilling one, despite the hardships they were forced to endure. Richard Powell's health declined over the years following his stroke, and he died in January of 1848 at the age of 53.

In 1849, *The Saturday Evening Post* published a story believed by many to be the first commercially published account of the "Bell Witch." The story implicated Elizabeth as having been the culprit behind the "Bell Witch" disturbances. This angered her to the point that she threatened the publication with a libel suit if it did not retract its statements. A public apology and retraction of the comments appeared in a later edition of *The Saturday Evening Post,* and as such, the case never went to trial.

Elizabeth Powell remained in the Cedar Hill area for many years after her husband's death and had the reputation of being a very witty and personable lady. Later in life, she gained considerable weight and a number of health problems befell her as a result. She was ultimately forced to move to Yalobusha County, Mississippi in 1874. She lived out her final years with a daughter, Eliza Jane Powell, who had moved to the area from Tennessee about 1849.

It was said that Elizabeth Powell refused to discuss Kate with people outside the family all the way up to the time of her death. It has also been said that she was terrified of sleeping alone and that she always slept between the wall and another person. Elizabeth "Betsy Bell" Powell died on July 11, 1888 at the advanced age of 82 years. She is buried in Long Branch Cemetery near Water Valley, Mississippi along with Eliza Jane Powell and a son-in-law, Z.Y.X. Bell.

This is the grave of Elizabeth "Betsy Bell" Powell. The gravestone in the picture is the original, and contains a beautifully designed inscription. After this picture was taken in 1999, the original stone was replaced with a generic stone.

Dean

Dean, John Bell's most prized slave, often reported encounters with Kate. His encounters included being followed by a black dog with two heads, being turned into a mule, and having his head split open by a large rabbit.

He carried a large scar on his head after the incident with the rabbit, and often told people it was the work of Kate. It is believed that his scar was really the result of a severe beating he received at the hands of a local planter who "rented" him from John Bell to do some farm work. Bell was reportedly outraged by the planter's cruelty and pursued legal action as a result.

An honest and dependable field slave, Dean was noted for his precision with the axe. Despite his small frame, Dean could take one side of a tree against any two men on the other side and cut a deeper kerf. His axe reportedly even split a dog's head open, causing it to appear to him with two heads from that point forward. It was also his axe that he was looking for when Kate reportedly turned him into a mule.

Dean, who also mastered the Bells' wagon from North Carolina to Tennessee, was one of two slaves who moved to Tennessee with the Bells. The other slave was Chloe, his mother, who was 42 years of age at the time. Chloe had worked for Lucy Bell's father, John Williams, in North Carolina before being given to the Bells upon his death.

It is presumed that Dean and his wife are buried in two of several unmarked slave graves in the old Bell cemetery near Adams, Tennessee. They have many descendants living in the same area today. The exact date of Dean's death is unknown.

Richard Powell (1795-1848)

Born in Halifax County, North Carolina, Professor Richard Rowell Ptolemy Powell figured prominently into the legend of the "Bell Witch" because of his having taught several of the Bell children and his admiration and later marriage to Elizabeth Bell.

After receiving an advanced education in his native North Carolina, Powell moved to Tennessee about 1815 and settled near the village of Nashville. As he explored teaching opportunities in Nashville, he

learned of the flourishing, Red River community in Robertson County and the need for a schoolmaster there. He left Nashville and moved some fifty miles to the northwest, settling in the Red River community near the Bell farm. [59]

Powell began teaching in a small schoolhouse located on a tract of land donated by James Johnston, only a few yards from John Bell's east property line. In addition to his classroom activities, Powell privately tutored some students in their homes. Having taught several of the Bell children, he became good friends with John and Lucy Bell.

Powell developed a fondness for Elizabeth Bell as she matured into adolescence. Despite his more

[59] Richard Powell's photo from *Authenticated History of the Bell Witch*, M.V. Ingram, 1894.

frequent visits to the Bell home and the compliments he often paid her, Elizabeth was already involved in a courtship with Joshua Gardner, a well-respected and close neighbor whose age was much closer to hers. Both the Bell and Gardner families were pleased with Elizabeth and Joshua's courtship; however it seemed that neither Powell nor Kate were fond of it.

Elizabeth broke off her engagement to Joshua Gardner on Easter Monday of 1821 after Kate's pressure had begun to take an emotional toll on her. Richard Powell visited Elizabeth frequently during her ensuing period of grief, often reciting poetry to help lift her Spirits. A courtship gradually evolved between the two, lasting three years until their marriage on March 21, 1824.

Richard Powell's marriage to Elizabeth was not his first. Powell earlier married Esther McKenzie Scott of Dickson County, Tennessee, who was 18 years his senior. Powell never mentioned his first marriage, but did refer to it in his personal diary.

"Richard R. P. Powell and Esther Scott was married on the Seventh Day of December, Eighteen Hundred & Fifteen, in the Twentieth year of my Age, on the day before my Birthday. It being Thursday." [60]

In the years following Powell's marriage to Elizabeth Bell, his involvement in society and politics increased — eventually requiring him to give up his

---

[60] Digitized image courtesy of Phillip C. Norfleet, used by permission.

job as schoolmaster to pursue a career in politics. Powell was elected and served as Sheriff of Robertson County between 1830 and 1833; and was elected to the Tennessee House of Representatives in 1833. He represented Robertson County in the 20th Tennessee General Assembly. Powell made a name for himself as a lawmaker of great ability, and gained wide popularity in Tennessee. In addition to this coveted office, Powell also had been a Captain in the Tennessee State Militia, a census enumerator, and a Justice of the Peace. [61]

Powell's personal diary alluded to earlier was his "Ciphering Book," a 271-page collection of advanced math problems, genealogical notes, and other information. It is believed that many of the math problems in Powell's "Ciphering Book" were created by his father, Richard Powell, Sr., who was a well-educated man. According to dates listed in his "Ciphering Book," Richard Powell solved many of the math problems between 1812 and 1822. The "Ciphering Book" makes no mention whatsoever of the "Bell Witch" disturbances or any problems associated with Elizabeth Bell.

---

[61] A biographical sketch of Richard Powell from the Tennessee Legislative Encyclopedia is included in Appendix C.

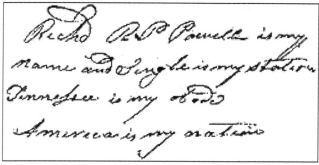

"Richard R. P. Powell is my name, and Single is my station. Tennessee is my abode, America is my nation."

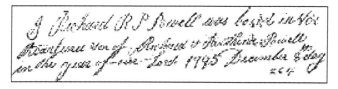

"I Richard R. P. Powell, was born in North Carolina, Son of Richard and Parthenia Powell, in the Year of our Lord 1795, December 8th day." [62]

At the height of his political career, Powell suffered a massive stroke that rendered him unable to fend for himself and his family. The Powells purchased a keelboat to ship goods to New Orleans in hopes of being able to raise money to meet their family's financial needs. On the night before the first shipment was to have set sail, all loaded goods were lost when a misguided steamboat crashed into the vessel as it was moored in Clarksville, Tennessee waiting for daybreak.

---

[62] Digitized images of Powell's writings courtesy of Phillip C. Norfleet, used by permission.

The substantial monetary loss and Powell's inability to earn a living left his family broke and destitute. A number of Powell's friends, including a certain "Joshua Gardner," then of Henry County, Tennessee, drafted and submitted a petition to the Tennessee State Legislature seeking financial assistance for Powell and his family. The petition was rejected. [63]

Richard Powell's condition slowly worsened until his death in 1848. Powell is buried in the Cedar Hill community of Robertson County, Tennessee.

Richard Powell was never around when Kate put on demonstrations, and neither spoke nor wrote of her. Interestingly, there are several accounts that allege Powell was involved with the occult. One such account describes an incident that took place at the schoolhouse involving Calvin and John Johnston.

While walking down the road by the schoolhouse one evening, Calvin and John Johnston noticed the glare of a candle burning inside. Having some time to spare, they decided to pay Professor Powell a visit. After several knocks without a response, they entered the door. Unable to find Powell, they stood and waited for him next to his desk and casually glanced down at the many books.

Powell soon arrived, running quickly to his desk where he hurriedly put away a book that had been left open. Calvin Johnston apologized, stating that he was "just glancing" and had not read the book. Powell replied, saying that the book was an old, Latin book and not important. [64]

Well-versed in both Latin and Greek, Calvin Johnston later commented that nothing he saw in the book, which he was unable to decipher, appeared

---

[63] Richard Powell's petition to the Tennessee State Legislature for financial relief is included in Appendix B.

[64] Source does not wish to be disclosed.

to be Latin or Greek. Could this book have been a *grimoire,* or "Book of Shadows" that has been used for centuries as a tool for tracking the progress and effectiveness of conjurations, spells, and potions?

Most who know anything about Powell would logically assume that the mysterious book was his "Ciphering Book." The author has reviewed Powell's "Ciphering Book" in meticulous detail, and has concluded that its contents are easily decipherable, including the occasional usage of Greek symbols in applicable math problems. As such, the author does not feel that the book seen by Calvin and John Johnston was Powell's "Ciphering Book."

Another account of Richard Powell's alleged involvement with the occult comes from a descendant of Joshua Gardner's younger brother, John A. Gardner. [65]

Several children, including some of the Gardner and Bell family, were walking home from school late one afternoon when they began discussing a difficult problem that Professor Powell had tried to explain in class that day. As it would turn out, the children would become more confused and return to the schoolhouse to ask Powell for clarification.

They found the door locked but clearly heard the sound of Professor Powell's voice coming from inside upon returning to the schoolhouse. They did not listen for long before realizing that Powell was speaking in a language completely unknown to them. Powell's speaking ceased and he opened the door upon hearing the children knock. When asked about his speaking episode, he said that he must have been daydreaming and that no one else had been present.

For several months there was considerable talk throughout the community, especially among the

---

[65] Source does not wish to be disclosed.

children, about Professor Powell's performing "incantations" in the schoolhouse. According to the story, Powell severely punished several of his students upon learning of their conversations about his actions.

Other than the writings of those who related these accounts first-hand and passed them down through many generations, and reports of his alleged study of occult-related topics while in North Carolina, very little evidence suggests that Powell was involved with the occult.

Jesse Bell (1790-1843)

Kate once "checked on" Jesse Bell and reported to his mother, Lucy Bell, that he had returned safely from a business trip and was at home reading by candlelight. Upon visiting his parents and siblings the following morning, he remarked that his front door mysteriously opened and shut as he read a book the night before. It was Jesse Bell's wife, Martha, whom Kate gave a pair of black stockings as a "gift" and asked that she be buried in them.

The eldest of John and Lucy Bell's children, Jesse Bell was born in Edgecombe County, North Carolina, where he spent his early childhood before moving to Tennessee with his family. He joined the Tennessee Militia in 1814 and fought in the Creek Indian War and the battles of Horseshoe Bend and New Orleans under the indirect command of Major General Andrew Jackson. [66]

He married Martha Gunn, daughter of the Reverend Thomas Gunn, in September of 1817. Jesse and Martha Bell's family, which ultimately consisted of nine children, lived in Robertson

---

[66] *Tennessee Military Service Records*, State Library and Archives, Nashville.

County, Tennessee up until the 1837-1842 period when they moved to Panola County, Mississippi. [67]

They settled and developed farmland in the present-day community of Eureka, about seven miles east of Batesville, Mississippi. Jesse and Martha Bell's first child, John Thomas Bell, was the patriarch of the Mississippi Bell Witch legend discussed in Appendix I. Their third child, Sarah Elizabeth Bell, married her first cousin, Jesse Bell Porter, a son of Alex and Esther Porter.

Jesse Bell died in 1843 while visiting friends in Christian County, Kentucky near the present-day town of Hopkinsville. His place of burial is unknown; however, there exists a gravestone in a Hopkinsville, Kentucky cemetery bearing the faint inscription of the name "Bell," and listing 1843 as the date of death. [68]

One of Jesse Bell's direct descendants has pointed out the possibility that he could have been buried in the Bell family cemetery at Red River because of its close proximity to Hopkinsville. Although no visible markers exist suggesting this was the case, it is nevertheless a very strong possibility.

Martha Gunn Bell died in 1881, and is buried along with several of her children in Long Creek Cemetery in Panola County, Mississippi. It remains unknown to this day whether she was buried in the black stockings as Kate requested.

---

[67] Time frame arrived at by examining real estate, tax, and census records.
[68] Riverside Cemetery, Hopkinsville, KY.

Located in Panola County, Mississippi, Long Creek Cemetery is where a number of Jesse Bell's descendants are buried, including the woman asked by "Kate" to be buried in black stockings, Martha Gunn Bell. Long Creek Cemetery is also where much of the Mississippi version of the legend allegedly took place.

Esther Porter (1800-1859)

It was Esther Bell Porter who witnessed the terrifying apparition of the "witch family" bouncing on saplings in the field across from her home.

Born in Halifax County, North Carolina, Esther Bell was the eldest of John and Lucy Bell's two daughters. After arriving in Tennessee with her family in 1804, she spent her childhood at the Bell farm on Red River. Esther was the first of John Bell's children to wed, marrying Alexander Bennett (Alex) Porter in July of 1817.

During the 1836-1840 period, the Porters moved to Panola County, Mississippi, settling near the present-day town of Oakland. [69] They had 12 children, several of whom died at birth or at very young ages. Esther Bell Porter died in 1859, and is allegedly buried in Union Hill Cemetery near Oakland, Mississippi. [ii]

John Bell, Jr. (1793-1862)

John Bell, Jr. was Kate's harshest critic by far. While others around the community and in the Bell household seemed terrified by Kate's presence, John Jr. was never at a loss for words. He yelled, cursed, challenged her, and consistently maintained that he knew what she was and was not afraid of her in any way. Kate took notice of his boldness, often stating that he was a very smart man and that she had considerable respect for him.

It was with John Bell, Jr. whom Kate intelligently debated and shared her predictions of major world events during her 1828 return-visit to the Bell farm. It is also believed that John Jr. was the first person Kate visited upon her return-visit, and that it was he and his best friend, Frank Miles, whom she bade her last farewell.

In his later years, John Bell, Jr. spent two days describing in meticulous detail his private conversations with Kate as his son, Dr. Joel Thomas Bell, listened and took notes. The younger Bell later shared this information his son, Dr. Charles Bailey Bell, who included much of it in his book, "The Bell Witch – A Mysterious Spirit," published in 1934. [ii] Recent findings indicate that these conversations might have been a hoax, the reasons for which will be discussed in a future edition of the book you are reading.

---

[69] Time frame was arrived at by comparing tax and real estate records in both states.

John Bell, Jr. spent his early childhood in Halifax County, North Carolina and moved to Tennessee with his family in the winter of 1803-1804. He later joined the Tennessee Militia and fought in the battles of Horseshoe Bend and New Orleans along with his brother, Jesse, under the indirect command of Major General Andrew Jackson. [70]

In 1815, John Jr. and his brother Drewry, along with Alex Gunn, used flatboats to carry goods from nearby Port Royal to the southern markets of Natchez and New Orleans. They sold scrap wood from their boats to finance their trip home along the Natchez Trace.

In November of 1828, John Bell, Jr. married Elizabeth Gunn and built a house just south of the original Bell home. They raised six children and amassed over 600 acres. He also served as a magistrate for several years.

The flat gravestone in the foreground marks the grave of John Bell, Jr.

He died from pneumonia on April 8, 1862, and is buried along with his wife and several of their

---

[70] *Tennessee Military Service Records*, State Library and Archives, Nashville.

children in a small cemetery near where their house once stood. ᵏᵏ The house burned sometime after Bell's death, but its remnants are still evident today in the form of charred bricks and stones.

Drewry Bell (1796-1865)

Drewry Bell was one of the first people to experience an apparition of Kate, which came in the form of a giant, mysterious bird sitting on the fence by the lane leading from the main road to the Bell home. As he began shooting at the creature, it vanished and was never seen again. This apparition occurred only a short time after his father, John Bell, encountered the mysterious, "dog-rabbit" in a corn row – which is widely believed to have been the first known apparition of Kate.

It is said that Drewry Bell lived his entire life in constant fear of Kate, and harbored very bitter feelings toward her because of his younger sister's trials and tribulations. Although he seldom spoke of Kate, he often referenced the physical and emotional torment his sister experienced and the evil, demented force responsible for it.

The third son of John and Lucy Bell, Drewry was born in Halifax County, North Carolina and spent his early childhood there before moving to Tennessee with his family. A lifelong bachelor, Drewry Bell made his home across the Red River from the Bell farm in the years following Kate's visit. He became a successful farmer and amassed six slaves to help him. It is not clear whether he owned the land he lived on, as the 1830 Federal Census lists him as owning no land, but six slaves.

Drewry Bell's slaves built their own place of worship near his home, and named it "Bell's Chapel."

After Bell's death, the church was physically moved across the Red River and put on land situated just across Keysburg Road from the present-day driveway of the Kirbys and Bell Witch Cave. A new building has long since been erected, however the frame and boarding of the original building still stands in a thicket adjacent to the modern building.

Drewry Bell died on New Year's Day of 1865, and is presumably buried along with his parents and several siblings in the old Bell cemetery near Adams, Tennessee. In his will, he left Elizabeth twenty-five dollars — five times the money he left each of his other siblings. It is interesting to note that four of the six siblings Drewry Bell left money to were already deceased at the time his will was written and dated, September 2, 1864. [71]

Zadok Bell (1803-1826)

Zadok Bell had no known encounters with Kate. Born in North Carolina just before his family's emigration to Tennessee, he would have been fourteen years old at the time the disturbances began. Given that he was being educated to become a lawyer, it is possible that he spent some of his adolescent years in a boarding school; however, the author has no proof of this.

Zadok completed his advanced education and became a bright lawyer, marrying Katherine Lawrence in Rutherford County, Tennessee in July of 1821 and moving to the "Montgomery Settlement" in southern Alabama soon thereafter. Aware that the Apalachee Indians had relinquished most Florida panhandle territories, he moved to Florida with hopes of setting up a successful law practice. ·He

---

[71] *Robertson County TN Will Book 17*, pp. 644-645.

settled in an area known as the Tallahassee Settlement, which was established in April of 1824 when seven men camped near the present-day capital. [72]

After spending less than a year in the Tallahassee Settlement, Zadok Bell moved back to Alabama where he died of Yellow Fever in a sweeping epidemic that struck the region in 1826. It is widely believed that Zadok Bell is buried in the old Bell cemetery near Adams, Tennessee; however, a small amount of research performed by the author indicates that he is actually buried near Montgomery, Alabama.

Richard Williams Bell (1811-1857)

Although only six years old when Kate's disturbances began, Richard Williams Bell vividly remembered the many terrible encounters that he, his parents, and siblings had with Kate. He is credited with authoring the only known eyewitness account of the disturbances.

In 1846, Bell journalized the disturbances in a comprehensive manuscript that he later passed on to his son, Allen Bell, who later circulated it among his closest family members. In the late nineteenth century, Martin Ingram incorporated Richard Williams Bell's manuscript into his book, "Authenticated History of the Bell Witch," where it appears as a single chapter entitled, "Our Family Trouble." Both the inclusion of Bell's manuscript and the book's 1894 publication date reflect Ingram's honoring the Bell family's request that the account not be published until after all of John Bell's immediate family had died. "Our Family Trouble" was also published by Mini-Histories in 1985.

---

[72] *Route Guide – The Sunset Limited*, Amtrak, 2000.

The second youngest child of John and Lucy Bell, Richard Williams Bell was born at the Bell farm in Robertson County, Tennessee. He spent his entire life as a successful farmer in the Red River area and was married three times – to Sallie Gunn, Susan Gunn, and Elizabeth Orndorf. Among his three wives, two of whom were daughters of the Reverends Thomas and James Gunn, he had two children.

He purchased a tract of land atop the hill at Brown's Ford Bluff from his brother, Joel Egbert Bell, in 1855, where he remained until his death two years later. His son, Allen Bell, then inherited the land. This land is not far from where the original Bell home stood, and is directly above the Bell Witch Cave. Many strange things have happened on this land and in the house that once stood there.

Richard Williams Bell died in 1857 at the young age of 46 years, and is buried along with his parents and several siblings in the old Bell cemetery near Adams, Tennessee.

Joel Egbert Bell (1813-1890)

Although too young at the time of the disturbances to remember many details, Joel Bell later became very knowledgeable about Kate by listening to his mother and siblings tell of their remarkable encounters with her.

After the original Bell house was razed, Joel Bell used some of the logs and stones to build his house on Brown's Ford Bluff, a hill overlooking the Red River about a half-mile from where the original Bell house stood and directly above the Bell Witch Cave. A number of strange things happened in this house.

During the winter of 1852, Dr. Henry Sugg experienced an incident where Kate shook and rattled the vials in his medicine bag as he tended to a sick child at this house. Three years later, Joel Bell moved to nearby Springfield and sold the land and house to Richard Williams Bell, who in turn left it to his son, Allen Bell, when he died in 1857. About 1861, Allen Bell was discharged from the Confederate Army due to illness. While recuperating at his home, he was visited one night by Reynolds Powell, son of Elizabeth and Richard Powell. The two men reported being harassed by Kate up until the wee hours of the next morning.

Over the course of many years, Joel Bell cultivated a good friendship with Martin Ingram, author of the book, "Authenticated History of the Bell Witch," and shared many stories about Kate with him.

The youngest child of John and Lucy Bell, Joel Egbert Bell was born at the Bell farm in Robertson County, Tennessee and spent his childhood and many of his adult years in the area. He married twice and had fourteen children.

Bell moved his family to nearby Springfield in 1855, where he spent the remainder of his life as a successful farmer and well-respected citizen. Joel Egbert Bell died in 1890, and is buried in a rural area just outside Springfield, Tennessee.

Joshua Gardner (1800-1884)

One of nine children, Joshua Gardner was born in Robertson County and spent his childhood on a farm situated along present-day State Route 256.

Although he had very few direct encounters with Kate, Gardner figures prominently into the legend by virtue of having been Elizabeth "Betsy" Bell's suitor and fiancé during the terrifying period of Kate's disturbances. Kate strongly disapproved of Elizabeth and Joshua's engagement, and voiced her disapproval to Elizabeth every time she got the chance.

Kate, despite never having said anything bad about Gardner himself, provided Elizabeth no reason for her disapproval of their engagement other than, "You will not have happiness with Joshua Gardner, and future generations will see it true." After giving the matter much thought and enduring considerable agony, Elizabeth finally broke off the engagement.

Not long after that fateful day in 1821, Joshua Gardner wrapped up his affairs and left the area, settling in Henry County, Tennessee where in 1829 he married Sarah Donelson and had two children. Joshua became a successful farmer and served as a magistrate for several years.

Joshua Gardner's younger brother, John, became the first president of the Nashville and North Western Railroad, which is now part of the CSX Railroad. John Gardner had a successful political career, serving as a state Senator for several years and later attending the 1870 Tennessee Constitutional Convention.

Joshua Gardner left Henry County, Tennessee in 1840 and settled in Weakley County near Gardner's Station, a small town named for his younger brother. He purchased 228 acres of land and began farming it, using his profits to purchase additional land that was once estimated to have been more than 1,800 acres.

Although Easter Monday of 1821 was the last time Joshua Gardner and Elizabeth Bell ever saw each other, he became friends with Richard Powell and even signed a petition to the Tennessee State

Legislature requesting financial assistance for Powell's family after a series of misfortunate events. The author feels that it was not Richard Powell whom Gardner was concerned about, but the well-being of his lost love, Elizabeth.

After Sarah Donelson's death, Gardner remarried and continued farming successfully up until his death in 1884. Joshua Gardner is buried in Weakley County, Tennessee near the present-day town of Dresden. [73]

Reverend Sugg Fort (1776-1829)

Reverend Sugg Fort was Pastor of Red River Baptist Church during the time of the Bell disturbances, and with other clergymen in the area, tried to determine Kate's identity and purpose while comforting the Bell family as much as possible.

The youngest of nine children born to Elias and Sarah Sugg Fort, Reverend Fort was born in Edgecombe County, North Carolina and moved to Tennessee with his family in 1788, settling between the Red River and Elk Fork Creek in what would later become the northwestern end of Robertson County. His father, Elias Fort, was actively involved in the Tar River Association, a religious advocacy group in North Carolina whose membership included the church John and Lucy Bell attended, Union Baptist Church, before they moved to Tennessee.

Reverend Sugg Fort married Elizabeth Diggs in December of 1801, and they had two children before her death in February of 1805. He never remarried. During this time, Elias Fort was the Pastor of Red River Baptist Church while two of his sons, Sugg and Josiah, served as clerks of the church. Around

---

[73] Joshua Gardner's photo from *Authenticated History of the Bell Witch*, M.V. Ingram, 1894.

1816, Sugg Fort became the Pastor of Red River Baptist Church.

Over the years, mainly as a result of his father's having known the Bells in North Carolina before they moved to Tennessee, Reverend Fort developed a good friendship with John Bell and his family, often visiting and holding prayer meetings in their home. The same could not be said about Reverend Fort's older brother, Josiah, however.

At a church service in August of 1815, a deacon was unable to distribute communion because John Bell had privately expressed to him his dissatisfaction with Josiah Fort. [74] Because both men were at the table and prepared to partake of the elements, the deacon refused to proceed because not all present were in fellowship with one another. Confusion arose among those prepared for communion and several, including John Bell, got up and went home.

The church conducted a private hearing some weeks later to determine why "Brethren Bell & Fort do not appear to be in fellowship." [75] The outcome of this hearing is not documented in the church minutes; however, at the church's next meeting, Josiah Fort requested and received a letter of dismission from the church and joined nearby Drake's Pond Baptist Church. He would eventually return to Red River Baptist Church, but not until after John Bell's death.

Despite the issue of John Bell's excommunication from the church in 1818, Reverend Fort continued to maintain the good relationship with Bell and his family that they cultivated and enjoyed over the years. Reverend Sugg Fort died in 1829, and is

---

[74] *Red River Baptist Church Minutes (1791-1826)*, pp. 165-166.
[75] *Red River Baptist Church Minutes (1791-1826)*, pp. 167-169.

buried in one of the three Fort cemeteries in Robertson County, Tennessee.

Reverend James R. Gunn (1772-1845)

It was Reverend James R. Gunn who asked Kate the question, "Who are you and what do you want?" in such a manner that a truthful answer was the only option. Kate's answer to his question, "I am nothing but old Kate Batts' witch, here to torment Ol' Jack Bell to his death," is what earned the Spirit the nickname, "Kate."

Reverend James Gunn was the younger of the two Gunn brothers who pioneered Methodism in the Red River area during the early Nineteenth Century. He was born and spent his childhood in Virginia, where he and his brother, Thomas, were licensed to preach in May of 1789. He moved to Caswell County, North Carolina in 1791.

The son of Episcopalians, Reverend James Gunn was married twice and had a total of seventeen children, three of who (Joseph, E.W., and William) followed in his footsteps and became Methodist ministers. He moved to Robertson County, Tennessee in 1811, settling in the Red River area near the Bell farm. He helped establish and then began preaching at nearby Bethel Methodist Church, which was in addition to riding the "circuit" and preaching at other Methodist churches in Tennessee and southern Kentucky. Along with his brother, Thomas, Reverend James Gunn founded Ebenezer Methodist Church (now known as Cedar Hill Methodist Church) in 1833. Many of the churches he helped to establish still exist today.

Reverend James R. Gunn died of a probable stroke in 1849 after spending the last eight months of his life confined to a bed.

Reverend Thomas Gunn (1770-1859)

Along with his brother, Reverend Thomas Gunn pioneered Methodism in the Red River area during the early Nineteenth Century. He was born and spent his childhood in Virginia, where was licensed to preach in May of 1789. [76] He moved to Caswell County, North Carolina in 1791.

In the spring of 1812, Reverend Gunn moved to the Red River area and settled in Logan County, Kentucky where he remained four years before moving to Robertson County, Tennessee. He was married twice, and three of his five children married into the Bell family.

Despite having a dislocated hip from being thrown by a horse in 1840, Reverend Thomas Gunn continued preaching fervently in his trademark, "hellfire and brimstone" manner – often traveling long distances and suffering great pain to deliver the word. Four years later, he was stricken with palsy and suffered a serious head injury that rendered him invalid for the remainder of his life. Reverend Thomas Gunn died in May of 1859 at the advanced age of 89 years, and is buried in one of the two Gunn cemeteries near Adams, Tennessee. [77]

---

[76] *McFerrin's History of Methodism in Tennessee*, 1886.
[77] Information about the Gunns was obtained from the Bible of Reverend James Gunn and information provided to the author by Nancy Williams Lewis, a direct descendant of the Gunns.

James Johnston (1759-1851)

No man or family was closer to John Bell's family during the disturbances than James Johnston and his two sons, John and Calvin. James Johnston was the first person outside the Bell family whom John Bell confided in about Kate's disturbances. Johnston and his wife were the first people outside the Bell family known to have had an encounter with Kate.

The first question that Johnston asked Kate, "In the name of the Lord, who and what are you, and what do you want?" would turn out to be the most popular question asked of Kate throughout the period of the disturbances. Johnston first thought the disturbances were a practical joke being played by the Bell children or others in the community; however, he changed his mind after spending several nights at the Bell home. He learned that the entity causing the disturbances possessed an intelligence all its own.

James Johnston was a very devout Christian. Despite his inability to read or write, he was considered by many to be an expert on Christianity and the Bible. Because the Bible says that both good and bad Spirits exist, and that trafficking with the evil supernatural is possible, Johnston often expressed his strong belief that the disturbances were being caused by "An evil Spirit, a demon, just like in the Bible!" His sons, John and Calvin, also shared this belief.

The Johnstons had the most commonly misspelled surname in the entire "Bell Witch" legend, "Johnson." The correct spelling is "Johnston," with the Scottish pronunciation silencing the "t." The first Johnstons to settle in America came from Annandale, Scotland by way of County Tyrone in Northern Ireland, settling in Pennsylvania before moving southward to Virginia and the Carolinas as land grants became available. Born in Pennsylvania in 1759, James Johnston was the youngest child of John and Mary Patterson Johnston.

After spending his early childhood in Pennsylvania, he moved to Caswell County, North Carolina with his parents and siblings. After reaching a suitable age, Johnston joined the North Carolina Continental Line and fought in the Revolutionary War. He married Rebecca Porter in July of 1780, and they had nine children before her death in 1802. In 1800, James Johnston and his family migrated to Robertson County, Tennessee as his brother did twenty years earlier.

Because of the treacherous terrain and Native American conflicts in the Cumberland Gap and Tennessee River areas at the time, Johnston brought his family and belongings to Tennessee by way of Georgia. In addition to his concerns about providing a safe and smooth passage for his family, Johnston was also concerned about protecting a priceless china cabinet that he had decided to carry on the journey. Because of James Johnston's awareness of the possible dangers along the way and his efforts to avert them, a very old and priceless china cabinet sits today in the dining room of a private residence near Adams, Tennessee.

Johnston and his family settled on 1,000 acres of land that he received as a grant for serving in the Continental Army. The Johnston farm was situated along the Red River just east of present-day Adams, Tennessee and encompassed both sides of Sturgeon Creek. About two years after the death of his first wife, Johnston married Jane Marvlin Greer. Having no children of their own, they adopted Jane's niece, Parthenia "Theny" Thorn, of Stewart County,

Tennessee. Born on Christmas of 1804, "Theny" Thorn lost her parents at an early age and had been placed in the care of her aunt, Jane Greer. [78] She always referred to James and Jane Johnston as her parents.

James and Jane Johnston subscribed to the doctrine of the Cumberland Presbyterian Church. Because there was no Cumberland Presbyterian Church in the area, they joined the Methodist Church because they felt part of their Christian duty was to be active members of some church. James Johnston died in April of 1850 at the advanced age of 91 years, and is buried along with his two wives and many relatives near Adams, Tennessee. [79]

John Johnston (1783-1874)

Like his father, John Johnston often sat up nights and talked to Kate so the Bells could sleep. Despite her insistence that his motives were less than

sincere, Kate frequently engaged John Johnston in fascinating and thought-provoking conversation.

During one discussion, he asked Kate what his Dutch step-grandmother in North Carolina said when one of her slaves did something wrong. Using the woman's own voice and Dutch accent,

---

[78] Theny Thorn's birth date obtained from her gravestone.
[79] Correspondence with Mr. Jim Brooks, a direct descendant of the Johnston family.

Kate replied, "Hut, tut. What has happened now?" "Hut tut" is a Dutch term meaning "No-no," and is used as a chiding expression — almost a term of endearment. Johnston later told others about this astonishing encounter, describing how quickly Kate returned the correct phrase and how perfectly she imitated his step-grandmother.

On another occasion, Kate allowed John Johnston's brother, Calvin, to shake her hand. After learning of this incident, Johnston repeatedly begged Kate for the opportunity to shake her hand. She continually refused, stating that he was only "out to get her" and that his brother's intentions had been sincere. [80]

One of the most significant things that John Johnston learned about Kate was that she could not fully read minds, as some people believed. He asked her on several occasions what he was thinking. He said that while her guesses were sometimes close, she never gave the right answer.

During one of their discussions, Kate became angry with Johnston and threatened to kill him. On his way home the following morning, he noticed what looked like the shadow of a long, sharp knife behind him. He thought to himself, "If the Lord wants me to die, then I will die; I will not run."

He stood still in his tracks to see what fate would deal him. The "knife" never disappeared, and after taking the time to analyze his surroundings, he realized that the "knife" was actually the shadow of a blade from a corn stalk, blowing in the wind. After this incident, Johnston hypothesized that many so-called "encounters" with Kate were logical things such as the shadow of the corn blade, but that most

---

[80] John Johnston's photo from *Authenticated History of the Bell Witch*, M.V. Ingram, 1894.

people ran away without taking the time to observe their surroundings and determine the true cause.

John Johnston was born and spent his childhood in North Carolina before moving to Robertson County, Tennessee in 1800 with the rest of his family. In 1810, he married Martha Johnston, his first cousin and the daughter of James Johnston's brother, William, who moved to the area about 1780. John and Martha Johnston had eight children, one of whom was Nancy Johnston, the baby who was spanked by Kate. Like John Bell's eldest sons, John Johnston was a member of the Tennessee Militia and fought in the battles of Horseshoe Bend and New Orleans. John Johnston died in March of 1874 and is buried along with his relatives near Adams, Tennessee. [81]

Calvin Johnston (1796-1859)

Daniel Calvin Johnston was the man who Kate allowed to shake her hand. He often spoke of the incident, describing Kate's hands as being "fragile and velvety." Kate thought a great deal of Calvin Johnston, often using him as a basis for comparison when telling others of their faults, exclaiming, "There is no finer man in this country than Calvin Johnston."

Born in North Carolina, Calvin Johnston was a toddler when his family moved to Tennessee in 1800. He spent his childhood on the Johnston farm in Robertson County, Tennessee, where he developed a keen interest in Latin and horticulture. He married Francis Porter, a first cousin, in 1823 and had one child.

He built a large brick home on his father's farm

---

[81] Correspondence with Mr. Jim Brooks, a direct descendant of the Johnston family.

and spent most of his adult life there. It is believed that the house was built around 1841, with that being the date carved into a stone window lintel. In 1850, four years after the death of his first wife, Johnston married Elizabeth Holland. They had no children of their own.

Contrary to the way in which Calvin Johnston is portrayed by many authors and historians, he was in fact a very enlightened and innovative man, much more so than many of his peers.

One of his greatest achievements was his creation of a raised writing system for the blind, which enabled them to read written materials with their fingers. After perfecting his system, Johnston traveled to New Orleans to apply for a patent. Upon his arrival, he learned that a Frenchman named "Braille" had received a patent for the same type of writing system only a week earlier.

A horticulture enthusiast, Johnston collected specimens of all wild plants and flowers in the area  and pressed them in a book, listing both the Latin and common name of each. Vanderbilt University in nearby Nashville learned of Johnston's book and asked that it be donated because of its stunning accuracy and potential as a learning tool. His descendants decided to retain the book, and it is still in their possession today. Calvin Johnston's interest in horticulture is still evident today, not only in the form of his book, but also in the flowers he planted many years ago. He loved buttercups and liberally planted them around the site of his home and the grave of his nephew. Although the buttercups around his home site are long gone, the ones he planted on his nephew's grave still bloom each year. The variety growing on the grave is very old and no longer obtainable, which leads many to believe that these are the same buttercups planted by Johnston many years ago. The variety contains some green, but mostly "butter and egg" colors.

Both Calvin and John Johnston were subscribers to *The Scientific American,* one of the earliest scientific magazines to be published in this country, all the way back to the early 1830's. The family still has some very early copies of the magazine, which belonged to the Johnston brothers of long ago. Calvin Johnston died in 1859, and is buried near Adams, Tennessee. [82]

His gravestone reads, *"Remember mortal man, as you pass by. As you are now, so once was I. As I am now, so you must be. Prepare for death and follow me."*

---

[82] Correspondence with Mr. Jim Brooks, a direct descendant of the Johnston family.

Many of those who figured prominently into the legend of the "Bell Witch" rest in this cemetery located in rural Robertson County. Those buried here include the Johnstons, David and Parthenia "Theny Thorn" Gooch, William Porter, and many others.

Appendix B:

Richard Powell's Petition to the Tennessee State Legislature for Financial Relief

31 October 1837
Petition Number 54-1837-01

To the Legislature of the State of Tennessee now in session:

Your petitioner Richard R. P. Powell a citizen of the County of Robertson and state aforesaid begs leave humbly to state to your honorable body that tho he has enjoyed the advantages of health and body vigor and the helpings of prosperity, yet he is now struggling against chill adversity. He would further represent that by his own virtuous industry and economy he so far succeeded in life as to raise himself from the shades of poverty to the sunshine of a reasonable affluence supporting and rearing at the same time a wife and a numerous offspring and flattered himself that he had so far gained the advantages of the world that he could close the evening of life in quiet and ease. But at a moment when those fond anticipations were freshest and fairest, promising the fruition of all earthly happenings, the destroyer came - that monsterful disease overtook him - that blight and mildew came upon him. He fell a victim to a paralysis of the right side of his whole frame and while the physical man was thrown from its lofty heights, the intellectual throne was likewise sapped til altogether have decayed and are crumbling.

Your petitioner thinks that his acquaintances and countrymen will bear witness that he, when he was himself, possessed some humble merit and he is the more inclined to this belief from the circumstances of the past testimonials beyond that of words that he was repeatedly in his county for years elected sheriff and also as their member to the Legislative body, that responsible station which you now fill.

Your humble petitioner will no further trouble you with a preface but will come to the catastrophe. Your petitioner fell not only a victim to disease but likewise to his own unskillfullness and want of judgment and the artifices of the cunning and uncharitable. He is now desolate, disrobed of his estate and left penniless with a wife and many children dependent upon the poor effects of your humble petitioner.

Your petitioner will endeavor not to fatigue you with the details of his woes - suffice to say they are not the offspring of crime but the calamity of disease and affliction. Having thus addressed myself to your charity and discretion allows your humble petitioner to ask at your hands the humble privilege of retailing such small quantities of merchandise, as his limited circumstances assisted by his wife may enable him through the kindness of friends may procure free of taxation that the small profit rising there from may be the means of supporting the family of your humble petitioner which he is desirous to rear up in a respectable circle of life. That could your honorable body consistent with good feelings and the constitution of the government make to your humble petitioner some small donation to aid him in a small commencement. Your petitioner having some knowledge of merchandise. You would incur all the good feelings of your humble petitioner and family with a sincere hope that your charity will ever be remembered by an all wise who is able to add to the blessings of the charitable.

Your humble petitioner would trouble your honorable body with short history of one of his calamities that in order to enable him to circumvent the embarrassments incurred in consequence of this affliction he purchased a keel boat and loaded the same with the most valuable products of our country to the amount of $10,000 and had her launched at the landing at Clarksville nearly ready to set sail to the southern market where your petitioner had every reason to believe he would from the profits arising there from be fully enabled to relieve himself from every embarrassment and leave him in affluent circumstances. But to the sad misfortune of your petitioner, before he had set sail a steam boat came along in the night time and ran afoul of the boat of your petitioner and sunk her with his loading which was destroyed and lost which proved the destroyer of the remaining estate of your humble petitioner to the amount of $6000. The premises considered your humble petitioner submits his case to the mercy of your honorable body. [83]

---

[83] From Tennessee Legislative Records; provided electronically by Mr. Phillip C. Norfleet, webmaster of The Bell Witch Folklore Center, http://members.zoom.com/bellwitch001

Appendix C:

Biographical Sketch of Richard Powell from the Tennessee Legislative Encyclopedia

HOUSE, 20th General Assembly, 1833-35; representing Robertson County. Born in Halifax County, North Carolina, December 8, 1795; son of Richard Rowell Ptolemy and Parthenia Powell; grandson of John Powell. He was married (1st) on December 7, 1815, to Esther Scott; no further record of her. Powell removed to Robertson County. Schoolmaster; was teacher to his second wife. Married (2nd) on March 21, 1824, to Elizabeth Bell (1806-1888), daughter of John and Lucy (Williams) Bell, of Robertson County (with whose family the "Bell Witch" legend is concerned). Their children are variously identified as Susan Amanda, Emily Caroline, Permelia Adeline (Mrs. W. M. Gardner), Eliza Jane (Mrs. Zadock R. Bell), DeWitt Williams, Virginia Reynolds, Tennessee Bell, and Leftrick Reynolds Powell. One source states that a son, Sam Powell, was killed in the Civil War, but the reference is probably to Reynolds Powell, who was killed during the Civil War. Representative Powell was sheriff of Robertson County, 1830-33; census enumerator, justice of the peace, and captain in the state militia, he died January 13, 1848, and is buried near Cedar Hill, Robertson County. His widow was living with her two younger children in Robertson County in 1850; she later removed to Panola County, Mississippi; died near Water Valley, Yalobusha County, on July 10, 1888; buried near that place. Richard Powell was a brother of Mathew Powell, sometime member Tennessee General Assembly.

Sources: *Springfield Record*, March 1, 22, August 16, 1886; Albert Virgil Goodpasture, *Goodspeed History of Tennessee - Robertson County*, p. 837; M.V. Ingram, *Authenticated History of the Bell Witch*; Charles Bailey Bell, M.D., *The Bell Witch - A Mysterious Spirit*; *Robertson County Deed Book 3*, p. 150; Information furnished by Ralph L. Winters, Historian – Clarksville, TN; Mrs. A. E. Clement, Nashville, TN; and Mrs. Clyde Herring, great-granddaughter; *U.S. Census*, 1830, 1850, Robertson County, TN; Hoffman, *Genealogical Abstracts of Wills - 1758-1824, Halifax County, North Carolina*, pp. 70-71, 155. [84]

---

[84] From Tennessee Legislative Encyclopedia; provided electronically by Mr. Phillip C. Norfleet, webmaster of The Bell Witch Folklore Center, http://members.zoom.com/bellwitch001

Appendix D:

Early History of Robertson County, Tennessee

THE EARLIEST INHABITANTS of Tennessee that we know much about were the Mound Builders. Archaeologists recognize two major mound-building cultures – the Woodland and the Mississippian.

The Mississippian culture came into existence around 750 AD. Although most Mississippian groups buried their dead in cemeteries, the Woodland-type burial mounds were sometimes used. At larger Mississippian settlements, the elite families were sometimes buried in special mounds along with their elaborate possessions that represented their status in society. These burials took place from about 1000 to 1500 AD, when the Mississippian culture was at its peak.

The Mississippian culture was still flourishing when early Spanish explorer Hernando de Soto visited the area in the 1540-1541 period. By the middle of the seventeenth century, mound building had ceased and the Mound Builders (as we knew them) became extinct. Other nations, such as the Cherokee, Chickasaw, Creek and Choctaw, were descended from the Mound Builders.

Most of Tennessee was hunting ground for these groups many years before the white settlers arrived. Most permanent Cherokee settlements were in eastern Tennessee near the Tennessee and Holston Rivers. Permanent Chickasaw settlements were in northern Mississippi and western Tennessee, the Choctaws had permanent settlements in northeastern Mississippi and southwestern Tennessee, and the Creeks lived primarily in Alabama. By 1776, most Native American tribes in the area had decided to reclaim their land – now occupied by white settlers.

The first known white settler in Robertson County was Thomas Kilgore, who in 1778 built a fort on the banks of the Red River near Cross Plains. It is also believed that Ezekiel Polk, grandfather of President James Knox Polk, settled on Sulphur Fork Creek near the Red River about two years later; however, Native American hostility was so great in the area that he remained for less than a year. Albert Virgil Goodpasture relates the following detailed account of Thomas Kilgore's early settlement:

"The first settlement in Robertson County {The facts in regard to Kilgore's settlement were condensed from the articles written by Dr. J.S. Mulloy, for the Springfield Record} was made by Thomas Kilgore on the waters of the Middle Fork of Red River, three-fourths of a mile west of Cross Plains. The Legislature of North Carolina passed a preemption law securing to settlers of Tennessee 640 acres of land, provided the settlement was made prior to 1780.

In the spring of 1778, Kilgore left North Carolina with some ammunition, some salt, and a few grains of corn. Traveling on foot, he passed through East Tennessee and plunged into the wilderness beyond. Guided alone by the sun and the North Star, he pushed on, seeing no white people until he reached Bledsoe's Lick, where he found a colony of six or eight families. After resting a few days, he went on some twenty-five miles west where he located.

As a safe hiding place from the Indians, he selected a cave a mile west of where Cross Plains now is. It had a bold stream of water running from it into the Middle Fork of Red River, and by wading through the stream he could enter the cave without leaving a trail.

In the spring of 1779, with a few families besides his own, he returned to the spot where he had passed the previous summer. A stockaded fort, "Kilgore's Station" was at once erected to protect them from the Indians. This fort was situated on a commanding eminence, about three-fourths of a mile from Cross Plains. Kilgore's Station, from that time for years, was a landmark in the overland emigration to Tennessee.

Thomas Kilgore, after living half a century on the land which he had acquired by his heroics, died at the advanced age of one hundred and eight years." [85]

A number of families settled in the area over the next few decades, including the Forts, Gunns, Gardners, Norfleets, Bells, Gooches and others. During this time, "war parties" ravaged the early frontier – killing white settlers and burning their homes. Despite the signing of a peace treaty as early as 1777, the brunt of attacks on the early settlers of Robertson County did not come until the early 1780's, when several renegade groups of Cherokees and Creeks formed what became known as the

---

[85] Albert Virgil Goodpasture, *Goodspeed History of Tennessee – Robertson County*, 1886, p. 829 [Edited by Pat Fitzhugh].

Chickamauga Nation, whose purpose was to reclaim their land despite the existence of peace treaties.

After a failed attack on Fort Nashboro, which later became known as Nashville, the Chickamaugans headed north and raided early settlements all along the Red River, carrying out brutal and relentless attacks that often signaled the demise of the settlements and their inhabitants. This series of attacks marked the beginning of a reign of terror that lasted almost a decade.

Over time, many of the settlers armed themselves and casualties gradually lessened. The fall of the Chickamauga Nation began in 1792, after its chief allegedly had a heart attack and collapsed after a prolonged and drunken war dance. Another chief soon replaced him, and the brutal attacks continued over the next two years. The new chief finally sued for peace and signed a treaty in 1794, after which time the attacks in middle Tennessee subsided greatly.

Most of the area along the Red River is in present-day Montgomery and Robertson Counties, although the area was originally part of Tennessee County, North Carolina before Tennessee became a state in 1796. The new state was divided into counties and Robertson County was named for James Robertson, the founding father of nearby Nashville.

During the time of John Bell, Robertson County had a population of 9,938. [86] The primary goods produced in early Robertson County were whiskey and cotton. Albert Virgil Goodpasture describes the importance of these staples in Robertson County's early economy in his book, *Goodspeed History of Tennessee – Robertson County*:

---

[86] Albert Virgil Goodpasture, *Goodspeed History of Tennessee – Robertson County*, 1886, p. 836.

"The manufacture of whisky and brandy has always been an important industry in Robertson County. In the earlier days, small distilleries were found in almost every hollow, and it is said that on some streams there was a stillhouse every 100 yards.
These establishments had a capacity of not more than thirty or forty gallons per day, and the whisky was manufactured by what is known as the 'sour-mash' process. The honesty and care used in making the whiskey gave it a high reputation, which it has since maintained.
One of the first distilleries in the county was erected near Cross Plains by Daniel Holman, about 1798. In the same year, another distillery was built near Turnersville by Mr. Grider. The Woodards were also among the first distillers of the county.
During the first fifty years after the settlement of the county, cotton was a crop of some importance. Nearly every farmer raised enough to clothe his own household, and after the invention of the gin, considerable quantities were shipped. Among the gins and presses in use in 1804 were those of Archer Cheatham, in Springfield, and John McMillan, near Cross Plains. The cultivation of cotton began to decline about 1830, and it was not long until its production practically ceased." [87]

Cotton was later replaced by tobacco as the county's most prized crop. Over the years, Robertson County earned its reputation as the dark-fired tobacco capital of the world.

---

[87] Albert Virgil Goodpasture, *Goodspeed History of Tennessee – Robertson County*, 1886, p. 828 [Edited by Pat Fitzhugh].

Appendix E:

The Town of Adams, Tennessee

ADAMS IS LOCATED about 10 miles northwest of Springfield, Tennessee and 7 miles south of Guthrie, Kentucky. The town, first called "Red River Station," was changed to "Adams Station" in honor of a local merchant, landowner and railroad stockholder, Reuben Adams, when the first railroad depot and post office were built in 1860. [88] The Edgefield and Kentucky Railroad connected nearby Guthrie, Kentucky with the Edgefield community just north of present-day Nashville.

The town was first incorporated on November 10, 1869. The first Charter was repealed in 1899, and the town did not incorporate again until the 1908-1909 period. [11] The size of the town was measured as, "120 rods in each direction from the center of the depot." [89]

The town's first newspaper, "The Adams Enterprise," was started by Charley Willett and remained in circulation for about six years. Willett later became a professional baseball player, a successful attorney, the Mayor of Adams, and a Tennessee State Senator.

Adams Station became known simply as "Adams"

---

[88] Albert Virgil Goodpasture, *Goodspeed History of Tennessee – Robertson County*, 1886, p. 832.
[89] Ralph Winters, *Historical Sketches Adams, Robertson County and Port Royal/Montgomery County TN*, 1978, p. 47.

on February 10, 1898, and the Edgefield and
Kentucky Railroad became known as the Louisville
and Nashville Railroad when the trunk line was
extended from Guthrie to Louisville, Kentucky. [90]

Located along what was the main railroad and
highway between Nashville and Louisville for many
years, Adams was a thriving town with many
residents and businesses. Tennessee historian Albert
Virgil Goodpasture describes Adams during its
heyday:

"The first store-house was built and occupied by
Adams & Holloway, who carried on a grocery
business. At about the same time, B. O.
Crenshaw opened a drygoods store. During the
Civil War, nearly all buildings were destroyed. In
1866, only three dwellings remained in the town.
About 1865 C. M. Brown & Co. established a
general merchandise business in the depot. A
little later, Capt. Thomas Mallory built a
storehouse on the lot now occupied by J. C.
Moody's drug store, and a business was
conducted there under the firm name of J. E.
Ruffin & Co.
The present business interests of the town are
represented by J. E. Gaines, W. S. Miller and
Redding & Cobb, drygoods; J. C. Murphey and
Winters & Head, groceries; W. H. Howsley,
general merchandise; J. S. Moody, drugs; Crouch
& Co., and Hallums & Edwards, tobacco dealers;
G. A. Farmer, flouring-mill; Alsbrooke &
Robinson, Blacksmiths; and J. T. Bell and J. C.
Moody, physicians [Editor's Note: J.T. Bell was
Dr. Joel Thomas Bell, son of John Bell, Jr.].

---

[90] Ralph Winters, *Historical Sketches Adams, Robertson County and Port
Royal/Montgomery County TN*, 1978, p. 44.

The town has two churches, Methodist and Missionary Baptist. The school under the principalship of S. A. Link is one of the best in the county." [91]

The railroad's abandonment of passenger service through Adams and the construction of Interstate 24, both occurring in the Twentieth Century, took a heavy toll. A number of businesses were forced to

close, and most buildings in what was once the central business district have long since been destroyed or boarded up.

Adams' best-known citizen was (is) none other than the "Kate." Small signs at the east and west city limits along Highway 41 say, "Welcome to Adams," and display a carved-out picture of a witch riding a broom.

Coming into Adams from the east on Highway 41, the first landmark one will see is Bellwood Cemetery, which is situated on the right-hand side of the highway. Towards the back of the cemetery lies a monument dedicated to John Bell and his descendants, which reads:

John Bell 1750-1820 and his wife Lucy Williams
Pioneer Settlers from Halifax & Edgecombe Co., N.C.
Their children were
Jesse, John Jr., Drewry, Benjamin, Esther, Zadok,
Elizabeth, Richard Williams and Joel Egbert

---

[91] Albert Virgil Goodpasture, *Goodspeed History of Tennessee - Robertson County,* 1886, p. 845 [Edited by Pat Fitzhugh for clarity, grammar and spelling].

John Bell, Jr. 1793-1862 and his wife Elizabeth Gunn
Their children were
Sarah Williams, Joel Thomas, Zadok, Martha Miles,
Mary Allen and John

Joel Thomas Bell 1831-1910 and his wife Laura
Virginia Henry
Their children were
John Thomas, Flora Adeline, Sarah Elizabeth, Boyd
Minerva, Charles Bailey and Mary Allen

Inscription on the Bell monument at Bellwood Cemetery.

About a quarter-mile west of Bellwood Cemetery is the Bell School Antique Mall, located in the Bell School building on Highway 41. Here, you will find countless antiques – anything from churns to furniture, and old books and postcards to authentic soldier uniforms. Upstairs is where the "Bell Witch

Opry" was held on Saturday nights for many years. The Opry has since been moved to the old gym on the first floor to provide access to handicapped persons.

The antique mall is owned by James Humphries, who possesses a wealth of knowledge about antiques and the area's history. On several different occasions, Humphries has experienced strange and unexplainable encounters while working at the antique mall.

The old Bell School building is also home to the Adams Museum and Archives. Dedicated on July 4, 1996, the museum boasts lots of documents, pictures, and relics that pertain to the town's past, including a number of documents and pictures pertaining to the Bell family. The museum's curator, Tim Henson, is very knowledgeable about the town's history and the legend of the "Bell Witch." The author feels that a trip to Adams is not complete without visiting the Bell School Antique Mall and museum, where one might run into Mr. Henson or Mr. Humphries.

Owned by the City of Adams, the old Bell School building was built in 1920 to replace another building that was built in 1913 but burned in 1919. The Bell School and was the only school in northwestern Robertson County up until 1949, when Jo Byrns School was built. Bell School remained open as a junior high school up until 1975.

The Bell School Building in Adams, Tennessee.

Behind the old Bell School building stands an authentic log cabin built in the early Nineteenth Century, which acted as a tenant house on the Bell farm for a number of years. After the deaths of his parents, Joel Egbert Bell inherited the northwestern portion of the Bell farm where the cabin was located. Although it is fairly common knowledge that the logs from the original Bell home were used to build structures on Joel Bell's land, the question of whether any of these logs became a part of the preserved log cabin remains unanswered.

The first answer one might arrive at is "no," because the cabin was built between 1810 and 1820, many years before the original Bell home was razed in 1843. By examining the situation more closely, one will learn that the cabin's additional half-story was not added until many years after its original construction. There exists the possibility that the logs used to construct the second story were once a part of the original Bell home.

In a report issued in January of 1996 by Steve Rogers of the Tennessee Historical Commission, the following observations of significance were noted:

"...the Bell house is an early log structure. I would guess the house was built between 1810-1820..." "In fact, a portion of one of the cut joists was used as chinking to fill a hole on the rear of the house. This alteration may represent a major remodeling of the structure, changing it from a one story to a one and a half story house by raising the walls and adding a stairs and second story floor."

The land on which the log cabin was first situated changed hands from Allen Bell to Levi Smith in the 1870's. In 1941, Smith's great-grandsons, George S. and Theo Dickinson, Jr., also direct descendants of James Johnston, acquired the land allowed the cabin to be used as a tenant house up until 1966. mm The cabin stood vacant until 1982, when Theo Dickerson, Jr. donated it to the Tennessee-Kentucky Threshermen's Association, at which time it was moved to its present-day location behind the old Bell School building. [92]

---

[92] Information and report excerpts come from the memorandum, *The Bell Log House*, by Emerson A. Meggs, July 11, 1996.

The Bell Log Cabin, which is located behind the Bell School building in Adams, Tennessee.

Just west of the old Bell School building on Highway 41 is Keysburg Road, which leads to nearby  Keysburg, Kentucky. The Bell Witch Cave is approximately one mile down this road from Adams-proper. The cave is currently open daily for tours between May 1st and October 31st, with only weekend tours between Labor Day and Halloween. On the last few nights leading up to Halloween, the cave owners offer haunted hayrides, psychic readings, books, and a full-service concession stand in addition to tours of the cave. The cave is subject to temporary closures due to floods or drought conditions, so it is advisable to check before going. [nn]

Two major events are held each year in Adams: The Tennessee-Kentucky Threshermen's Show and the Bell Witch Bluegrass Festival.

Now in its 31st year, the Threshermen's Show boasts antique tractors and farm equipment, as well as arts and crafts booths, tractor and mule pulls, pony rides, square dances and other family activities. This event is held every July on the grounds of the old Bell School. The Bell Witch Bluegrass Festival, now in its 22nd year, is the second oldest such competition in Tennessee. Each year, bluegrass musicians from all over the southeast converge on the grounds of the Old Bell School to "pick and grin."

Just as it was during the time of John Bell, the Red River bottomland boasts large corn and tobacco fields as far as the eye can see. During late summer, the aroma of freshly cut tobacco being dried in the area's many tobacco barns fills the air. The terrain is mostly flat, with dense forests covering the rolling hills.

The Red River is much smaller now than it was in the days of John Bell. Only small canoes and rafts now use the river that once carried steamboats from Port Royal to markets such as Natchez and New Orleans. Despite the river's many changes, the magical melodies played by its ripples are as delightful today as they were when Elizabeth Bell, Joshua Gardner, and others walked its banks nearly two centuries ago.

The Red River

Appendix F:

The Primitive Baptists

THE AUTHOR CANNOT OVER-EMPHASIZE the importance of understanding the religious beliefs and principles from which many theological conflicts (discussed earlier) arose during the John Bell era. Moreover, he feels this discussion is warranted because it will help the reader to better understand the profound social and personal impact these conflicts had on those living in the Red River community of Robertson County at the time.

The author has provided the following discussion of the Primitive Baptist faith because Red River Baptist Church was closely aligned with its beliefs, most notably Calvinism, during the time of John Bell. Text from the London Baptist Convention of 1644, to which Red River Baptist Church subscribed, and John Calvin's doctrine of Predestination, are presented in Appendices G and H, respectively.

Primitive Baptist ancestors have been called by various names over the ages. The name *Primitive Baptist* became popular in the early 1800's, when the term *primitive* conveyed the idea of originality rather than backwardness.

Primitive Baptists claim the scriptures as their sole rule of faith and practice, and therefore are not bound to creeds of faith. However, churches and associations among Primitive Baptists have summarized their interpretation of scriptures in various *Articles of Faith.* Primitive Baptists claim primary descent from certain Baptist churches in Wales and in the Midlands of England. The views of these Baptists are summarized in the 1655 Midland Confession of Faith. The Particular Baptists of London are also part of Primitive Baptist heritage. Their most important confessions of faith were the London Confessions of 1644 and 1689. The 1644 confession better represents Primitive Baptist views than the 1689 confession.

Primitive also conveys the idea of simplicity. This describes the Primitive Baptists, whose church services consist of nothing more than preaching, praying, and singing. The *Black Rock Address of 1832* will acquaint the reader with the circumstances that lead to the division between Primitive and other Baptists earlier in the Nineteenth Century.

Primitive Baptists view scriptures as the divinely inspired word of God, and as the sole rule of faith and practice for the church. It is also believed that the scriptures have been divinely preserved over the ages, and that the 1611 *King James Version* is the superior English translation of the scriptures. This preference is based upon evidence indicating the superiority of its base manuscripts and evidence indicating the superior scholarly abilities of its translators.

Paul claimed that all scripture is given by inspiration of God (II Tim 3:16). Accordingly, Jesus said that scripture can not be broken (Jn 10:35). Such infallibility could only occur in writings under the power of full inspiration.

The assertion of full inspiration does not necessarily imply that the Spirit masked or overrode the writing styles or personalities of the writers; however, it does imply that the informational content of the scriptures is of God.

All books of the *King James Bible* are regarded by

Primitive Baptists as scripture. The books of the Old Testament are known to be scripture because Jesus and the apostles quoted them as such. The books of the New Testament are known to be scripture because of Jesus' promise that special inspirational guidance would be upon the apostles (Jn 14:26, Jn 16:13). This pertains to Paul, also, as implied by Peter (II Pet 3:15-16).

Primitive Baptists believe that scriptural precedent should resolve issues of practice not explicitly addressed by scriptural commandment, where possible. Primitive Baptists are not inclined to treat scriptural practices as mere cultural fashions of biblical times, and will do so only where this is obvious (I Cor 9:19-23).

The scriptures offer two alternate titles for preachers, *bishop,* and *elder* (I Tim 3:1-7, Tit 1:5-9, I Pet 5:1). The importance of using these titles was evidenced by Jesus' condemnation of the Pharisees for taking aggrandizing titles to themselves (Mt 23:5-12).

That *elder* refers to gospel preachers is evidenced by the fact that both Peter and John claimed this title for themselves (I Pet 5:1, II Jn 1, III Jn 1). That *bishop* and *elder* refer to the same office is proven by the interchanged usage of these terms in Tit 1:5-9. Primitive Baptists typically refrain from the usage of *bishop* because of the misimpression that would be conveyed under modern connotation.

The term *reverend* is used only once in the scriptures, where it has direct reference to God (Ps 111:9). Primitive Baptists believe that men are therefore unworthy of wearing this title. Though a minister can be a *father* in certain respects (I Cor 4:15), this term is never used as a title in the scriptures. In fact, Jesus commanded to call no man your *father* upon the earth (Mt 23:9).

The term *apostle* is used by the scriptures to mean a minister who is an eyewitness to the sufferings and resurrection of Christ (Acts 1:1-3, Acts 1:21-26, I Cor 9:1, I Pet 5:1).   In addition, *apostles* were granted special powers not possessed by *elders* (Acts 8:18, II Cor 12:12, Heb 2:3-4). Primitive Baptists believe that any man claiming this title for himself today does so in error.

Primitive Baptist *elders* are chosen by the individual congregations from male members who have proved to be faithful to the church and its principles. These men are given the opportunity to speak over a trial period to determine if they have a gift to preach. This trial period typically lasts from one to five years. The other elders ordain those judged by the congregations to satisfy scriptural qualifications for the ministry.

All Primitive Baptist *elders* are expected to be self-educated in the Word of God, and expected to seek the counsel of experienced *ministers* about questions of scriptural interpretation and other matters church matters.

Appendix G:

The London Baptist Confession of 1644

A CONFESSION OF FAITH of seven congregations or churches of Christ in London, which are commonly, but unjustly, called Anabaptists; published for the vindication of the truth and information of the ignorant; likewise for the taking off those aspersions which are frequently, both in pulpit and print, unjustly cast upon them. Printed in London, Ann. 1646.

But this I confess unto thee, that after the way which they call heresie so worship I the God of my Fathers, believing all things that are written in the Law and the Prophets, and have hope towards God, which they themselves also allow, that there shall be a resurrection of the dead both of the just and unjust - Acts XXIV, 14-15.

For we cannot but speak the things that we have seen and heard - Acts IV, 20. If I have spoken evil, bear witness of the evil; but if well, why smitest thou me - John XVIII, 23. Blessed are ye when men revile you, and say all manner of evil against you falsely for my sake. Rejoice, etc. - Matt. V, 11-12; XIX, 29.

Appendix H:

Calvin's Doctrine of Predestination

THE COVENANT OF LIFE not being equally preached to all, and among those to whom it is preached not always finding the same reception, this diversity discovers the wonderful depth of the Divine judgment. Nor is it to be doubted that this variety also follows, subject to the decision of God's eternal election.

If it be evidently the result of the Divine will, that salvation is freely offered to some, and others are prevented from attaining it...this immediately gives rise to important and difficult questions, which are incapable of any other explication, than by the establishment of pious minds in what ought to be received concerning election and predestination...a question, in the opinion of many, full of perplexity; for they consider nothing more unreasonable, than that of the common mass of mankind, some should be predestinated to salvation, and others to destruction.

But how unreasonably they perplex themselves will afterwards appear from the sequel of our discourse. Besides, the very obscurity, which excites such dread, not only displays the utility of this doctrine, but shows it to be productive of the most delightful benefit.

We shall never be clearly convinced as we ought to be, that our salvation flows from the fountain of

God's free mercy, till we are acquainted with His eternal election, which illustrates the grace of God by this comparison, that He adopts not all promiscuously to the hope of salvation, but gives to some what He refuses to others.

Ignorance of this principle evidently detracts from the Divine glory, and diminishes real humility. But according to Paul, what is so necessary to be known, never can be known, unless God, without any regard to works, chooses those whom He has decreed. "At this present time also, there is a remnant according to the election of grace. And if by grace, then it is no more of works; otherwise, grace is no more grace. But if it be of works, then it is no more grace; otherwise, work is no more work."

If we need to be recalled to the origin of election, to prove that we obtain salvation from no other source than the mere goodness of God, they who desire to extinguish this principle, do all they can to obscure what ought to be magnificently and loudly celebrated, and to pluck up humility by the roots. In ascribing the salvation of the remnant of the people to the election of grace, Paul clearly testifies that it is then only known that God saves whom upon which there can be no claim.

They who shut the gates to prevent anyone from presuming to approach and taste this doctrine, do no less injury to man than to God; for nothing else will be sufficient to produce in us suitable humility, or to impress us with a due sense of our great obligations to God. Nor is there any other basis for solid confidence, even according to the authority of Christ, who, to deliver us from all fear, and render us invincible amidst so many dangers, snares, and deadly conflicts, promises to preserve in safety all whom the Father has committed to His care.

I. Whence we infer, that they who know not themselves to be God's peculiar people will be tortured with continual anxiety; and therefore, that the interest of all believers, as well as their own, is very badly consulted by those who, blind to the three advantages we have remarked, would wholly remove the foundation of our salvation. And hence the Church rises to our view, which otherwise, as Bernard justly observes, could neither be discovered nor recognized among creatures, being in two respects wonderfully concealed in the bosom of a blessed predestination, and in the mass of a miserable damnation.

But before I enter on the subject itself, I must address some preliminary observations to two sorts of persons. The discussion of predestination...a subject of itself rather intricate...is made very perplexed, and therefore dangerous, by human curiosity, which no barriers can restrain from wandering into forbidden labyrinths, and soaring beyond its sphere, as if determined to leave none of the Divine secrets unscrutinized or unexplored.

As we see multitudes everywhere guilty of this arrogance and presumption, and among them some who are not censurable in other respects, it is proper to admonish them of the bounds of their duty on this subject. First, then, let them remember that when they inquire into predestination, they penetrate the inmost recesses of Divine wisdom, where the careless and confident intruder will obtain no satisfaction to his curiosity, but will enter a labyrinth from which he will find no way to depart.

For it is unreasonable that man should scrutinize with impunity those things which the Lord has determined to be hidden in himself; and investigate, even from eternity, that sublimity of wisdom which God would have us to adore and not comprehend, to promote our admiration of His glory. The secrets of His will which He determined to reveal to us, He discovers in His word; and these are all that He foresaw would concern us or conduce to our advantage.

II. "We are come into the way of faith," says Augustine; "let us constantly pursue it. It conducts into the king's palace, in which are hidden all the treasures of wisdom and knowledge. For the Lord Christ Himself envied not His great and most select disciples when He said, 'I have many things to say unto you, but ye cannot bear them now.' We must talk, we must improve, we must grow, that our hearts may be able to understand those things of which we are at present incapable. If the last day finds us improving, we shall then learn what we never could learn in the present state."

If we only consider that the word of the Lord is the only way to lead us to an investigation of all that ought to be believed concerning Him, and the only light to enlighten us to behold all that ought to be seen of Him, this consideration will easily restrain and preserve us from all presumption. For we shall know that when we have exceeded the limits of the word, we shall get into a devious and darksome course, in which errors, slips, and falls, will often be inevitable.

Let us, then, in the first place, bear in mind, that to desire any other knowledge of predestination than what is unfolded in the word of God, indicates as great folly, as a wish to walk through unpassable roads, or to see in the dark. Nor let us be ashamed to be ignorant of some things relative to a subject in which there is a kind of learned ignorance. Rather let us abstain with cheerfulness from the pursuit of that knowledge, the affectation of which is foolish, dangerous, and even fatal.

But if we are stimulated by the wantonness of intellect, we must oppose it with a reflection calculated to repress it, that as "it is not good to eat much honey, so for men to search their own glory, is not glory." For there is sufficient to deter us from that presumption, which can only precipitate us into ruin.

III. Others, desirous of remedying this evil, will have all mention of predestination to be as it were buried; they teach men to avoid every question concerning it as they would a precipice. Though their moderation is to be commended, in judging that mysteries ought to be handled with such great sobriety, yet, as they descend too low, they have little influence on the mind of man, which refuses to submit to unreasonable restraints. To observe, therefore, the legitimate boundary on this side also, we must recur to the word of the Lord, which affords a certain rule for the understanding. For the Scripture is the school of the Holy Spirit, in which, as nothing necessary and useful to be known is omitted, so nothing is taught which is not beneficial to know.

Whatever, therefore, is declared in the Scripture concerning predestination, we must be cautious not to withhold from believers, lest we appear either to defraud them of the favor of their God, or to reprove and censure the Holy Spirit for publishing what it would be useful by any means to suppress. Let us, I say, permit the Christian man to open his heart and his ears to all the discourses addressed to him by God, only with this moderation, that as soon as the Lord closes his sacred mouth, he shall also desist from further inquiry. This will be the best barrier of sobriety, if in learning we not only follow the leadings of God, but as soon as he ceases to teach, we give up our desire of learning. Nor is the danger they dread, sufficient to divert our attention from the oracles of God.

It is a celebrated observation of Solomon, that "it is the glory of God to conceal a thing." But, as both piety and common sense suggest that this is not to be understood generally of every thing, we must seek for the proper distinction, lest we content ourselves with brutish ignorance under the pretext of modesty and sobriety. Now, this distinction is clearly expressed in a few words by Moses "The secret things," he says, "belong unto the Lord our God; but those things which are revealed belong unto us, and to our children forever, that we may do all the words of this law." For we see how he enforces on the people attention to the doctrine of the law only by the celestial decree, because it pleased God to promulgate it; and restrains the same people within those limits with this single reason, that it is not lawful for mortals to intrude into the secrets of God.

IV. Profane persons, I confess, suddenly lay hold of something relating to the subject of predestination, to furnish occasion for objections, cavils, reproaches, and ridicule. But if we are frightened from it by their impudence, all the principal articles of the faith must be concealed, for there is scarcely one of them which such persons as these leave unviolated by blasphemy. The refractory mind will discover as much insolence, on hearing that there are three persons in the Divine essence, as on being told, that when God created man, He foresaw what would happen concerning him. Nor will they refrain from derision on being informed that little more than five thousand years have elapsed since the creation of the world. They will ask why the power of God was so long idle and asleep.

Nothing can be advanced which they will not endeavor to ridicule. Must we, in order to check these sacrileges, say nothing of the Divinity of the Son and Spirit, or pass over in silence the creation of the world? In this instance, and every other, the truth of God is too powerful to dread the detraction of impious men; as is strenuously maintained by Augustine, in his treatise on the Perseverance of the Faithful.

We see the false apostles, with all their defamation and accusation of the true doctrine of Paul, could never succeed to make him ashamed of it. Their assertion, that all this discussion is dangerous to pious minds, because it is inconsistent with exhortations, shakes their faith, and disturbs and discourages the heart itself, is without any foundation. Augustine admits, that he was frequently blamed, on these accounts, for preaching predestination too freely; but he readily and amply refutes them.

But as many and various absurdities are crowded upon us here, we prefer reserving every one to be refuted in its proper place. I only desire this general admission, that we should neither scrutinize those things which the Lord has left concealed, nor neglect those which He has openly exhibited, lest we be condemned for excessive curiosity on the one hand, or for ingratitude on the other.   For it is judiciously remarked by Augustine, that we may safely follow the Scripture, which proceeds as with the pace of a mother stooping to the weakness of a child, that it may not leave our weak capacities behind.

But persons who are so cautious or timid, as to wish predestination to be buried in silence, lest feeble minds should be disturbed, with what pretext, I ask, will they gloss over their arrogance, which indirectly charges God with foolish inadvertency, as though He foresaw not the danger which they suppose they have had the penetration to discover.   Whoever, therefore, endeavors to raise prejudices against the doctrine of predestination, openly reproaches God, as though something had inconsiderately escaped from Him that is pernicious to the Church.

V. Predestination, by which God adopts some to the hope of life, and adjudges others to eternal death, no one, desirous of the credit of piety, dares absolutely to deny.   But it is involved in many cavils, especially by those who make foreknowledge the cause of it. We maintain, that both belong to God; but it is preposterous to represent one as dependent on the other.

When we attribute foreknowledge to God, we mean that all things have ever been, and perpetually remain, before His eyes, so that to His knowledge nothing in future or past, but all things are present; and present in such a manner, that He does not merely conceive of them from ideas formed in His mind, as things remembered by us appear present to our minds, but really beholds and sees them as if actually placed before

Him.   And this foreknowledge extends to the whole world, and to all the creatures.

Predestination we call the eternal decree of God, by which He has determined in Himself what would have to become of every individual of mankind.   For they are not all created with a similar destiny; but eternal life is fore-ordained for some, and eternal damnation for others.   Every man, therefore, being created for one or the other of these ends, we say, he is predestinated either to life or to death.   This God has not only testified in particular persons, but has given a specimen of it in the whole posterity of Abraham, which should evidently show the future condition of every nation to depend upon His decision.   "When the Most High divided the nations, when he separated the sons of Adam, the Lord's portion was His people; Jacob was the lot of His inheritance."

The separation is before the eyes of all: in the person of Abraham, as in the dry trunk of a tree, one people is peculiarly chosen to the rejection of others: no reason for this appears, except that Moses, to deprive their posterity of all occasion of glorying, teaches them that their exaltation is wholly from God's gratuitous love.   He assigns this reason for their deliverance, that "He loved their fathers, and chose their seed after them." More fully in another chapter: "The Lord did not set His love upon you, nor choose you, because you were more in number than any people; but because the Lord loved you."   He frequently repeats the same admonition: "Behold, the heaven is the Lord's thy God, the earth also, with all that therein is.   Only the Lord had a delight in thy fathers to love them, and He chose their seed after them."

In another place, sanctification is enjoined upon them, because they were chosen to be a peculiar people. And again, elsewhere, love is asserted to be the cause of their protection. It is declared by the united voice of the faithful, "He hath chosen our inheritance for us, the excellency of Jacob, whom He loved." For the gifts conferred on them by God, they all ascribe to gratuitous love, not only from a consciousness that these were not obtained by any merit of theirs, but from a conviction, that the holy patriarch himself was not endued with such excellence as to acquire the privilege of so great an honor for himself and his posterity. And the more effectually to demolish all pride, he reproaches them with having deserved no favor, being "a stiff-necked and rebellious people."

The prophets also frequently reproach the Jews with the unwelcome mention of this election, because they had shamefully departed from it. Let them, however, now come forward, who wish to restrict the election of God to the desert of men, or the merit of works. When they see one nation preferred to all others...when they hear that God had no inducement to be more favorable to a few, and ignoble, and even disobedient and obstinate people...will they quarrel with him because he has chosen to give such an example of mercy? But their obstreperous clamors will not impede this work, nor will the reproaches they hurl against Heaven, injure or affect his justice; they will rather recoil upon their own heads. Lo, this principle of the gracious covenant, the Israelites are also recalled whenever thanks are to be rendered to God, or their hopes are to be raised for futurity.

"He hath made us, and not we ourselves," says the Psalmist: "we are His people, and the sheep of His pasture." It is not without reason that the negation is added, "not we ourselves," that they may know that of all the benefits they enjoy, God is not only the Author, but derived the cause from Himself, there being nothing in them deserving of such great honor. He also enjoins them to be content with the mere good pleasure of God, in these words: "O ye seed of Abraham His servant, ye children of Jacob His chosen." And after having recounted the continual benefits bestowed by God as fruits of election, he at length concludes that He had acted with such liberality, "because He remembered His covenant."

Consistent with this doctrine is the song of the whole Church: "Thy right hand, and Thine arm, and the light of Thy countenance, gave our fathers the land, because Thou hadst a favor unto them." It must be observed that where mention is made of the land, it is a visible symbol of the secret separation, which comprehends adoption. David, in another place, exhorts the people to the same gratitude: "Blessed is the nation whose God is the Lord; and the people whom He hath chosen for His own inheritance." Samuel animates to a good hope: "The Lord will not forsake His people, for His great name's sake; because it hath pleased the Lord to make you His people." David, when his faith is assailed, thus arms himself for the conflict: "Blessed is the man whom Thou choosest, and causest to approach unto thee; he shall dwell in Thy courts."

But since the election hidden in God has been confirmed by the first deliverance, as well as by the second and other intermediate blessings, the word choose is transferred to it in Isaiah: "The

Lord will have mercy on Jacob, and will yet choose Israel;" because, contemplating a future period, He declares that the collection of the residue of the people, whom He had appeared to have forsaken; would be a sign of the stable and sure election, which had likewise seemed to fail. When He says also, in another place, "I have chosen thee, and not cast thee away," He commends the continual course of His signal liberality and paternal benevolence. The angel, in Zachariah, speaks more plainly: "The Lord shall choose Jerusalem again;" as though His severe chastisement had been a rejection, or their exile had been an interruption of election; which, nevertheless, remains inviolable, though the tokens of it are not always visible.

VI. We must now proceed to a second degree of election, still more restricted, or that in which the Divine grace was displayed in a more special manner, when of the same race of Abraham God rejected some, and by nourishing others in the Church, proved that He retained them among His children. Israel at first obtained the same station as his brother Isaac, for the Spiritual covenant was equally sealed in him by the symbol of circumcision. He is cut off; afterwards Esau; lastly, an innumerable multitude, and almost all Israel. In Isaac the seed was called; the same calling continued in Jacob.

God exhibited a similar example in the rejection of Saul, which is magnificently celebrated by the Psalmist: "He refused the tabernacle of Joseph, and chose not the tribe of Ephraim, but chose the tribe of Judah;" and this the sacred history frequently repeats, that the wonderful secret of Divine grace may be more manifest in that change. I grant, it was by their own crime and guilt that Ishmael, Esau, and persons of similar characters, fell from the adoption; because the condition annexed was, that they should faithfully keep the covenant of God, which they perfidiously violated. Yet it was a peculiar favor of God, that He deigned to prefer them to other nations; as it is said in the Psalms: "He hath not dealt so with any nation; and so for His judgments, they have not known them."

But I have justly said that here are two degrees to be remarked; for in the election of the whole nation, God has already shown that in His mere goodness He is bound by no laws, but is perfectly free, so that none can require of Him an equal distribution of grace, the inequality of which demonstrates it to be truly gratuitous. Therefore Malachi aggravates the ingratitude of Israel, because, though not only elected out of the whole race of mankind, but also separated from a sacred family to be a peculiar people, they perfidiously and impiously despised God their most beneficent Father.

"Was not Esau Jacob's brother? Saith the Lord: yet I loved Jacob, and I hated Esau." For God takes it for granted, since both were sons of a holy father, successors of the covenant, and branches from a sacred root, that the children of Jacob were already laid under more than common obligations by their admission to that honor; but Esau, the first-born, having been rejected, and their father, though inferior by birth, having been made the heir, He proves them guilty of double ingratitude, and complains of their violating this two-fold claim.

VII. Though it is sufficiently clear, that God, in his secret counsel, freely chooses whom He will, and rejects others, His gratuitous election is but half displayed till we come to particular individuals, to whom God not only offers salvation, but assigns it in such a manner, that the certainty of the effect is liable to no suspense or doubt.

These are included in that one seed mentioned by Paul; for though the adoption was deposited in the hand of Abraham, yet many of his posterity being cut off as putrid members, in order to maintain the efficacy and stability of election, it is necessary to ascend to the head, in whom their heavenly Father has bound His elect to each other, and united them to Himself by an indissoluble bond. Thus the adoption of the family of Abraham displayed the favor of God, which He denied to others; but in the members of Christ there is a conspicuous exhibition of the superior efficacy of grace; because, being united to their head, they never fail of salvation.

Paul, therefore, justly reasons from the passage of Malachi which I have just quoted, that where God, introducing the covenant of eternal life, invites any people to Himself, there is a peculiar kind of election as to part of them, so that he does not efficaciously choose all with indiscriminate grace. The declaration, "Jacob have I loved," respects the whole posterity of the patriarch, whom the prophet there opposes to the descendants of Esau.

Yet this is no objection to our having in the person of one individual a specimen of the election, which can never fail of attaining its full effect. These, who truly belong to Christ, Paul correctly observes, are called "a remnant," for experience proves, that of a great multitude the most part fall away and disappear, so that often only a small portion remains. That the general election of a people is not always effectual and permanent, a reason readily presents itself, because, when God covenants with them, He does not also give the Spirit of regeneration to enable them to preserve in the covenant to the end; but the eternal call, without the internal efficacy of grace, which would be sufficient for their preservation, is a kind of medium between the rejection of all mankind and the election of the small number of believers.

The whole nation of Israel was called "God's inheritance," though many of them were strangers; but God, having firmly covenanted to their Father and Redeemer, regards that gratuitous favor rather than the defection of multitudes; by whom His truth was not violated, because His preservation of a certain remnant to Himself, made it evident that His calling was without repentance. For God's collection of a Church for himself, from time to time, from the children of Abraham, rather than from the profane nations, was in consideration of his covenant, which, being violated by the multitude, He restricted to a few, to prevent a total failure. Lastly, the general adoption of the seed of Abraham was a visible representation of a greater blessing, which God conferred on the few out of the multitude.

This is the reason that Paul so carefully distinguishes the descendants of Abraham according to the flesh, from His Spiritual children called after the example of Isaac. Not that the mere descent from Abraham was a vain and unprofitable thing, which could not be asserted without depreciating the covenant; but because to the latter alone the immutable counsel of God, in which He predestinated whom He would, was of itself effectual to salvation. But I advise my readers to adopt no prejudice on either side, till it shall appear from adduced passages of Scripture what sentiments ought to be entertained. In conformity, therefore, to the clear doctrine of the Scripture, we assert, that by an eternal and immutable counsel, God has once for all determined, both whom He would admit to salvation, and whom He would condemn to destruction. We affirm that this counsel, as far as concerns the elect, is founded on His gratuitous mercy, totally irrespective of human merit; but that to those whom He devotes to condemnation, the gate of life is closed by a just and irreprehensible, but incomprehensible, judgment. In the elect, we consider calling as an evidence of election, and justification as another token of its manifestation, till they arrive in glory, which constitutes its completion. As God seals His elect by vocation and justification, so by excluding the reprobate from the knowledge of His name and the sanctification of His Spirit, He affords an indication of the judgment that awaits them.

Here I shall pass over many fictions fabricated by foolish men to overthrow predestination. It is unnecessary to refute things, which, as soon as they are advanced, sufficiently prove their own falsehood. I shall dwell only on these things which are subjects of controversy among the learned, or which may occasion difficulty to simple minds, or which impiety speciously pleads in order to stigmatize the Divine justice. [93]

---

[93] John Calvin, *The Institutes of the Christian Religion.*

Appendix I:

The Bells in Mississippi

MUCH HAS BEEN SAID about the Bells who moved to Mississippi and had various encounters with Kate. As was mentioned earlier, the families of Jesse Bell and Alex Porter moved to Mississippi in hopes of escaping from Kate. It is unclear if this was the real reason, for they did not move until many years after Kate had left the Bell home in Tennessee. The families who moved to Mississippi were still not free from Kate, however. Those who moved to Mississippi were tormented just as they were in Tennessee many years beforehand.

Unlike most accounts of Kate in Tennessee, the Mississippi accounts are undocumented and the product of stories passed from generation to generation – pure folklore. This is not to say that the Mississippi accounts are false, but that no "hard evidence" exists to substantiate their occurrence. We do know by examining the public records of Mississippi that Jesse Bell, Alex Porter (and his wife, Esther Bell), and later, Elizabeth (Bell) Powell, did in fact emigrate to and live in Mississippi after the hauntings in Tennessee.

While the Porters experienced very few encounters with Kate after moving to Mississippi, the same cannot be said of Jesse Bell's family, who were frequently subjected to Kate's tricks. A number of their descendants in the area today still experience unexplainable encounters they believe to be the doings of Kate.

The most popular Mississippi account of Kate deals with the daughter of John Thomas Bell (son of Jesse Bell), who fell in love with a farm overseer who died at the height of their affair. After the overseer's death, strange things began to happen on the farm and around the small community of Eureka, just outside present-day Batesville.

The farm overseer had been interested in Bell's daughter since he first started working on the farm. Over time, he watched her mature into a beautiful, young woman. As she matured, the overseer spent more and more time with her – walking her to the outbuildings and helping with chores, taking her fishing at nearby Long Creek, and occasionally helping her with schoolwork. Over the course of time, a deep love fell between the two and they became inseparable.

Both knowing that Bell would strongly disapprove of their relationship because of their ages and the business relationship he had with the overseer, they decided to keep it a secret – hoping to marry once she became older and he could find work on some other farm. Several of the farmhands noticed the seeming attraction between the two but never said a word. Before long, Bell himself began to notice that something seemed to be going on between them. Anywhere he saw one, the other would be nearby – and always with a seemingly good excuse for being there. The relationship between Bell's daughter and the farm overseer was short-lived, however.

One late-summer afternoon, the overseer went to an outbuilding to fetch some nails for one of the new farmhands. Not having a candle with him, he methodically ran his hands up and down the shelves looking for the right sized nail. As he reached both arms over his head to feel along the top shelf, he suddenly felt a strong blow to his stomach, followed by an intense, "stinging" sensation.

In pain, he stepped backwards and out the door where in the daylight he saw two small streams of blood coming from his stomach. He grew very weak as he stood in the hot sun, eventually dropping to his knees as his vision became blurred and his breathing more labored; he knew that whatever hit him had poisoned him in some way. Now too weak to yell for help, the overseer tried crawling to the wall of the outbuilding in hopes of hitting it to get someone's attention.

Through a one-inch opening between the wall of the outbuilding and the ground slithered a copperhead over six feet in length and as big around as a man's arm. It became obvious that the snake had been coiled up on one of the shelves and bitten him when he came too close. He knew it would be of no use to get help at that point. The end was near. As soon as he had finished saying his final prayer to God, a young woman who appeared to be Bell's daughter appeared.

"It's over, love," the farmhand whispered in a weak and feeble voice; "I went to get some nails and a snake bit me, right in the stomach. Come be with me, my dearest; if I have to die, then I want it to be nowhere but in your arms." "And I suppose you want to be in my arms as you burn and rot in Hell," the young woman exclaimed in a raspy, low-pitched voice that nobody had ever heard before. The young woman that the farmhand thought was his sweetheart continued, "Oh, you thought you knew who I was, you old rascal. But, sometimes looks can be deceiving, can't they!" "Who are you?" asked the farmhand as he began slipping into a coma. "I was once a young woman, just as Miss Bell is now, back in the days of her grandfather, Ol' Jack Bell. You are no better of a man than he was; and as my name, Cypocryphy, implies, I have the gift of prophecy. I know you don't know what I am talking about, but I know that you are no good, never will be, and will destroy the life of Miss Bell if I let you."

A strong rush of energy went through the overseer as he jumped to his feet, grabbed the woman by the throat, and said, "Why no, the lovely Miss Bell is mine and I will have her join me as I burn in Hell, all the while watching you suffer for the sins you committed against me and Miss Bell's grandfather, John Bell. I will see you in Hell." The overseer then fell – dying before he hit the ground. Meanwhile, back at the Bell home, Bell's daughter awoke from what seemed to have been a deep trance and sensing that something didn't feel right.

John Thomas Bell remarked that he hadn't seen the overseer all afternoon and that he was getting worried. "Have you seen Gardner around here anywhere?" Bell asked his daughter. "Why no, father, but I am very worried that something is wrong." "Why do you say something is wrong? You've been asleep all afternoon!" "Father, I don't know, but I can just sense it." Bell then had two of the slaves light torches and mount their horses to go and look for the overseer. The slaves returned about three hours later with the overseer's body in tow.

One morning in the early fall, several months after the death of his overseer, Bell was walking around the farm inspecting the fence when he heard the voice of the deceased overseer. "Mister Bell, I don't have to tell you who I am because you already know. And you also know why I am here" "I have a good idea," replied Bell. "You know that your daughter and I had very strong feelings for one another," the voice exclaimed, "and my death means nothing because I have unfinished business here on earth." "And just what unfinished business is that?" Bell inquired. "Your daughter, Mr. Bell; your daughter." "What about her!" Bell inquired angrily. The voice replied, "We were to have been married. We talked about it all the time and decided not to tell you until we felt the time was right. But because of my death, I must have her right now if we are to spend eternity together."

"You are a sick, demented soul!" Bell exclaimed, "you think you can just come out of your grave and marry my daughter? No, you can't. You are a ghost, and probably burning in Hell if the truth be known!" "You are right," said the voice, "I can't marry her as she is now, and I want to take her so she can be with me." "You will not!" Bell yelled. "Are you telling me that you won't let me unite with your daughter, Mr. Bell?" "That's right, you good-for-nothing scoundrel. You leave me, my family, and especially my daughter alone; otherwise I will chase you straight to Hell and destroy you!" "Ok, Mr. Bell," exclaimed the voice. The voice was not heard again, and Bell quickly made his way back to the farmhouse where he remained for several weeks.

Over the next few weeks, Bell's daughter grew ill. She lay in agony week after week, growing weaker and more incoherent with each passing day. She failed to respond to medication, and the family doctor, not really knowing what was wrong with her, was unable to give a prognosis. Her mysterious illness progressed as time went on, and she soon fell into a coma. She occasionally regained her consciousness, but only long enough to speak of the deceased farm overseer and the love that she never got to share with him.

One day in the late fall, Bell's daughter appeared

to have regained both her consciousness and energy. Although too weak to rise up from the bed, she lay there smiling and laughing with her sparkling eyes wide-open. She refused to acknowledge the presence of her family in the room, and laughed even harder when they tried to communicate with her. Finally, late that afternoon, the girl spoke. In the same tone as "Cypocryphy," she exclaimed, "I am going, I am going, to love HIM, HIM, HIM, HIM," then, with a smile on her face, she closed her eyes and died.

As the girl was being carried from her home down Eureka Road to nearby Long Creek Cemetery, a large, black bird wearing a bell around its neck flew just above the wagon. Ringing in a low, sad tone, the bell continued until the funeral procession arrived at the cemetery and the girl was being laid to rest. The large bird then circled the cemetery until the last person left – all the while laughing in the deceased overseer's voice. The bird finally flew away and was never seen again.

On many occasions after the girl's death, people reported having strange and unexplainable encounters in the area. Cows were found mysteriously dead, blood flowed from water taps, fresh milk went sour for no apparent reason, and people often became afflicted with short, unexplainable illnesses.

It has been reported that some descendants of John Thomas Bell know in advance when a visit will come from the Spirit world, and will gather at a particular relative's house to wait. [94] Very few descendants in the area today will share information about the "Bell Witch," whether it is the Tennessee version of the legend or the Mississippi version.

---

[94] Source does not wish to be disclosed.

Appendix J:

Frequently Asked Questions

OVER THE MANY YEARS he has researched the legend of the "Bell Witch," the author has been asked literally thousands of questions about the subject, from the most valid to the most absurd. Some questions are asked more than others, and require a great deal of research to answer intelligently.

The author has documented and provided answers to the most popular questions he is asked concerning the "Bell Witch," below. Most of these questions are impossible to answer from a factual standpoint, and as such are provided only as the author's opinion based on his research.

Why was Kate kind to Lucy Bell but hateful towards John and Elizabeth?

Why Kate was kind to Mrs. Bell but hateful towards John and Elizabeth is one of the most puzzling questions associated with the legend and has been asked many times.

The only reason Kate gave for her seeming kindness to Mrs. Bell was that "Luce" was a good woman. The author feels there was more to Kate's treatment of John Bell's immediate family than someone's having been a "good" or "bad" person.

There are different kinds of torment, some of which can be "masked" to create the proverbial, "wolf in sheep's clothing" effect. The author feels that Kate's torment was inflicted equally among John Bell and his immediate family members, following the "path of least resistance" to each family member's soul. While Elizabeth and John Bell bore the brunt of Kate's *physical* torment, Mrs. Bell received an equal share of torment at the *emotional* level. Regardless of Kate's kind gestures towards Mrs. Bell, her being forced to witness the day in and day out torture of her husband and daughter undoubtedly took a strong emotional toll on her.

Some people can endure more *physical* pain than *emotional* pain, and vice versa. When a person's threshold in one of these areas is exceeded, the person "snaps," and suffers irreparable emotional damage – even if it was the *physical* threshold that was exceeded. The lower of these two thresholds in a person becomes the path of least resistance to their soul. Elizabeth, John, and Drewry Bell were weaker on the physical end than the emotional end; and as such, Kate followed their paths of least resistance by physically tormenting them. This is not to say that they were "frail" by any means, only that *physical* pain would take a greater long-term toll on them than *emotional* pain would.

The author feels that Mrs. Bell had a very high *physical* threshold. Think about it — she had experienced the pain of giving birth to a number of children. By contrast, Elizabeth did not experience childbirth until well after the disturbances ceased, meaning that at the time of the disturbances, her *physical* threshold was much lower than her mother's. Mrs. Bell's lowest threshold was *emotional* in nature; and for that reason, Kate tormented her from that angle — pursuing her soul through her own path of least resistance. Let us now look at another example of *physical* and *emotional* thresholds.

John Bell, Jr. begged Kate on many occasions to physically abuse, and even kill him, if it would result in his family's deliverance from her reign of terror. Kate always responded by saying that she could inflict more pain on John Jr. by making him watch members of his family suffer than by launching a physical attack on him. John Jr. stood about 6'3 and weighed nearly 200 pounds. In the Tennessee Militia, he trained hard and fought at Horseshoe Bend and New Orleans.

It almost goes without saying that his strong *physical* threshold was greater than his *emotional* threshold; hence, Kate's decision to force him to watch while members of his family suffered physical pain. His *emotional* side was clearly the path of least resistance to his soul.

Kate's giving Mrs. Bell grapes and hazelnuts, singing hymns to her, and regularly conversing with her were, in the author's opinion, her way of invoking a false sense of security to "cover up" the severe emotional damage that was really being inflicted upon Mrs. Bell. Moreover, the author feels that this "smokescreen" was put up as an act of diversion to gain Mrs. Bell's trust and respect so that her *emotional* side would be easier to conquer.

The others who Kate treated kindly were very close to John Bell and his family – James Johnston, Calvin Johnston, the Reverends, and of course, William Porter. Despite her perceived kindness towards these men, would Kate's tormenting the Bell family not have taken some degree of emotional toll on them as well? The author feels that Kate's perceived kindness to those outside but close to the Bell family was an attempt to earn their respect so they might eventually accept her ramblings and turn against John Bell. This never happened, however; all of the men mentioned above displayed their friendship and allegiance to John Bell and his family up until the very end.

Do John and Lucy Bell have any descendants in the Robertson County area today?

John and Lucy Bell have a number of descendants, stretching from Tennessee to Mississippi, and from Texas up through the Midwest. There are several descendants of John and Lucy Bell living in Robertson County, Tennessee today; however, the author has chosen not to list their names in this book as a matter of respect for their privacy.

Some Bell descendants believe that "something" was wrong in the home of John Bell, some do not believe anything was wrong, and other Bell descendants refuse to discuss the matter altogether. The author wishes to state that after having met and conversed with a number of John and Lucy Bell's descendants, he sees nothing at all strange or otherwise "different" about them – they are all fine and well-respected citizens of their communities, and are to be commended for their diplomatic handling of all the disinformation currently in circulation regarding the "Bell Witch."

What remains of the Bell farm today?

Very little is left of John Bell's plantation. A newer road roughly follows the old main road, which was the Springfield and Brown's Ford road. Now located in the middle of a field and a good distance from the nearest road, all that remains of the original Bell home is a hole where the cellar was, a few rocks from the original foundation, and some small trees growing around the hole. The old well is nearby, and the cemetery is on a small hill overlooking the old homesite. The cemetery is not marked in any way, nor is there a road leading to it. The only headstone is the replacement of John Bell's original headstone, which was taken in 1951.

A section of the old Springfield and Brown's Ford roadbed, which was a major road during the days of John Bell.

Can One see where the Bell home stood?

The old Bell farm is on private property, and entry without written permission from the private organization that owns it is forbidden. Moreover, even if one had permission, it would be difficult to visit the old homesite and cemetery without possibly damaging crops. The area is being used as farmland.

Appendix K:

Common Myths

A S WAS MENTIONED in *Appendix J*, there is an abundance of misinformation circulating in regards to the "Bell Witch." When the facts of a case are not crystal-clear or readily available, there exists the possibility that some will, as opposed to doing research, make hasty generalizations and arrive at fallacious conclusions about the case. Add to this the many years over which the legend has been told in different and often conflicting versions. The end-result is a plethora of information believed by many people, but which lacks any authoritative foundation.

In general, very few people are familiar with the facts behind the legend of the "Bell Witch," and as such, it logically follows that very few generalizations and "theories" regarding the legend are built upon a foundation of hard, documented evidence.

Facts, in and of themselves, do not make a story. Moreover, they serve as a general foundation and the glue that holds the story together. The more facts there are behind a story, the more credible the story is. The case of the "Bell Witch," differs significantly from many other cases of hauntings in that the characters, places, and dates have been proved. Unfortunately, however, it is from this very information that the most popular misinformation concerning the "Bell Witch" evolved – simply because people did not research the facts.

Add to this the fact that because the "Bell Witch"

legend involved so many characters, places and times, even those who have done extensive research sometimes confuse or forget the facts. The situation that exists today, that there are as many versions of the "Bell Witch" legend as there are people who tell it, is the end-result. Some myths regarding the "Bell Witch" are more common than others; and in most cases, researching the facts pertaining to people, places, and times can easily dispel these myths. When the facts are understood clearly and put into place, peoples' generalizations and "theories" regarding the "Bell Witch" tend to become very similar. Below, the author will address some of the more common myths about the "Bell Witch."

Kate Batts was the "Bell Witch"

Many books and other published accounts of the Bell disturbances suggest that they were the work of Kate Batts, an eccentric neighbor of the Bells. The primary reason stems from the Spirit's telling Reverend James Gunn that it was "Ol' Kate Batts' Witch." Moreover, this is how the Spirit earned its nickname, "Kate."

After this revelation to Reverend Gunn, which was only one of many such false revelations, stories began to develop which would support the Spirit's claim of having been Kate Batts' "witch." These stories arose undoubtedly because of Kate Batts' nature and character, which we discussed earlier in this book.

The most common "theory" about Kate Batts being the "Bell Witch" stems from an alleged dispute between John Bell and Mrs. Batts over the sale of a slave. There was not, in fact, any such dispute between John Bell and Kate Batts. According to official records, the slave dispute was between John

Bell and a "Benjamin Batts" around June 1, 1816. [95] Benjamin B. Batts and his family and lived more than one mile from Kate and Frederick Batts, and was not closely related to them. [96] [00] Benjamin B. Batts, whose wife was named Olive, died in 1842 and is buried in the Batts Cemetery just south of Adams, Tennessee. In addition to Benjamin B. Batts' son, Benjamin F. Batts (1841-1861), there was also another Benjamin B. Batts, born in 1809.

Evidence establishing the fact that the dispute was with Benjamin Batts, and census data showing that Frederick and Kate Batts did not even own any slaves during the time in question, are readily available. [97] The author feels that with this abundance of validated evidence, and no evidence whatsoever connecting Kate Batts with the slave dispute, that no such dispute ever took place between John Bell and Kate Batts.

Another popular "theory" supporting the notion that Kate Batts was the "Bell Witch" suggests that John Bell and Kate Batts' dispute was over the sale of real estate when they both still lived in North Carolina. While official records show that both families once lived in the same area of North Carolina, and that John Bell was involved in a number of real estate transactions there, the author has found no record of any real estate transaction between John Bell and Kate or Frederick Batts. Until such evidence can be found and validated, this "theory" is false.

Another "theory" suggests that John Bell was a wealthy bachelor and the owner of the first business

---

[95] *Red River Baptist Church Minutes (1791-1826)*, p. 180.
[96] Ralph Winters, *Historical Sketches Adams, Robertson County and Port Royal/Montgomery County TN*, 1978, p. 158.
[97] See state and federal census information at Robertson County Archives, Springfield, TN.

in Adams, and that because of Fredrick Batts' paralysis, Kate Batts desired to aggressively pursue a romantic relationship with Bell. According to this "theory," he did not agree and Kate Batts "haunted" him as a result. While Frederick Batts was indeed an invalid and Kate Batts may very well have desired such a relationship, John Bell was not a bachelor and he did not own any businesses in Adams. As is the case with the two preceding theories, this "theory" is false.

Two records exist that prove John Bell was married to Lucy Williams Bell. One of these is the will of her father, John Williams, which names John Bell as being her husband. The other record is John Bell's estate settlement document showing Lucy Bell as the recipient of the dower portion of his estate. [98] John Bell did not own a business in Adams. Adams did not come into existence until 40 years after his death. The only businesses in the area other than stillhouses and mills were located in Port Royal, some seven miles away.

Another "theory" suggests that John Bell locked Kate Batts in a smokehouse and let her hang until she was dead. Kate Batts outlived both John and Lucy Bell by a number of years. Like the others, this "theory" is false.

Because of her nature and character, and the Spirit's claiming to have been her "witch," Kate Batts was nothing more than the most convenient and logical scapegoat.

---

[98] *Robertson County Will Book 3*, pp. 267-268.

Nestled among a clump of trees and dense undergrowth is the Batts Cemetery near Adams, Tennessee – a large, overgrown cemetery that reminds us of a long-forgotten era. Several of the most prominent figures in the "Bell Witch" legend, such as Benjamin Batts, rest here.

Elizabeth Bell was Abused by Her Father

There is no way to prove nor disprove that such abuse took place; however, the author's extensive research has not yielded anything that would lead a reasonable person to suspect that John Bell abused her.   Even if the author's research did yield something that supports this claim, this "theory" would still be fallacious in that even if abuse could be proved, there is sill no proof that such abuse actually evoked a poltergeist.

While parapsychologists and students of the paranormal tend to agree that emotional trauma, especially on the part of an adolescent or pre-adolescent person, is one way in which poltergeists can be evoked; it is still not the only way. In the many eyewitness accounts and interviews of those who encountered the Bell disturbances published in the Ingram book, Elizabeth Bell was always described in a high-Spirited, congenial, happy and good light – none of the signs that would indicate the presence of severe emotional trauma.

Another thing to take into consideration when discussing the abuse "theory" is that many factors were present, any one of which could have caused emotional trauma in the Bell home. John Bell, Jr., Drewry Bell, and Jesse Bell were in the military and had fought in several wars, undoubtedly having seen many of their friends die right before their very eyes. John Bell had become afflicted with a medical condition that nobody could diagnose and was barred from the same church at which he was an elder. This was also at a time when there was a great deal of theological turmoil in the Baptist and Presbyterian faiths — Calvinism versus Arminianism and Old Sides versus New Sides. And finally, the series of earthquakes that took place several years earlier in west Tennessee brought about fear among families all over the area, including the Red River Settlement.

It is the author's opinion that these events would be just cause for emotional trauma on the part of anyone, and that there exists no evidence whatsoever supporting the notion that Elizabeth Bell was abused by her father and evoked a poltergeist as a result. pp

The Legend Was Made Up

This myth stems from the allegation that the Bells made up the stories in hopes of attracting attention to Adams so the railroad would come through.

During the days of John Bell, the area was known simply as "Red River." Adams did not come into existence until the 1858-1860 period, almost 40 years after the Bell disturbances took place. But most importantly, talks of a railroad between Edgefield (Nashville) and Guthrie, Kentucky did not even begin until 1855, nine years after Richard Williams Bell wrote his manuscript and six years after the Saturday Evening Post Article pertaining to the "Bell Witch."

The author has found no evidence that suggests a railroad was being talked about in the Red River community between 1817 and 1828.

If you stand in front of a mirror, something bad will happen to you.

This myth actually comes from the legend of *Bloody Mary*, and not the "Bell Witch." The author did in fact try this technique as a child, and something bad did happen to him as a result. After turning around some thirty times, he became dizzy, fell, and hit his head on the corner of the bathtub.

Appendix L:

Information about the "Bell Witch" on the Internet

THE INTERNET provides a wealth of information pertaining to the "Bell Witch." While some sites contain only short accounts of the legend, others are devoted entirely to the legend and the history surrounding it. As is the case with other informational mediums, the Internet contains an abundance of disinformation about the "Bell Witch."

Below, the author lists two of the many Internet sites he considers to be of good informational value to those wishing to learn more about the "Bell Witch" or the history of the Bell family.

The Bell Witch Folklore Center

http://bellwitch02.tripod.com/
Designed and managed by Phil Norfleet (whose ancestors knew and lived near the John Bell family), this well-researched site provides visitors not only an overview of the legend, and very thorough information about the Bell family and others who figured prominently into the legend. The Bell Witch Folklore Center provides genealogies of various families associated with the legend, reviews of books and essays written about the legend, and a digitized version of Martin Ingram's book, "Authenticated History of the Bell Witch." All information is presented in a clear and easy-to-read fashion.

Walter Bell's Bell Witch Page

members.aol.com/wbell27598/genpages/bellwitch.html
Part of his larger genealogy site, Walter Bell's well-presented page provides visitors with a well-written overview of the legend, a list of books pertaining to the legend, links to other "Bell Witch" Internet sites, and links to his Bell family genealogy page. A direct descendant of John Bell, Walter provides extensive information about his family's history.

Author's Notes

[a] Some accounts list Arthur Bell as being John Bell's father (not grandfather); however, the author has not found any evidence supporting this.

[b] Although George B. Hopson was referred to as "Dr. Hopson," he did not receive his medical degree until 1822, two years after the death of John Bell.

[c] In addition to his work with the church, Josiah Fort was very active in civic affairs. He became one of Robertson County's first trustees in 1796, and was in that same year appointed to serve as one of the county's three presidential electors. Ten years later, he was appointed by the General Assembly to serve as a trustee of "The Liberty Academy," a local school that was proposed and mulled over until 1811 but never materialized. See: Albert Virgil Goodpasture, *Goodspeed History of Tennessee – Robertson County*, 1886, pp. 837-838, 860.

[d] Drake's Pond Baptist Church adhered to Calvin's doctrine of Predestination and Red River Baptist Church adhered to the Arminian doctrine after the Baptist denominational split.

[e] A person who was alive at the time of the disturbances alleged later in life that John Bell, Jr. shared the matter of the Spirit with his closest friend, Frank Miles, in confidence shortly after the apparitions began – thus breaking the imposed vow of secrecy.

[f] An examination of John Bell's estate settlement yields persuasive evidence of his wealth. See: *Robertson County, Tennessee Will Book 3*, pp. 267-268, 503.

[g] In the days of John Bell, the term, "witch" was widely misunderstood. As a result, the term was often applied to anything considered by most as being "spooky," "ungodly," or otherwise unexplainable. In addition to being applied to those who allegedly possessed supernatural powers (witch doctors), the term also comprises, in part, the name of this legend - "The Bell Witch." Although the world has now advanced beyond this unenlightened state, the stigma associated with the term "witch," still remains.

[h] Loosely stated, *usury* is the practice of charging an excessive rate of interest on borrowed money. The Robertson County Circuit Court records of that era no longer exist, so it is not possible to ascertain the type of punishment, if any, Bell received as a result of his conviction.

[i] After leaving Red River Baptist Church, Josiah Fort was received into membership at nearby Drake's Pond Baptist Church by letter of dismission. During the spring of 1816, Red River Baptist Church sent

a letter to Drake's Pond Baptist Church expressing a desire to meet with church leaders to discuss "matters of grief" regarding Josiah Fort that they (Drake's Pond Baptist Church) should be made aware of. Details of the grievance are sketchy at best; however, Josiah Fort was received back into the fellowship of Red River Baptist Church several years later. See: *Red River Baptist Church Minutes (1791-1826)*, pp. 172-173, 201.

[j] Major Garaldus Pickering became the schoolmaster in the Red River community when Professor Richard Powell resigned his post to pursue a career in politics. Pickering educated John Bell's two youngest sons, Richard Williams Bell and Joel Egbert Bell.

[k] According to legend, if a rabbit found near the Bell farm has a black spot on the bottom of its left hind foot, it is said to be a manifestation of the Spirit. When such a rabbit is found, the foot is to be cut off and placed in a hip pocket, and then the rabbit's body is to be buried on the north side of an old log.

[l] "Pots" was the nickname given to Martha Bell by Kate.

[m] Anky's real name was "Anica." See: *Robertson County, Tennessee Will Book 3*, p. 503.

[n] The author has located no official records of Esther Scott's birth and family. Two second-hand accounts suggest that she was born in September of 1777 to James Hayes and Elizabeth McKenzie of Dickson County, Tennessee, eighteen years before Richard Powell's birth in 1795.

[o] The hill above Brown's Ford Bluff is a Native American burial mound.

[p] James Allen Bell was discharged from the Confederate Army on May 4, 1862 at Cumberland Gap, due to physical disability. His company commander certified, "He has acted well and truly the part of the soldier. I have unbounded confidence in his patriotism and devotion to the interest of his country." In his career, James Allen Bell was a Justice of the Peace (1860), president of the Robertson County Agricultural and Mechanics Association (1872), and served in the Tennessee House of Representatives, representing Robertson County in the 39th General Assembly (1875-1877). See: Microcopy, *TN Confederate Service Records*, roll 159. See also: Albert Virgil Goodpasture, *Goodspeed History of Tennessee – Robertson County*, 1886, p. 1129.

[q] Leftrick Reynolds Powell died November 30, 1864 in the Civil War battle of Franklin, Tennessee. Other losses in the company included Jeremiah Batts, III., who died on December 9, 1864 of wounds suffered in the Battle of Franklin, and Benjamin F. Batts, who died of pneumonia in Knoxville, TN in 1861. James Long, who was later promoted to the rank of Colonel, died at Jonesboro. See: Albert Virgil Goodpasture, *Goodspeed History of Tennessee – Robertson County*,

1886, p. 857. See also: *11th TN Vol. Infantry, Confederate Service Records*, TSLA.

ʳ A house was built on the hill above the spring in the early 1900s, and water was pumped up to the house from the spring – making it the first house in the community with running water.

ˢ John Bell's gravestone was replaced by Leslie Covington in 1957, and has since remained in the old Bell cemetery.

ᵗ Some of the logs salvaged from this old building were later used in the construction of a log cabin that stands behind the Bell School Antique Mall and Adams Museum in Adams, Tennessee. Therefore, it is possible that 'some' of the logs used to build this log cabin were originally part of John Bell's house.

ᵘ The term *orb* is generally associated with white or orange, semi-transparent spheres of electromagnetic energy that sometimes appear in photographs but which are invisible to the naked eye. Believed by many to be manifestations supernatural energy, white orbs denote positive energy whereas reddish-colored orbs denote negative energy.

ᵛ The term, *witch head*, when used in the context of this discussion, refers to the head and face of a traditional "witch," as viewed by the public in general; i.e., a round forehead, pointed nose and chin, etc.

ʷ The "mist picture" mentioned in the last paragraph of this account was taken at the crest of the sinkhole just a few feet from the tree where Elizabeth Bell and her brothers, in the early 1800s, encountered the crying, lifeless body of a young woman hanging from a tree.

ˣ Upon a later revisit to Bellwood Cemetery, it was discovered that the graves mentioned in this account were no longer there. Others have also reported the "disappearing graves" phenomenon at Bellwood Cemetery.

ʸ It has often been said that two of the Bells' sons, Benjamin and Zadok, are buried in the old Bell cemetery; however, the author has sufficient reasons to believe otherwise. At the time of his death, Zadok Bell was living in Montgomery, Alabama. Transporting bodies of the deceased was not done as a rule. We know that Benjamin Bell died at a very young age, and was definitely alive at the time the will of John Williams, Lucy Bell's father, was written in or slightly before 1792. Since the Bells moved to Tennessee in the winter of 1803-1804, the author believes that Benjamin Bell died in the late 1790's and is buried in North Carolina - most likely in Edgecombe or Halifax County.

ᶻ As noted elsewhere in this book, it is believed by one descendant that John and Lucy Bell's eldest son, Jesse, was buried in the old Bell cemetery also because he died in Christian County, Kentucky, which is near Adams, Tennessee. Whether he is buried in the old Bell cemetery or underneath an old headstone at Riverside cemetery in Hopkinsville, Kentucky that bears the faded name, "Bell" and the correct year of his death, is not known and probably never will be.

aa There is a discrepancy between the birth dates listed for Elizabeth Gunn Bell on her gravestone and in the public records. The former states 1806 and the latter states 1807.

bb The author has not ascertained the date or cause of the fire, and few remnants of John Bell Jr's house remain today.

cc It is a violation of federal law to deny any individual, at any time, access to any graveyard, regardless of whether it is situated on public or private property. The law creates a de facto *public easement* to all graveyards. This law is not well known, and the author strongly discourages people from visiting graveyards on private property without first obtaining permission as a matter of courtesy.

dd Some Native American researchers have labeled this apparition as the Spirit, "Trickster." Interestingly, this type of apparition also matches the "trick" stage of poltergeist progression.

ee *Gehenna* is more commonly known as "Hell."

ff Demons and Spirits are not one in the same.

gg We know this was around the 1819 period because, when bringing hazelnuts to Mrs. Bell, Kate remarked to Mrs. Bell that a baby, Nancy, was just born to John and Martha Johnston. This story comes from Richard Williams Bell's manuscript, *Our Family Trouble.* Johnston family genealogical records show that Nancy Johnston was born on June 6, 1819. According to the legend, Kate brought fruit to Elizabeth Bell and her friends at her thirteenth birthday party the same year. She was born in January of 1806, which would have made her thirteen years of age in 1819.

hh A number of books and essays on the "Bell Witch" have discussed possible "theories" regarding the benevolence achieved as the result of John Bell's death; however, none of these can be substantiated.

ii The author has visited and scoured Union Hill Cemetery in Oakland, Mississippi on several occasions and has yet to locate the graves of Esther Bell Porter and her husband. Two different records indicate this is the place of burial, however. It can only be presumed that their graves are no longer marked.

jj The whereabouts of the notes taken by Dr. Joel Thomas Bell and later used in his son's book are unknown to the author. Locating and proving the authenticity of these notes would undoubtedly lend additional credibility to Dr. Charles Bailey Bell's book.

kk Although John Bell, Jr. died on May 8, 1862, a poster announcing the estate sale of "John Bell, Jr., deceased," was dated May 5, 1862.

ll The town has been incorporated three times since its original incorporation in 1869. The most recent incorporation occurred in 1963, under the name, "The City of Adams."

mm Theo Dickerson, Jr. was a professional jockey between 1934 and 1942. He rode "Blue Marvel," a winner at Boston's Suffolk Downs on May 24, 1938.

nn Information about the Bell Witch Cave's hours and admission prices, along with a contact phone number, can be found on various Internet sites.

oo There was thought to be a relation between John Bell's family and the family of Jeremiah Batts, who was not directly related to Kate Batts. It is reported that Jeremiah Batts' wife, Elizabeth Williams, was a sister of Lucy Williams who married John Bell.

pp Several books, articles and other works have introduced evidence supporting the notion that Elizabeth Bell was abused by her father; however, all such evidence to date has been unsubstantiated.

INDEX

INDEX

QUEEN OF THE HAUNTED DELL

'Mid woodland bowers, grassy dell,
By an enchanted murmuring stream,
Dwelt pretty blue-eyed Betsy Bell,
Sweetly thrilled with love's young dream.

Life was like the magic spell,
That guides a laughing stream,
Sunbeams glimmering on her fell,
Kissed by lunar's silvery gleam.

But elfin phantoms cursed the dell,
And sylvan witches all unseen,
As our tale will truely tell,
Wielded sceptre o'er the queen.

From *An Authenticated History of the Bell
Witch*, M.V. Ingram, 1894.

About the Author

THE PUBLISHED AUTHOR of books, magazine articles, and syndicated columns, Pat Fitzhugh has researched the legend of the "Bell Witch" for more than twenty years. In addition to lecturing and giving interviews, he has written two books and countless magazine articles on the subject. A native Tennessean, Pat Fitzhugh has held public office and holds degrees in accounting and information systems management. He enjoys train travel and the Mississippi Delta blues scene in his limited spare time. Fitzhugh lives in Nashville, Tennessee, and runs the Bell Witch Web Site at http://www.bellwitch.org.

About the Artist

KRIS STUART-CRUMP (Christabel) was born and raised in Middle Tennessee. She is an artist, writer, and animal-lover who comes from a musical family. Her art career began the day she first picked up a crayon, and continues to be her biggest obsession next to music. The legend of the Bell Witch has always been her favorite piece of Tennessee history. Kris resides in Nashville, Tennessee.

Made in the USA
Lexington, KY
01 March 2013